Clausewitz Reconsidered

Clausewitz Reconsidered

H. P. Willmott and Michael B. Barrett

PRAEGER SECURITY INTERNATIONAL
An Imprint of ABC-CLIO, LLC

A B C CLIO

Santa Barbara, California • Denver, Colorado • Oxford, England

Library of Congress Cataloging-in-Publication Data

Willmott, H. P.
   Clausewitz reconsidered / H.P. Willmott and Michael B. Barrett.
     p. cm.
   Includes bibliographical references and index.
   ISBN 978-0-313-36276-7 (hard cover : alk. paper) — ISBN 978-0-313-36286-6
(pbk. : alk. paper) — ISBN 978-0-313-36277-4 (ebook)   1. Clausewitz, Carl von, 1780–1831.
Vom Kriege.   2. Military art and science.   3. War.   I. Barrett, Michael.   II. Title.
U102.C6643W55   2010
355.02—dc22   2009029803

14   13   12   11   10   1   2   3   4   5

This book is also available on the World Wide Web as an eBook.
Visit www.abc-clio.com for details.

ABC-CLIO, LLC
130 Cremona Drive, P.O. Box 1911
Santa Barbara, California 93116-1911

This book is printed on acid-free paper ∞™

Manufactured in the United States of America

Clausewitz wrote that war is an instrument of policy and, given the time and context of his studies, war was an instrument of state policy.

But in 2004, there were as many as 60 wars being fought around the world, and few of these were wars between states; indeed, in a considerable number of these conflicts one of the parties was not what may be considered polities.

In that case, one is left to ponder the relevance of Clausewitz and *On War*.

Contents

Preface and Acknowledgments

The origins of this book lie in the time that H. P. Willmott spent as a member of the faculty in the Department of Military Strategy and Operations at the National War College in Washington in 1992–1994. There, in Course II that dealt with the theoreticians of war, he was introduced to Clausewitz as the answer to all questions: he was the writer who initiated military thought, provided comprehensive analysis of war in his own time, and left a legacy that provided the start point, the terms of reference, for all subsequent knowledge and understanding of war, and for military planning.

The treatment thus afforded Clausewitz and *On War* did not commend itself to Willmott. *On War* may well provide a start point for the study of war, but the status of sacred text, when aligned with what amounted in intellectual terms to a fawning sycophancy, did not commend itself to Willmott who resolved, at some time in the future, to work on an historical analysis that would attempt to examine and explain war in the two centuries that have passed since the time that Clausewitz lived and fought. The objective was not to try to displace *On War* but to supplement it and for obvious reason. The place that Clausewitz and his book commands in terms of military art and science is secure and not to be shouldered aside by some pretentious tome and author: *On War* is endowed with status and relevance that means its place in history and in war is assured, though perhaps the process is but little understood. Clausewitz's relevance lies in the fact that, in the midst of a quarter century of all but continuous and immensely destructive warfare that seemingly toppled the *ancien régime* and all that it held sacred, he saw that war, seemingly so chaotic, was or should be an act of rational behavior, that is, policy conducted by other means. The following two centuries have allegedly followed this latter notion but more often than not in the breach rather than the observance, for example, the Western

Front battles of 1916–1917, the air campaign against Germany 1942–1945, the counter-insurgency campaign in Algiers 1956–1958. These, and other, points present themselves for consideration and in part provide the rationale for a subsequent study that could do no more than complement *On War* in terms of examination of conflict and related matters that have been set in place since the time of the French Revolutionary and Napoleonic Wars.

A number of books, different establishments and courses, and a proliferation of professional problems ensured that more than a decade passed before Willmott was able to turn attention to this study, and when he did so he found himself at The Citadel, the Military College of South Carolina, where among his colleagues for the year he found a certain Brigadier General Michael Barrett. Barrett and Willmott were possessed of very different interests and commitments but shared a certain skepticism with reference to the treatment afforded Clausewitz and *On War* in general and with reference to contemporaneous U.S. military practice. Thus was born an association that over the years very slowly pieced together a tome that hopefully reflects the better elements of their respective academic and military backgrounds, brings together learning and standards of two very different societies and cultures, and, hopefully, embraces a shared modesty and proper reticence.

For Barrett, the proddings of Willmott in many conversations and the questioning from students over the course of three decades of teaching, asking the inevitable why, deserve acknowledgement as the reason for this look at the fundamentals of war. Over the years, many colleagues and friends have offered encouragement and friendship, and in naming a few, I run the risk of leaving out many, who hopefully will understand the limitations of memory. Specifically, the late Joseph F. Tripp, John S. Coussons, Wm. G. Nichols, W. B. Moore, Jr., Isaac S. and Cam Metts, Carey and Nancy Rushing, Patrick and Jennie Speelman, and Kyle Sinisi. On the home front, my son and wife, Michael M. and Sara M. Barrett, have always stood behind whatever I have done, and their love and encouragement are instrumental.

For Willmott, specific acknowledgement needs be made to certain individuals who have afforded advice, support, and comfort not simply in the writing of this screed but at a time of very considerable personal and professional misfortune and without whose quiet companionship what was bad might well have been nigh-impossible. Among those I would acknowledge my debt of gratitude to Patrick Birks, Anthony Clayton, Bernard Cole, Michael Coles, Paul Harris, Nigel and Martine de Lee, William Spencer and Andrea Johnson and family, John Andreas and Tine Olsen, Gerard Roncolato, Jack and Gee Sweetman, Tohmatsu Haruo, Spencer C. and Beverly Tucker, and Steven Weingartner and to Ken Franklin, Andrew Orgill, and John Pearce. To all of these people I would simply state my thanks and appreciation for help and camaraderie that are beyond my poor powers to acknowledge properly.

Book I

On Clausewitz and *Vom Kriege*

CHAPTER 1

The Clausewitzian Context: The Modern Era

On War must be one of the most irritating books ever written, and for two very obvious reasons: first, no matter how carefully and painstakingly one studies its contents, every time one opens its pages one finds something that one had never previously noticed, and, second, it is a book that if it did not give rise to the comment, "more quoted than read," then most certainly it could well have done so.[1] But one would suggest that even Clausewitz (1780–1831), if he were allowed the indulgence of considering the treatment afforded *On War*, would have just cause for irritation. At a wholly personal level he could not but be flattered by the treatment afforded the book and himself, but one would suspect that his reasoned response would be somewhat different, and again on two counts. First, *On War* was clearly written in an attempt to explain, not to describe, and in a very obvious sense it sought to present questions and to provide the basis of understanding. But so much of recent and present treatment of *On War* starts from a premise that Clausewitz himself would question: most certainly the status of holy writ and the mantle of uncritical acceptance of self-evident truths are ones with which Clausewitz, intellectually, would be uncomfortable. Second, despite the acclaim afforded *On War*, there is no escaping the fact that the analysis is dated and much of its contents have been overtaken by events. And the simple fact is that there have been such massive changes in terms of war and warfare, the nature and conduct of war, and the state and society, that there is a need for a recast *On War* that may serve as the basis of understanding conflict at the present time.

If one is permitted, one would give but one example of the manner in which *On War* is dated, and it is perhaps the one element of Clausewitz's writing with which most people with an interest in matters military will be familiar, namely the concept of the trinity. The idea of a trinity is very much 18th century, the period of the Enlightenment, the Age of Reason, and, of course, it also has a religious base, and one that was consciously and deliberately employed by Clausewitz: if the individual could grasp the idea of the Holy Trinity in terms of the relationship of parts and their combining to make up the whole, then the individual could grasp the idea of war as a trinity. But Clausewitz was very much the product of his time: the whole rationale for *On War* lay in the attempt, and the need, to analyze war in order to understand the changes that the French Revolutionary and Napoleonic Wars represented. But if Clausewitz had been a product of the 19th century it is more than likely that a pair rather than a trinity, or perhaps a pair of pairs rather than a single pair, would have provided the basis of analysis, and in any case one would suggest that the idea of a trinity is something of a disservice to the cause of understanding for a reason that may not appear obvious. The outcome of war may indeed be the product of violence, chance, and reason, and most certainly does involve (or more accurately at the time of Clausewitz's writing did involve) the state direction of policy, the professional qualities of the army, and the attitude of the people. But, and leaving God out the equation, the concept of a trinity naturally invokes one image, the image of the triangle, and specifically the image of the equilateral triangle with the obvious implication being the equality of importance and contribution of the constituent parts. That, of course, was not what Clausewitz stated or indeed intended with reference to war. Perhaps the best representation of the Clausewitzian trinity is the screen saver ubiquitous to most computer monitors, with the triangle portrayed in perpetual motion, moving through three dimensions and with sides and angles constantly moving and changing relative to one another, one being of specific importance and relevance at one time and another on a different occasion but always related to the others.

One would suggest, moreover, that Clausewitz and his concept of war is peculiarly 18th century in the sense that the latter is curiously antiseptic and possessed of a simplicity that, if it did not die in the 19th century, most certainly was killed in the 20th. The basis of this statement lies in the fact that, for Clausewitz, war was an instrument of state policy and there was a clear distinction between war and peace. The 19th century saw many changes but one would suggest that its impact in terms of war was two-fold. The 19th century was about the cultivation of hatred, the 20th century about the reaping. The 19th century played host to an increasingly assertive nationalism and racism, but the real point in terms of Clausewitz and war was the fact that this century saw the emergence of the concept of struggle as the permanent feature of existence—between classes, according to Karl Marx (1818–1883) and Friedrich Engels (1820–1895), for existence *per se*, according to Charles Darwin (1809–1882) and Herbert Spencer (1820–1903), and between races, according to Arthur de Gobineau (1816–1882) and Houston Stewart Chamberlain (1855–1927)—and this basically rendered war and peace as nothing other than parts of a struggle with the obvious implication: if war was merely an instrument of policy in the process of struggle then so, too, was peace, and if both were instruments of policy then war and peace were one and the same or, perhaps more carefully, the two sides of a single coin. Vladimir Ilyich Lenin (1870–1924) most definitely recognized and embraced this idea, one that has survived the demise of the state that he and his comrades created.[2]

But, one would suggest, this is a matter that runs hand-in-hand with other items that one would consider, for the purposes of convenience, to be "errors of omission," though in reality they are not; Clausewitz could not concern himself with such matters as strategic nuclear deterrence, air power, and the impact of the Information Revolution, and for obvious reason that needs neither definition or elaboration on this second page. But there is one matter that, if only for convenience, may be defined herein, and that is the example provided by Japan's defeat in the Second World War in terms of Clausewitzian analysis. Clausewitz provided explanation of Japan's defeat in the Second World War, a hundred years before it happened, and did so in one sentence:

The first, the grandest, the most decisive act of judgement which the Statesman and General exercises is rightly to understand (the nature of) the War in which he engages, not to take it for something, or wish to make of it something, which (it is not and) it is impossible for it to be.[3]

Now, in a sense, this comment can be used to explain any and every defeat and in that sense does not provide complete explanation,[4] but in another sense it does offer the basis of explanation: Japan initiated two wars, one in China in 1937 and the other in the Pacific and southeast Asia in 1941, neither of which she understood in terms of the nature of her enemy and of the conflict thus initiated. But in Clausewitz's writing, the clear point is the implication of the relationship between victory in war and military success, that victory on the battlefield is the *sine qua non* in terms of the realization of the state's objectives in the prosecution of a war. In one sense, this cannot be disputed though it does need be noted that a state (or group of states) might win the campaign(s) yet still not win the war in which it found itself, 1991 being an obvious example in which victory in war proved elusive despite overwhelming victory by force of arms in the campaign. But in terms of Japan and the Second World War, it is possible to argue that Japan's national defeat was assured if not from the time of the attack on the U.S. Pacific Fleet at Pearl Harbor then certainly from November 1943 and the start of the American offensive across the central Pacific. But if one accepts this argument, and the indisputable fact is that with the move into the Gilbert and Ellice Islands, the Americans initiated a process that the Japanese could not counter or even check, there is no escaping the fact that Japan's losses to date had been minimal. Between 7 December 1941 and 19 November 1943 the Japanese losses in the Pacific and southeast Asia theaters could not have totaled much more than three or four divisions, but if the point of argument is shifted to naval losses then the situation is really little different.

Between these dates the Imperial Navy lost 4 fleet and 2 light carriers, 2 sea-plane carriers, 3 battleships, 4 heavy and 4 light cruisers, 47 destroyers, and 40 submarines from among its fleet units.[5] Such losses really were very light, and they are not substantially different from American losses of 4 fleet carriers, 2 battleships, 6 heavy and 3 light cruisers, 38 destroyers, and 24 submarines, to all causes and in all theaters in this same period.[6] In terms of fleet units, the losses incurred by the Japanese and U.S. navies were roughly the same, but if, as indeed was the case, on 19 November 1943 Japan stood on the brink of assured defeat just as certainly as the United States stood on the brink of assured victory, then one conclusion would seem to be obvious: if Japan's defeat was assured because and in spite of such modest losses, then quite clearly factors other than battlefield victories and the balance of losses were at work in deciding the outcome of this war.

Clearly the more obvious of these other factors can be stated with relative ease. In China, Japan *per se* was incapable of adopting and putting into effect a genuine political program that could have ensured Chinese popular support while the Japanese Army faced an impossible numbers-to-space problem and was incapable of defeating the Chinese nationalist regime. In the Pacific, the Japanese faced the impossible task of fighting two wars, a naval war and a maritime war, across distance and time against an enemy possessed of an industrial capability that ensured that she was able to bring overwhelming mass and firepower against an industrially inferior enemy that, by war's end, had lost all semblance of strategic mobility and had not simply entered end-run production but faced the certainty of collapse of imports and the onset of widespread disease and starvation. A Clausewitzian trinity that defined the elements of defeat and victory—the political, the economic, and the military—would certainly be a useful tool for the purposes of analysis, but, of course, Clausewitz, in writing *On War*, was not concerned with the result of a given war and the factors that made for decision, and this example is provided for one reason. *On War* is not concerned with the sinews of power any more than it is concerned with industry and technology as the basis of state power and battlefield results, but a political-economic-military formula is relevant in terms of providing a basis of analysis, and a basis of understanding, of at least some of the wars of the 20th century and of the situation in which we find ourselves at the present time.

If Clausewitz and *On War* are to serve as a basis of analysis, and a basis of understanding, of war and the situation in which we find ourselves at this time, then two points need be noted at the outset. The first, cited *en passant* at this stage of proceedings, is to note something that is so obvious that it is seldom properly addressed, and it is, very simply, that the greater part of *On War* is not concerned with war; it is primarily concerned with soldiering or what might be defined as campaigning. It is concerned with the minutia and the detail in the field rather than with war *per se*. The second point, being the more immediately relevant, can be defined simply: any examination of the nature of war as presented by Clausewitz in *On War* must initially examine war in that period in order to set in place the basis of understanding of Clausewitzian logic and analysis. But where one starts such an examination cannot be defined quite so simply.

One is assured that wherever one starts an examination of war in order to try to understand present reality is certain to be condemned as fundamentally flawed or totally mendacious, in the correct meaning of that word. Certainly any number of points of departure recommend themselves, and each and every one commands reason and justification, justification; suffice it to note that here are given a number of possibilities that are offered to the reader on the proper basis: for what they are worth, if anything, and for the reader to decide upon value.

Whatever date or event is given as the point of departure the basis must be European, and on two counts: first, Clausewitz was European and his experience of war was an experience of war fought in Europe between 1792 and 1815, and, second, and more importantly, there is no escaping the fact that the world in which we live is a world that has been shaped by a whole number of different forces but that Europe has been specifically important in the process. The emergence and the definition of the state, of nations, of capitalist social orders, are the products of Europe. Moreover, Europeans have drawn virtually every border in the world. We have a year, a day, and a concept of time that are peculiarly European concepts. For good or ill, the mark the world wears is the mark of Europe, and if we are to understand war and the world in which we live one must understand how, why, and when it was that the least of the continents was to shape the world.

The obvious question that this premise invites is to ask the question of when did modern Europe, and with it modern warfare, emerge. A mediaevalist might suggest the end of the 13th century, and for two obvious reasons: the introduction of gunpowder to Europe—Crécy-en-Ponthieu (25 August 1346) allegedly was the first European battle in which cannon were used—and, much more importantly, the rise of mercenary forces. This choice of date, the end of the 13th century, does seem a little early on any number of counts, most obviously in light of the fact that the Combat of the Thirty took place in 1351 and, not least, the life and career of Pierre Terrail, seigneur de Bayard (1473–1524), the embodiment of mediaeval chivalry, straddled the 15th and 16th centuries. It does seem somewhat inconsistent to date the end of the Middle Ages as 1300 and identify its personification two centuries later. But it cannot be denied that this date does have certain points to recommend it. There took place the Christian re-conquest of Spain and Portugal between 1150 and 1275, which resulted in the recovery of classical antiquity from Arab sources and herein were the seeds of the Renaissance; 1300 saw the publication of Dante's *The Divine Comedy*,[7] and the concept of a universe bound together by *faith* but structured by *reason* is at least half modern rather than mediaeval, and there were the changes wrought to agriculture and society as a result of global cooling in the first quarter and of the Black Death in the second quarter of the 14th century. Certainly one could cite the end of the 13th century as marking the emergence of modern Europe, but equally one could move noughts and present the end of the

14th century, or the end of the 15th century, as the suitable point of departure—
and one can suggest a whole series of specific events.

- 1354, which marked the last invasion of mainland Europe by a non-European army until 1943.
- 29 May 1453, which was a Tuesday, and the fall of Constantinople and the demise of the Eastern Empire. This was the date with which one was raised, the event that marked the end of the Middle Ages not least in terms of forcing Europeans to face westward in order to reach the east and to avoid the Ottoman Empire's control of the trade routes within the Middle East. Most certainly this was an event important in the sense that it marked the end of the existence of the one institution afforded continuity over a thousand years to Rome and thence to the classical period and the element of rationalism that preceded Christianity.
- The introduction of printing or rather Gutenberg's development of a printing press with movable type in or about 1454, which resulted in the publication of the Gutenberg Bible in 1457–1458 and, more importantly, was crucial over time in the diffusion of knowledge through the availability of the written word.[8]
- 12 October 1492, on which date the expedition commanded by Christopher Columbus (1451–1506) reached the Bahamas; subsequently the expedition reached Cuba and Hispaniola, this representing the European discovery of the new world to the west.
- 1494, which witnessed both the French invasion of Italy and the Treaty of Tordesillas.[9]
- 31 October 1517, when Martin Luther (1483–1546) nailed to the door of the Castle Church in Wittenberg the 95 Thesis that came to represent the challenge to church authority that was in turn to lead to the Protestant Reformation.
- September 8, 1522, on which date the *Victoria* completed the first circumnavigation of the world.[10]
- 24 May 1543, on which date into the hands of a dying Nicolaus Copernicus (1473–1543) was placed the first printed copy of *De Revolutionibus Orbium Coelestium*.
- 25 September–25 October 1555, in which brief period were witnessed first the conclusion of the Peace of Augsburg and second the abdication on the part of Emperor Charles V (1500–1558) as King of the Netherlands.[11]
- October 1556–January 1568, the period that marked the start of a process that can be defined as the emergence of state, as we presently understand that term, in the form of Spain (and the origins of the Dutch Revolt) as a direct result of Emperor Charles V's having initiated the process of division of Hapsburg lands between two branches of the Hapsburg family.
- And two events, selected simply as points of contrast, namely the battle of Lepanto (7 October 1571) and the defeat of the Spanish armada (1588), the battles that marked the end of major naval battle in the Mediterranean and the emergence in importance of the waters of northern Europe, and the juxtaposition of the galley and galleass and the galleon and what was to emerge over time as the line-of-battle ship.

It is not possible in these few lines to argue the merits of these various contenders, but it must suffice to note two matters. In the process of gradual change,

Europe in 1600, indeed Europe in 1500, was clearly very different from the Europe that began the Dark and Middle Ages, and obviously if one seeks to determine European change then the concept of Europe itself demands attention. In an obvious sense, it is possible to argue that there was no real concept of Europe, as distinct from Christendom or the legacy of Rome, before 28 May 1453 and really Europe in itself had no real form or identity until the discovery of the New World. In one very obvious sense the claims of the return of the Magellan's last surviving ship to Sanlucar de Barrameda after an absence of 3 years less 11 days as point of reference for the end of the Middle Ages would seem to be overwhelming, but the counter-arguments to this point, and indeed each and every point, speak for themselves.[12]

Certainly a very strong case can be made in terms of dating the emergence of modern Europe, the end of the Middle Ages, from the middle of the 16th century, specifically the abdication of the last catholic Emperor—catholic being used in the sense of universal. Charles V, the last emperor to be crowned by the pope and the only emperor to abdicate, is synonymous with the attempt to create an all-embracing empire, by faith attached to Rome. The failure of this attempt, and the division of Hapsburg lands between two lines of the dynasty, plus the fact that by 1556 Spain was in possession of an empire on which the sun never set, can be said to mark the end of the old mediaeval order. The Europe of 1600 was very different from the Europe of 1500, and perhaps this one act more than any other symbolizes the difference. One is only too aware that the argument can be reversed upon itself, that Charles V was not the last mediaeval but the first modern emperor in the sense that no mediaeval monarch could have considered the imperial effort that he initiated: the Middle Ages most certainly could never have provided the means that underpinned his effort. But 1555, specifically 25 October 1555 when, in Brussels, the Emperor announced his decision to divide his lands between the two branches of the family, in an obvious sense closed the door on the mediaeval world, and could for our purposes be identified as the chosen time, the point of departure between two ages, between the mediaeval and modern worlds. The most obvious point of weakness of this argument can be identified with Spain, which after 1556 was pulled in two very different directions, to the world beyond Europe but at the same time she was still tied to the Empire, Germany, Italy, and the Mediterranean.

There are other events that should intrude upon consideration, and two commend themselves: 1440 or thereabouts and the formation of the *compagnies d'ordonnance*, the raising of a professional guard and the re-organization of the French Army by *les Bureau frères*,[13] and 1494 and the French invasion of Italy with what was the first professional army to enter the field in Europe since Roman times. Obviously there is a certain logic should one choose to begin our search here, but to do so would raise the idea of "The Revolution in Military Affairs." One would admit to possession of a certain disdain for this concept. From Bailey's and many others', one via the Tofflers' three to Krepinevich's ten, historians, real and alleged, have been constantly identifying revolutions in military affairs at various stages in history—gunpowder, the long bow, 15th-century France, the Swedish system of the late 16th century via the changes of 1916–1918 to contemporary developments.[14] One wonders if the very term "Revolution in Military Affairs" is not much abused. Most of these revolutions have been associated with technological change, but no single development in itself changes the terms of reference of war or the conduct of operations. The introduction of a single weapon or system cannot be anything other than limited and local in terms of impact and effect. Moreover, the introduction of a new weapon to the battlefield is always evolutionary involving as it must the recognition of the need for this weapon, its production, and the development of organization and doctrine that govern its employment: to borrow an observation, technology alone does not a revolution make.[15] And nothing in war is wholly new. The Old Man in the Mountain and his Assassins in Alamut in the 12th and 13th centuries would recognize "Inside-Out Warfare" of the present time for what it is, as would any disciple of Sun Tzu with respect to his instruction to use disinformation and double-agents to paralyze the decision-making processes of an enemy.

But leaving that aside aside, the idea of "The Revolution in Military Affairs," specifically in terms of the rise of professional armies, clearly possesses a certain importance and relevance because in the aftermath of 1494 the enemies of France had no option but to follow suit. There was from this time a massive increase in the size of armies. In 1470 Spain had perhaps 20,000 men under arms, and hers was the largest army in Christian Europe. By 1630 Spain had an army of 300,000 men. In the middle of the 16th century, France had an army of perhaps 50,000 and by 1630 an estimated 150,000 soldiers. By 1630 field armies of 50,000 men were not uncommon, and in fact in 1630–1632 the Imperial and the protestant field armies in Germany each numbered about 130,000 men but even as one notes these figures a certain care needs to be exercised in examining this phenomenon. Spain, in effect, was bankrupted twice in the 16th century as a result of her military spending, and Spain was a rich and well administered state. By 1648, as a result of the impoverishment of Europe in the wake of the devastation of the Thirty Years' War, armies of 20,000 were large and the Imperial Army in 1648 mustered perhaps 9,000 troops. States could raise large numbers but could not administer them for the very simple and obvious reason that at this stage most had only very weak bureaucratic systems. Compounding this basic and inescapable fact of life was the parallel fact that Europe was for the most part bereft of adequate road and canal systems, and consequently supply for an army in the field was a somewhat hazardous, indeed not too far removed from a random, "liberating" process. Indeed, it is very tempting to suggest that there was only very limited means of command and control of armies in the field.

That, one would admit, is perhaps simplistic and an over-statement, but not by too much, and in any case it can be made here *en passant* and with E.&.O.E. added for our purposes.[16] But to return directly to 1494, the trouble with such a date is that it represents a type of military determinism that carries with it the implication that military changes drove other changes. Most certainly military changes were not divorced from other changes, but one would suggest that the other changes were more important in the re-shaping of the world and warfare. But leaving that point aside, one would suggest two dates for consideration as representing the dawn of the modern world and, with reference to the first, immediately there is a problem. We have something but we do not know when it happened and we do not know where it happened, but in or about 1470, and probably in northern Portugal, a European people discovered the means to sail against the wind.[17] This proved to be one of the most important and profound developments in history because it freed Europeans from Europe, it enabled them to reach out to the world beyond Europe. For over a thousand years Europe had been on the receiving end of successive invasions from Asia and Africa. It had been the anvil. Now Europe had the means to reverse the process; it was to be the hammer. The ability to sail against the wind meant that in time, and most certainly not immediately, it became easier to go around continents than across them, and this was a fact of life that was to become synonymous with European primacy in the world. That primacy was to begin to come to an end when the advantage held by maritime lines of communication over overland lines of communication ended, when, in the course of the 19th century, railways allowed size, as represented by continental land mass, to be used to real advantage for what was the first time.

The second date is exact: 23 June 1633, which is a date that most definitely can be represented as the date of the birth of modern Europe. Why? What happened on the 22nd? The answer is the recantation of Galileo Galilei of his belief in the Copernicus world system before the Inquisition. The question that we face is why the Roman Catholic Church brought the foremost scientist of the day before the Inquisition because, after all, the Copernican system had been generally accepted for the best part of a hundred years. The answer is that the Church was involved in a war—the Thirty Years' War (1618–1648)—and the Vatican adopted the ethics of the police state in order to prosecute not a war but what in effect were three wars—against heresy, against rationalism, and against the emerging nation-state. This effort to place faith and obedience before reason failed and in this failure the Thirty Years' War witnessed and played its full part in the final crumbling of the mediaeval world: by 1648 Europe had begun to assume a political shape that we would recognize today. Less the point be doubted, one would make reference to two matters that would seem to underline this argument that reference the significance of this event.

The first is Shakespeare (1564–1616), the very embodiment of English Protestant nationalism. But only 7 of his 27 plays are not set in the Mediterranean, and most of those that are set in the Mediterranean are set specifically in Italy.[18] Even for an Englishman in the reign of Elizabeth Tudor, in 1600 Italy and Rome still represented the "center of the world": by 1700 the Mediterranean was a backwater. The second is that when the news of Galileo's treatment reached Paris, a certain individual, reading the signs correctly, left the city, abandoned his current studies. He had been in the catholic armies in the initial phase of the Thirty Years' War but apparently fear of persecution led him to settle in the United Provinces and while there may be wonderment why anyone should want to leave Paris for the Netherlands, it was in the peace and tolerance afforded him in his new surroundings that this individual wrote the second-most important sentence ever written: *Cogito ergo sum* is the basis of rationalism and the modern world.[19] And it is with this war, of which Galileo's recantation forms the halfway point, and the system to which this war gave rise, that the next chapter concerns itself.

POSTSCRIPT

The basis of the argument that the recantation of Galileo before the Inquisition represents the link between the Middle Ages and the modern world is that with this was one episode in the process whereby Man replaced God at the center of the existence.

One set of illustrations perhaps provide an example of the change: the combined portraits of Michelangelo and Galileo. Galileo was born on 15 February 1564 and Michelangelo died on the 18th. The three days of common existence possess a symbolic value in terms of the end of the Middle Ages, the meeting place of Faith and Reason, though perhaps more appropriate might be not two but three portraits: those of Michelangelo, Galileo, and Sir Isaac Newton since their respective dates were 6 March 1475–18 February 1564, 15 February 1564–8 January 1642 and 25 December 1642–20 March 1727. All three lived to remarkable ages—into their 89th, 78th, and 85th years, respectively—and between them, with just the 11-month gap, they cover 252 years of history: from the Sistine Chapel to the prism, from a world formed by God to one dominated by Man.

And if someone can identify the point in time when the Television replaced Man at the center of existence then perhaps we might know when postmodernism began, whatever that dreadful phrase means.

CHAPTER 2

The Clausewitzian Context: War and the Westphalian System

According to Sir Rupert Smith, writing in *The Utility of Force,*

War no longer exists. Confrontation, conflict and combat undoubtedly exist all around the world—most noticeably, but not only, in Iraq, Afghanistan, the Democratic Republic of Congo and the Palestinian Territories—and states still have armed forces which they use as a symbol of power. None the less, war as cognitively known to most non-combatants, war as battle in a field between men and machinery, war as a massive deciding event in a dispute in international affairs: such war no longer exists. . . .

It is now time to recognize that a paradigm shift in war has undoubtedly occurred: from armies with comparable forces doing battle on a field to strategic confrontation between a range of combatants, not all of which are armies, and using different types of weapons, often improvised. The old paradigm was that of inter-state industrial war. The new one is the paradigm of war amongst the people.[1]

At various times individuals have made similar pronouncements or, indeed, pronouncements that would suggest that war had become so terrible that it would henceforth abolish itself,[2] but one would suggest that such comment, and specifically that by Smith, is fundamentally flawed. War most certainly exists at the present time, but the old paradigm was one that in the course of thousands of years of recorded history but briefly existed. At the present time we are host to a number of forms of war, most of which have existed over time but were removed from center stage as a result of a process that was peculiarly European and which emerged in the aftermath of the Treaties of Westphalia.

The Europe into which Clausewitz was born and in which he was raised was one shaped in very large measure by one war and the subsequent attempts to ensure that such a war, in terms of its nature but perhaps more importantly in terms of its conduct, was avoided in future. The war was the Thirty Years' War, 1618–1648, arguably Europe's last war of religion until the Nazi-Soviet conflict of 1941–1945, and most certainly this war was one of the worst of Europe's wars with the low point the sack of Magdeburg in 1631, though a certain care needs be exercised on this particular point: the Mongol destruction of Peking in April 1215, Baghdad in February 1258, and Delhi, Meerut, Aleppo, Damascus, and (for a second time) Baghdad between December 1398 and June 1401 were sacks that were infinitely more destructive and costly in terms of life than Magdeburg in May 1631.[3] But that caveat notwithstanding, the fact was that the Thirty Years' War had the most profound effects upon European development and for one reason: it was a conflict that resulted in the re-definition of the state and war and gave rise to deliberate restraint with reference to the nature and conduct of the state and of war.

The Thirty Years' War in many ways belies its name. It could be argued that this conflict was not so much a war but a brawl, but, leaving such a definition aside, most certainly it was a series of conflicts that merged together rather than a single war and that together devastated central Europe in general and Germany in particular. Such was the desolation and ruination of so much of Europe that in its aftermath the major powers, recognizing that Europe could not repeat the experience of this conflict, concluded that they had better attend to the future conduct of war. Consequently, in the decades that followed the treaties of Münster, Osnabrück, and the Pyrénées,[4] there was set in place a process that witnessed the very deliberate, albeit very imperfect, attempt to control war in terms of its nature and conduct, specifically to avoid the element of totality that is invariably associated with the Thirty Years' War even if the term "total war" had to await the period between the two world wars of the 20th century. In very large measure, this attempt was successful in terms of the creation of a system and ethic that enabled Europe over the following 140 years to avoid a repetition of wars of devastation that stood comparison with the Thirty Years' War.

What has become known as Limited War in the Age of Reason came to possess characteristics that linked war with the Westphalian state system that was slotted into place after 1648. The first of these related to the state itself and stemmed from the fact that after 1648 the concept of the state emerged with characteristics that commanded general acceptance over the next century. The Treaties of Westphalia accelerated the process whereby the state emerged as a definable entity. The word *état* entered the language about 1540 but certainly before 1618 the concept of the state was unintelligible to most Europeans. What little awareness of the state that existed was synonymous with individual rulers, and the distinction between the ruler and the state for the most part made little sense.[5] After the Thirty Years' War, the state began to emerge with a form and a popular identity that we would recognize today, and under the Westphalian system there came to be defined the concept of the state in terms of sovereignty, non-interference, and monopoly of force. In terms of war, the emergence of the state and its definition in terms of sovereignty and the monopoly of force within its borders were crucial and for obvious reason. If war was indeed the instrument of state policy then the state, and generally accepted terms of reference, had to exist.

In terms of the state and monopoly of force, and with it the sole attendant right to wage war, what emerged in the Westphalian system was recognition of state prerogatives, specifically in such matters as artillery, and unprecedented moves to define war as the *sine qua non* for its limitation and control. Before 1648 it was quite natural for states that were at peace with one another to conduct naval operations—particularly attacks on one another's shipping by commercial companies—and even to wage local undeclared wars on one another. Cross-border raiding was, if not an honorable occupation, then common in many parts of Europe.

Armed conflict in Europe before 1618 was all but endemic and existed at all levels within society. Warfare was generally regarded as a natural state, and as far as warfare was considered socially and philosophically it was generally regarded as a good thing, specifically in terms of confirming soldierly values and as a social cathartic in terms of the "lowest orders." Clearly, with a new restraint imposing itself after 1648, such matters had to change, most obviously in terms of two matters, first, the attempt to ensure that war, being a state activity, did not involve the mass of society and, second, the regularization of due process. Declarations of war and the denial of the right to wage proxy wars or to allow citizens and companies to conduct unofficial military operations were constituent parts of a slow but very deliberate attempt to regularize war to ensure that it was a state-directed and very deliberate, controlled process in which whatever private initiative was allowed—such as privateering—was brought within the proper context of state activity. Over time, practices were established whereby the state alone could sanction privateers by the issue of appropriate letters, and companies could not fight one another outside the context of properly declared war between states, but, inevitably, there were episodes when the states themselves broke the rules. Britain and France, for example, were to spar with one another for some two years in India and North America before they formally went to war with one another in 1756.

In such matters, the definition of aim, of over-arching principle, was clearly crucial, not least in terms of setting aside religion and God-given right in terms of purpose. The states of Europe, or at least Christian Europe, had in common monarchies and aristocracies, and working in favor of restraint was recognition that the monarchical principle demanded observation of norms lest people pick up bad ideas, England in 1649 setting a particularly unfortunate example in this matter. As a general rule this recognition of common identity came to encompass a lack of interest in destruction of an enemy but every interest in acquisition because, very simply, there was no point in seeking to acquire territories if their populations were to be killed and whole areas wrecked and devastated in the process; populations and territories had to be secured in working condition in order that they be positive assets. The proper treatment afforded civilian populations had its parallel in the proper treatment of prisoners and wounded.

This element of restraint in dealing with populations and territories that were subjected to campaigning went alongside restraint in dealing with domestic populations, one of the chief rationales of kingship in the post-Westphalian era being that it was increasingly identified with the least possible demands on society; good kings were those who imposed the least demands upon their people. This came to embrace a very deliberate attempt to isolate society from war and for one reason: war was the prerogative of the state and ruler. The view that the prosecution of war was not society's responsibility and that society should be as little involved as possible was one of the factors in the rise of professional armies, and the immediate point of comparison and contrast exists in the form of the mediaeval *levée* and the obligation of defense that had been placed on all men.

The emergence of professional armies and the concept of restraint in the conduct of war were linked, and for one very obvious reason: professional armies, representing investment over many years, were very costly and most certainly were too expensive to lose, particularly too expensive to lose in the course of a single afternoon. The emergence of professional armies, and specifically professional armies drawn from a state's own people rather than mercenaries, was necessarily a slow process but while such matters so important in terms of professional identity as uniforms, flags,[6] bands, and music were entering on the scene at this time—the first uniforms appeared as early as 1619—two developments were crucial. The state assumption of responsibility in terms of garrison barracks and magazines was specifically intended to ensure the proper control of soldiery[7] while the development of roads and canals in the 17th and 18th centuries made for the better provision of military formations in the field and hence concentration and effective control. The latter also meant that the new armies were limited in terms of speed of movement and of the distance from bases at which they could operate. Moreover, given the desire to secure territories—to make capital gains rather than impose some form of religious order or some other abstraction—the form of operations changed in terms of the primacy of siege and maneuver, and, consequentially, the primacy of engineers and gunners in terms of the emergence of a professional officer corps.

Inevitably, in setting out this account of proceedings there are the problems presented by the exceptions and those matters that fall outside the terms of reference thus defined. An obvious example in terms of speed and distance would be the march of King John III Sobieski's Polish Army and the relief of Vienna in 1683. In this episode, a Polish Army of some 30,000 officers and men marched a distance of 220 miles in 15 days and, linking with Austrian forces that had stood in defense of Pressburg and Imperial formations that had made their way from Germany, then fought and defeated what was not simply a Turkish army but what was the last Turkish, and Moslem, invasion of Christian Europe. It was also, in a very perverse sense, the last European effort against Islam.[8]

Consideration of the siege and relief of Vienna in 1683 permits the recounting of exceptions, those situations and circumstances in which the rules, as they came to evolve in the wake of the Westphalian peace, did not apply. The most obvious area, given the brief reference to the events of 1683, was in wars between Christian and Moslem. The siege of Vienna was noted for some particularly nasty treatment of prisoners by both sides, and the general viciousness of subsequent wars between Austria and the Ottoman Empire was noted in terms of the reality of the abrasive behavior of Austrian formations that had served in the Balkans when they came to Germany. But the rules of restraint were not observed in civil wars, which by their very nature were total wars, and the rules did not necessarily travel well. The Europeans, specifically the British and French, generally respected European conventions in their dealings with one another on the Indian sub-continent, where there were ancient civilizations, but very few rules were observed in North America. Moreover, of course, there were episodes even within Europe where the rules could be deliberately broken. The French devastation of the Palatinate in 1688–1689, and the allied devastation of Bavaria in 1704, were undertaken as quite deliberate acts of policy, and most certainly the former shocked Europe, and that shock was illustrative of the extent to which the concept of restraint had taken hold within 40 years of the end of the Thirty Years' War. Moreover, and inevitably, the rules could be broken *en passant*. The French behavior at Bergen-op-Zoom in 1747 and in Westphalia in 1759 was appalling. Russian behavior in Germany in 1758 and 1759 was almost as bad and, in August 1758, the Russian wounded on the battlefield at Zorndorf were buried alive by the Prussians. There is no ready explanation of these episodes though it need be noted that the French Army in 1758–1759 was a poor army, badly led, poorly administered, and ill-disciplined, and its behavior thus has some sort of context, but that most definitely was not the case in 1747. In the Seven Years' War (1756–1763), the Prussians and Russians really went for one another, but even if Zorndorf was a singularly nasty battle, this episode really was exceptional even by the Prussian and Russian (lack of) standards.

The Westphalian system imposed a certain order upon the conduct of states and the prosecution of war that lasted 140 years, though there were to be great changes in that time. By 1648, the state was in place and with borders from which it is possible to recognize certain basic similarities with the political map of Europe in 1919: by 1648 Europe was host to Austria, Denmark, England and Scotland, France, Poland, Portugal, Russia, Spain, Sweden with Finland, and the United Provinces. Perhaps more importantly, by 1648 there had been the start of the process of profound change in terms of the power structure of Europe. In the course of the Thirty Years' War, the power center of Europe shifted north of the Alps. The main focus of scientific enquiry was to be largely concentrated in northern Europe. Within a hundred years of the Treaties of

Westphalia, the political, intellectual, and scientific leadership of Europe had passed from southern, Catholic lands. Europe's primacy in the world was to lie in its scientific and technological superiority over the rest of the world and that superiority was increasingly concentrated in northern, Protestant Europe.[9]

In terms of power the post-Westphalian order saw the rise of the new, the decline of the old. England, and after 1707 Britain, emerged as a first-class rather than an occasional power, and the period also saw the rise of Russia—the treaty of Kiev in 1667 and the battle of Poltava in 1709 being of singular importance—and Prussia, which had emerged as a significant power before her initiation of the War of Austrian Succession, 1740–1748, saw her enter into first-class status. At the same time, Spain slipped from the ranks of the great powers. By the time of the Thirty Years' War she had fallen from her position as greatest of the European powers and indeed was fated to pass into secondary status. The Treaty of the Pyrénées in effect closed the door for the very simple reason that after 1648 nothing of any importance in terms of the European system and history happened south of the Pyrénées as the military center of gravity within Europe found itself a new home on the North European Plain. But the United Provinces and Sweden also passed from the first rank in this same period, and, with the rise of Prussia and Russia, the position of Poland, for a hundred years of liberal persuasion and standing aside from religious strife, became untenable, and perversely so: the hostile intent of her neighbors pointed Poland in the direction of a definition of nationalism that was synonymous with Catholicism and to a conformist pattern of behavior that she had previously eschewed.[10] It was not until 5 August 1772, however, that Poland's neighbors set about her dismemberment; after the second (23 January 1793) and third (24 October 1795) partitions she disappeared from the map.

In this period, indeed as a direct result of the exhaustion of Austria and Spain in the course of the series of wars after 1618, France emerged as Europe's leading power, a status that she was to enjoy until 1870. But French primacy within Europe was checked primarily because there was a gathering of enemies in order to preserve the balance of power. As early as 1673–1674 England was obliged to abandon her French alliance and after 1688 was to be at the forefront of France's enemies, and a token of this opposition was set out in the preamble of the Mutiny Act, which annually made provision for the army and which specifically stated that the English, later British Army, existed primarily in order to help maintain the balance of power within Europe. The significance of Britain's opposition to France was crucially important in terms of the sinews of war. After 1688, with Parliament assuming direct and sole control of national debt and taxation, Britain was able to generate credit on a scale that France, despite her greater area, population, resources, and overseas trade, simply could not match. In the 18th century, France of the *Ancien Régime*, distracted by the conflicting claims of the Rhine and her overseas interests, was gripped by a petrified social and economic system that marked out the path to the gathering crisis that finally broke in 1789. The simple fact was that Britain, with roughly two-fifths of the size and population of France, by virtue of her financial system was able to match France in terms of troops and warships. The French state was ever less able to generate resources effectively despite the scale and extent of national resources, and in this respect the French experience was untypical of the 18th century. French stagnation and decline were untypical in a Europe that witnessed the emergence of Enlightened Despotism, a concept that saw states take on the responsibility to ensure the commercial prosperity of their people. The interventionist state emerged in this period, but so, too, did capitalism, and, of course, the essence of capitalism lay in the assumption that the individual was the best judge of one's own interest. Politically and economically, capitalism was incompatible with Enlightened Despotism, but capitalist development points us in the direction of the fact that the landscape of the 18th century was to be dominated by three great revolutions: the American, French, and British.

Arguably the most important of these was the last one, which normally goes under the name of the Industrial Revolution, but the most significant in terms of war, in terms of both nature and conduct, was the French Revolution and for the very simple reason that its wars represented a break with what had been put in place over the previous decades. In terms not of war but of armies and the conduct of operations, what had developed in the period after 1648 were field armies generally stabilized around the 50,000 to 60,000 mark and committed to a very set process that was primarily devoted to maneuver and siege-craft. Battle tended to be elusive primarily because the search by both sides for advantage before action was joined precluded acceptance of battle by the other side, and for the most part armies were short-range, sustained from magazines and by canals, and which, because of problems of looting and desertion and the general problems of control of forces once committed to offensive operations, could only be held under close control by detailed administration of formations in the field. Perhaps somewhat curiously, this last aspect nevertheless involved a limited role for the state. For the most part states were content to allow the raising of forces and the provisioning of forces in the field to private individuals, and this was despite the abuse and corruption that followed as a result of such practice. It was not until 1762 that the French Army took responsibility for recruitment and it was not until the period of the French Revolutionary and Napoleonic Wars that states assumed direct responsibility for the feeding and provisioning of forces.

Reform was necessarily the by-product of defeat and the most significant changes that were effected were French and followed in the wake of the Seven Years' War, but the first changes, in themselves small, involved Austria in the 1740s and saw the first experiments with staff organizations. The next decade saw the Austrian introduction of what in effect were the first Quartermaster-General and Adjutant-General staff posts for individual armies.[11] The end of the Seven Years' War saw the first training of staff officers—specifically for what at the present time would be G-3 (operations) positions—by the French Army, and such was the innovation within the French Army at this time that in or about 1769 there was the composition of the first war plan, which interestingly was a French plan for the invasion of Britain. Far more basic were changes after 1776 affecting the artillery and the standardization of units and guns that were primarily the work of Lieutenant-General Jean Baptiste Vaquette de Gribeauval (1715–1789). The battery was established with eight guns while the guns themselves were standardized with 12-, 8-, and 4-pounders; howitzers and mortars came in a 6-in. variety. Improvements in metallurgy meant that the guns themselves were lighter and stronger than their predecessors, but after 1763 they came complete with new carriages, caissons, and harnesses and with new sights and incliners. At this same time there also appeared, for the first time, pre-packed shot and charges. Infantry changes within the French Army primarily concerned the line-*v.*-column argument, and exercises with mixed formations as well as a provisional drill-book in 1788 pointed to the path that was taken by revolutionary armies in the next decade. Moreover, the brigade of the 1700s had been largely replaced as standard field formation by the division of the 1760s, and quite clearly in the last years before the revolution, the French Army, with considerable prompting by Edmond Louis Alexis Dubois-Crancé (1747–1814), who was later to assume some degree of notoriety as one of the more extreme revolutionaries in the Third Estate, was working its way very tentatively to the all-arms corps. At the same time the Prussian Army sought to ensure proper and orderly supply by a fixed chain of command and responsibility downward, from field army to division to unit, that is, it was not the responsibility of the lowest level of command to ensure its own supply.

Obviously the point was that defeat spawned innovation and change, and most certainly many of the measures that commanded French military attention after 1763 were the direct result of the defeats that had been incurred in the Seven Years' War, which truly represented the low point of the French Army in the 18th century. These various changes were, for the most part, in the offing prior to 1789, at least in terms of general adoption, and the real point was that for the most part, in this period between 1648 and 1789, the state and military systems that emerged in the wake of Westphalia survived more or less intact. They survived, as noted in these pages, because of the investment in the system on the part of the powers, because the concept of restraint was so in accord with opinion in terms of reaction against past excesses and was in tune with the rationalism of the 18th-century Enlightenment, and because over time there came to exist a balance of power within Europe. The point of major change, primarily in terms of the nature of war, came as a result of a fact that can be stated very simply: in 1792, France, in the throes of a revolution, found herself involved in war with conservative, monarchical Europe and without a professional army in the field to meet those of her enemies. Revolutionary France, therefore, faced the problem of how to wage war in which her enemies held every *matériel* advantage, and she chose to anticipate the maxim that war is political in nature and that therefore political, not military, factors are the ultimate determinants of its outcome. Rather than seeking to isolate society from war, her response to this crisis was to render the effectiveness of her military response dependent upon the level of popular commitment to the struggle, and the whole point of the French effort is summarized in just one line of the greatest of all national anthems: *Aux arms, citoyens.*

Of course what one had here was a combination of the ideological and practical. France could not match the technique of her enemies and therefore had to rely on mass—vast numbers of semi-trained men, *enfants de la patrie*, the effectiveness of whom lay in their commitment and morale—in pursuit of victory. The issue between France and her enemies was how society was constituted, and the issue of legitimacy precluded limited warfare. War was no longer concerned with piecemeal annexations. The immediacy of the threat to the Revolution posed by the professional armies of monarchical Europe freed French commanders from many of the restraints upon the seeking of battle, specifically seeking battle through the conduct of offensive operations on enemy soil. What came into place was the combination of the politically revolutionary and the militarily offensive. Many examples could be used to prove the point, but one would suggest that the extent and nature of change can perhaps be glimpsed by a comparison between the Blenheim and the Austerlitz campaigns, between 1704 and 1805, and specifically the approach-to-contact phases that, in the case of the 1805 campaign, was the second of its four phases.

With reference to points of comparison, the 1704 march to the Danube was undertaken by an army that mustered 50 infantry battalions and 90 cavalry squadrons, a total of about 40,000 men. This force left Roermond, on the lower Meuse, on May 19 and arrived in the Ulm area on June 22. After having fought and prevailed at the battle of the Schellenberg on July 2, it then effected a *rendez-vous* with Austrian forces on August 12, one day before the battle of Blenheim was fought between an allied army that mustered some 56,000 men and a Franco-Bavarian army that totaled some 60,000 men. In 1805, the march to the Danube was undertaken by an army that mustered some 210,500 men organized into seven corps, each with a line of march within two days of support by a minimum of one of the other corps. This represented a total of 226 infantry battalions, 233 cavalry squadrons, 161 artillery and sapper companies, and 396 guns (with 6,430 horses) and the time-table was as follows: camp at Boulogne broken on September 2 and French forces crossed the Rhine on September 26 and the Danube on October 6. The Austrian force of some 30,000 men was obliged to capitulate at Ulm on October 17 and the French then moved to capture Vienna, declared an open city, on November 13. The battle of Austerlitz, the Battle of the Three Emperors, involving some 65,000 French and 73,000 Austrian and Russian officers and men, was fought on 2 December.[12] And lest the point be missed, Austria was obliged to sue for an armistice on 4 December and was forced into a series of major territorial concessions and to pay a major indemnity with the Treaty of Pressburg of 26 December; by comparison, the war of Spanish Succession lasted until September 1714.

Here in 1805 was a speed of an army on the march not equaled in Europe since Mongol invasions of the 13th century unless it was the Polish march to Vienna in 1683, and, of course, the real point of difference was not simply speed but speed and size. What we do see in these 1805 figures is the encapsulation of a transformation of war in terms of aim, popular participation, scale, and quickening tempo of operations, and the place that battle and maneuver played in the operational *repertoire*, and the contrast with the conduct of operations in the Age of Reason. Thus it is important to stress one fact, that here in these pages is a summary that cannot be anything more than a partial view of events with all the imperfections and inaccuracies thus entailed. One has been obliged to ignore much, most notably sea power, and there was a world beyond Europe, but what is provided here in these pages may serve as the basis of a guide to the campaigns of the French Revolutionary and Napoleonic Wars.

CHAPTER 3

The Clausewitzian Context: War and the French Revolutionary and Napoleonic Wars

It may seem strange to note but Clausewitz and *On War* commanded very little attention prior to 1871. *On War* was more or less compulsory reading for Prussian Army officers before that time but it commanded limited attention outside Prussia, not least because of the longevity of Antoine-Henri Jomini (1779–1869), whose accounts and analyses of the French Revolutionary and Napoleonic Wars provided a prescriptive formula that supposedly was a guarantee of success. It was only after the Prussian victories between 1864 and 1871, and acknowledgement on the part of von Moltke the Elder (1800–1891) of Clausewitz and his ideas, that *On War* began to command much in the way of attention outside Germany, and, of course, after the First World War such critics as Basil Liddell Hart (1895–1970) sought to discredit Clausewitz as having been instrumental in creating the conditions of deadlock that characterized the war on the Western Front.

One of the major difficulties that presents itself in any examination of the French Revolutionary and Napoleonic Wars is the Jominian legacy, and from the outset the fundamental distinction between Clausewitz and Antoine-Henri Jomini (1779–1869) needs to be made, and it consists of three separate but related parts. The first is that Clausewitz saw war as an art and Jomini saw war as a science, a point of contrast that was very real even if it does conjure up a somewhat incongruous image of a Swiss scientist and a Prussian artist. More importantly, and second, Clausewitz concerned himself with war; Jomini concerned himself with victory. And, third, it is not difficult to deduce what made for this difference, and it was the experience of war. Jomini defected from the French Army in 1813 and therefore was never on the losing side. His military experience was of victory, first in the French and then in the Russian armies. In professional terms, what must have been the formative experience for

Clausewitz had to be the Prussian defeats in the battles of Jena and Auerstadt on 14 October 1806. The whole of the Prussian system, in which Clausewitz had been raised and served, had been found wanting. When an enemy army, after winning two crushing victories in two separate battles on the same day, occupies one's capital, as was the case on 24 October, then it is clear that there is something very wrong with one's system. In the aftermath of such comprehensive defeat, defeat with no redeeming features, Clausewitz individually, indeed the whole of the Prussian military, had to go back to basics, and after Jena-Auerstädt and under the leadership provided by Major-General Gerhard von Scharnhorst (1755–1813) and Colonel August von Gneisenau (1760–1831), a new system, re-formed from the base up, was set in place and was to ensure that Prussia played a part, albeit a part grossly exaggerated in Western accounts, in the final French defeats in 1814 and 1815.

That definition of difference was presented in terms of "one of the major difficulties," and two more may be cited here at the outset. The first is the reputation of Napoléon Bonaparte (1769–1821). There can be no doubting a genius for war that clearly marked him as one of the greatest commanders of all time, but it is possible to raise two matters that need be considered in terms of proper assessment of man and worth. The first is the manner in which he stymied development within the military, specifically in terms of the development of staffs. The French Revolution gave rise to the first attempts by central authority to impose a staff system on individual armies, but the staff system was to be stunted as a result of Napoléon. His personal ability was such that the staff system was set back decades, except in Prussia. The problem herein primarily lies in the conflicting claims of the individual and the system and, of course, Napoléon belongs to the Great Man school synonymous with Thomas Carlyle (1795–1881). But it is perhaps worth noting that Napoléon abandoned no fewer than four armies—in Egypt in August 1799, in Russia in December 1812, at Leipzig in October 1813, and at Waterloo—and left them in the field facing defeat and in two cases annihilation. When historical reputation is placed on the scales it would seem that judgment should be tempered by what clearly is a moral dimension that has seldom commanded much in the way of attention over the years.

The second is in some ways the antithesis of the Great Man school, and it is the national perspective in the presentation of history. This is perhaps most marked in the English language, and, one would suggest, the prevailing interpretation of the French Revolutionary and Napoleonic Wars is the overwhelming importance of Britain in France's defeat and the crucial importance of Wellington and the British Army in Napoléon's final defeat at Waterloo on 28 June 1815. The interest of balance would suggest that proper consideration be given to the fact that the British Army lost more officers at the battle of Isandhlwana (22 January 1879) in the Zulu War than at Waterloo, and if the British Army was not without real achievement in the period of the French Revolutionary and Napoleonic Wars—in India and North America—the real point would seem to be that the British involvement in the Iberian peninsula after August 1808 was perverse evidence of lack of contribution. What happened south of the Pyrénees was largely irrelevant in terms of decision in European matters, and the fact that the British Army went to the Iberian peninsula was evidence of its total ineffectiveness in the real theaters of war, as witnessed by the disastrous and incompetently directed Walcheren expedition (July–October 1809).

The real point in terms of national contribution to Napoléon's defeats in 1814 and 1815 lies in one fact seemingly long forgotten and most definitely seldom appreciated, the *café bistro* phenomenon. The name means *coffee quickly*, and in Russian, because that was what Russian troops demanded when they reached Paris in 1814. Everyone knows about 1812 if only because of Pyotr Tchaikovsky (1840–1893) and his *Overture* (1880), but the fact was that the Russian Army fought its way from Moscow to Paris and is barely afforded any credit for having done so. It was the Russian Army that formed the cornerstone of the allied effort on the North European Plain in 1813 and 1814. It was the Russian Army that underpinned the Austrian and Prussian formations in Germany's War of Liberation while the final victory in 1814 was an allied victory, not one to which any single state had special claim. If the French Army had prevailed at Waterloo, where it should have won, it would have then faced a Russian Army that had turned back from Poland on its way home and was heading westward, and with a very pronounced sense of humor failure. Affording Russia due credit for anything is something that seems to have been virtually impossible for generations of Western historians, but the fact was that the Russians in 18 months advanced over a distance more than twice that registered by the British Army in more than five-and-a-half years—and the British victory at Toulouse came four days after Napoléon's abdication and some 11 days after allied forces entered Paris. The Peninsular War possessed little relevance in terms of the defeat of France in 1814 and 1815; the British contribution to allied victory, which was very real in terms of naval effort, continuity, and purpose, and support for allies, was not marked in the military field. The French defeat was registered primarily along the road that led from Moscow to Dresden to Leipzig to Paris; the British victories that were won in the south, astride the Pyrénees, represented a contribution—and a very modest contribution—to allied victory, not its cause. Napoléon was not defeated by the British, by Wellington, or as a result of the Peninsular War though one basic point needs be acknowledged: the level of French commitment south of the Pyrénees in 1813—about 175,000 troops—was most certainly not small but equally was not the margin between victory and defeat in Germany in that year, though the distraction for France was nonetheless very real indeed.[1] As always in such matters, it was pieces coming together, all the elements and different contributions slotting into place, which provide both the cause of events and a proper understanding of the result.

The French Revolutionary and Napoleonic Wars were very properly not two but a series of wars: the wars of the first (1792–1798), second (1798–1800), third (1805–1807), and fourth (1813–1814) coalitions that were punctuated by individual wars such as the Franco-Austrian War of 1809 and the Russian War of 1812, by the Peninsular War (1808–1814) and by the war at sea. The latter tends to be dominated by three battles, off Cape St. Vincent (14 February 1797), the Nile (1 August 1798), and Cape Trafalgar (21 October 1805), but it involved operations seldom afforded much in the way of historical attention, some of which seem somewhat surprising. For example, the British capture of Guadeloupe in the West Indies and Réunion and Mauritius in the Indian Ocean would seem that which might be expected given British supremacy at sea and control of the waters beyond Europe, but while the British occupied Corsica in August 1794 the fact was that Réunion and Mauritius were not taken until July and November 1810, respectively, and Guadeloupe, after having been taken and then lost by the British in 1794, was not secured until 6 February 1810. It does indeed seem extraordinary that the best part of 20 years were to elapse between the French declaration of war on Britain and the latter's capture of these French possessions. These operations go alongside other little known episodes such as the British occupation of the Cape settlement in September 1795 and in January 1806, Ceylon in February 1796, and the Dutch possessions in the Indies in September 1811, and operations against Spanish territories that resulted in defeats at Buenos Aires in August 1806 and again in August 1807. If nothing else, the British defeats in La Plata estuary were indicative of the limitations of sea power in dealing with a continental enemy, though in the event, the success of local forces in defeating the British proved crucial in terms of rejection of Spanish rule, which came just three years later.

The events at sea form no part of Clausewitz's *On War* and are cited here in order to permit one observation before full and proper consideration of events ashore. So much of British historiography has concerned itself with the person of Nelson and, of course, the importance of such victories as Trafalgar. But the British supremacy at sea was not the product of victories; the victories were the product of British supremacy. The superiority of the British state over continental enemies in terms of financial strength in depth was massive. In 1815 the British Navy had some 115 line-of-battleships, and, by a rough rule of thumb, four or five such ships carried the same number of guns as *La Grande Armée* possessed in September 1805. The British state could afford warships on a scale that no other state could match and in terms of training, experience, and seamanship the British outclassed each and every enemy that was met in these wars, French, Dutch, Danish, and Spanish and, when opportunity finally presented itself, American. In the course of the 18th century what had initially been a marginal English advantage, a first among equals relative to the Dutch and French, became an increasingly marked superiority, the evidence being the War of American Independence (1776–1783). It may be argued that in this war the British were checked at sea and lost the war, and indeed that was the case, but the real point was that despite lack of allies and a Franco-Spanish ability to devote all resources and attention to the war at sea, Britain fought her European enemies to a draw and was not subjected to invasion. Such was the measure of a superiority at sea that was basis of her victories in the French Revolutionary and Napoleonic Wars, conflicts in which her various enemies were not simply beaten but wholly out-classed.

With reference to events ashore, several matters would seem to be of specific relevance in terms of Clausewitzian analysis. The first is what can be termed the Napoleonic system, the salient feature of which was the primacy of the offensive, the basic objective of any operation being the breaking of the enemy will to resist by the destruction of the enemy means to resist. It was this point that, in association with the situation that prevailed in the years immediately after 1792, saw battle established as the *sine qua non* of offensive operations in the sense that it was the indispensable condition whereby victory might be secured. Tactically, this emphasis upon battle as the means of ensuring victory was primarily concerned with two features of operations, the frontal assault and the flanking attack, but it was tied to the second of these matters, namely the massive growth of artillery that, by 1809, permitted an establishment of a battery per battalion, a scale of artillery support for infantry that was unthinkable a hundred years earlier. To Napoléon, who was an artillery officer,

Fire must be concentrated on a single point and as soon as the breach is made the equilibrium is broken and the result is nothing,

that is, and to mix metaphors, what would be left of the enemy would be no more than flotsam and jetsam. Herein one can see the first line in what was to become the standard criticism of Clausewitz and *On War,* namely that it encouraged the search for concentration in order to secure overwhelming victory—the *Mahdi of Mass* syndrome—but Napoléon's conduct of operations, at least before 1811, invariably stressed the importance of deception and sound intelligence, and also (depending on circumstances and need) dispersal and concentration, and with the latter was the third matter, one that constituted fundamental change so obvious that it is seldom afforded due consideration.

The movement of the horizon represents perhaps the defining term of reference of battle, and it is easy to summarize battle throughout history. Up to this time battle had been fought within line of sight, at arm's length or at very short range, and within the hours of daylight of a single day. The various examples—and not just sieges—that would contradict this definition speak for themselves, suffice it to note that the introduction of the corps and separated lines of march for the first time presented an army undertaking an advance with a front. The idea of the movement of the horizon invariably is associated with aircraft and depth, but while time has shown that post-action analysis invariably discounts the claims of Air Force personnel to be able to make the ground move, the first movement of the horizon was lateral and not in depth. If one looks at the 1704 march, for example, it would be an exaggeration to state that the frontage of advance was one man, but the basic point is clear enough. By 1805 the frontage of Napoléon's army when it reached the Rhine extended from Mainz, at the juncture with the Main, to the Sélestat area, midway between Strasbourg and Colmar, across a front of about one hundred miles, and there was also a secondary force east of Frankfurt-am-Main. The French formations passed over the Danube across a front that reached from the outskirts of Ulm beyond Ingolstadt with two formations moving to secure Munich and provide flank protection while the greater part of French forces invested Ulm. Such deployment and movement across lateral distance were unprecedented,[2] and the key to its success lay in good-quality mapping (and thorough reconnaissance) that permitted proper identification of viable lines of advance, detailed and thorough administration in terms of supply, and the commitment of all-arms groups on lines of advance that were never more than two days march of support on the part of one or more sister formations.

Thus three matters, namely the Napoleonic system, artillery, and the movement of the horizon, have been noted, and two of the remaining three need to be addressed not least because they manifested themselves before Napoléon came to the fore. These related to communications and the very nature of the revolutionary army that France was obliged to put into the field in 1793, and on the first score the first years of revolutionary endeavor saw what amounted to an Information Revolution in France with the development, by *les Chappe frères*,[3] of a mechanical semaphore system with relay stations set some 10 to 20 miles distant. The first message was sent by this system from Paris to Lille in 1792 and in the following year Paris was informed of the checking of Prussian forces around Valmy within 90 minutes of the event. In 1794, Paris was informed of the capture of Condé-sur-l'Escaut, on the border with the Austrian Netherlands, in less than one hour, and by this time a complete message, with 36 signals, could make its way over the 138 miles from Paris to Lille in as little as 32 minutes. Within a few years France was literally covered with relay stations and her lead was followed throughout Europe. In Britain this French initiative was followed by, of all institutions, the British Navy with a direct signals link between London and Portsmouth.

The ability to pass messages across hundreds of miles in a matter of minutes represented an advance in terms of the enhanced power of the state that made for real change and difference from the past, but in terms of war in 1792–1794, the real point of change was moral and related to the fact that on 23 August 1793, when faced with defeat, France resorted to the *Levée en Masse*. It is one of those curious features of historiography that the battle of Valmy on 2 September 1792 is usually portrayed as one of the decisive battles of history.[4] Had she been defeated at Valmy then perhaps the revolution might have been overturned by a victorious conservative alliance that France had ranged against herself, but very seldom are single battles decisive—except to money-making publishers and hacks—and even less often are they turning points; there is seldom a single battle in which Fortune switched her allegiance, when the assured victory of one side became the assured victory of the other. But if Valmy was decisive then one is left to ponder upon the fact that in the following year, revolutionary France was faced with danger that clearly was greater and more direct than anything that she had faced in 1792, and most certainly Valmy did not represent to France's enemies a defeat from which, both individually and collectively, there could be no recovery.

But what was to save France in 1793 (and to which reference was made in the previous chapter) was the combination of numbers and motivation.* The *Levée en Masse* brought into the ranks something like a million men, of whom three-quarters were soldiers by summer 1794 and these were formed into no fewer than 11 armies.[5] This represented massive change in terms of numbers and quality of personnel, not least on account of an aristocratic officer corps having been consigned to History. What would be termed the emergence of meritocracy in terms of officer selection on the basis of ability and not birth and connection went hand-in-hand with a revolutionary ethic that afforded the individual soldier, hitherto not highly regarded, status that was identified with revolutionary cause and commitment. It was numbers on the battlefield, plus the offensive edge born of revolutionary fervor and endeavor, that provided the basis of French military effectiveness.

Outmatched in terms of professional technique in 1792–1794, this French military response with reference to motivation and numbers was arguably the single most important factor in French national survival in this crucial period of weakness and undoubtedly was critically important in providing the cutting edge of French military endeavor during the period of offensive operations that followed the battles of September 1793. The real period of success came in the course of 1794 and produced two results in the early months of 1795, namely the conquest of the Netherlands—in which the most famous single episode was the capture of an ice-bound Dutch fleet off Texel by French cavalry on 21 January—and Prussia's departure from the First Coalition at the Treaty of Basel. One is reminded of the comment attributed to General Maurice Sarrail (1856–1929), the French commander of Allied forces at Salonika between January 1916 and December 1917, that the experience of commanding coalition forces had served to lessen his previous admiration of Napoléon. Allies are not necessarily friends, a fact that is never more obvious than the approach of victory or defeat when the conflicting interests previously held in check by common need regain their importance. But allies are also not equal in terms of capacity to sustain a common effort, and the fact of the matter was that the Prussian defection was but the first in a series of departures from

---

*A certain care needs be exercised on this point. In many ways France's survival in these years of crisis owed more to the divisions of her various enemies, their lack of co-operation, and their failure to co-ordinate their military efforts. But the importance of French motivation and numbers cannot be gainsaid, and the fact was that French armies more than matched their enemies in terms of numbers and position in 1793–1794.

the war. The three treaties of Basel saw Prussia (5 April), Spain (22 July) and Hesse-Cassel (28 August)—and the Netherlands at the Treaty of Den Haag on 16 May—make their separate peaces with France that, in the process, was left in possession of the whole of the west bank of the Rhine. These treaties also pointed to the impermanence of alliances that was to be a recurring feature of events over the next two decades. French success in no small measure owed itself to the fact that she was not opposed by a series of coalitions but by successive collections of states.

What is so notable about the anti-French effort is Austrian persistence. One has expressed the argument that great powers are not powers that win wars but are powers that lose wars but keep going, the weakness of this premise being that on such criteria Austria would be the greatest of all the powers. Prussia was to emerge from the Napoleonic Wars, and specifically 1815, with a credit that was unequalled among the continental powers yet her involvement in the French Revolutionary and Napoleonic Wars was very short indeed. Austria was at war with France between 20 April 1792 and 17 October 1797 (the Treaty of Campo Formio), between 15 December 1798 and 9 February 1801 (the Treaty of Lunéville), between 2 September and 26 December 1805, between 9 April and 14 October 1809 (the Treaty of Schönbrunn), and after April 1813. She was, by some margin, the most persistent and determined of France's enemies on the continental mainland. It need be noted, though, that by 1813 the succession of defeats that she had incurred in the decade between 1799 and 1809, and the punishing series of treaties by which she had bought peace, had rendered her very vulnerable in terms of future survival should another defeat be incurred. Conversely, the French victory at Austerlitz, generally regarded as Napoléon's finest moment, needs to be considered very carefully in one respect: if indeed it was so overwhelming then the obvious question that presents itself is why there was any need to repeat it at Wagram, 5–6 July 1809. Defeats may possess elements of totality and permanence, but victories can never be anything other than transient.

France's final defeat was the product of two facts, national exhaustion and the gathering of a united continent against her. In the wake of the Russian *débâcle* there was a gathering of all the powers—Austria, Prussia, Russia, and Sweden—that among them ensured a margin of numerical superiority that only increased over time. *La Grande Armée* that invaded Russia in June 1812 consisted of an estimated 200,000 French, 100,000 Belgians and Dutch, 25,000 Italians, 24,000 Bavarians, 20,000 Saxons, 17,000 other Germans, 15,000 Swiss, and 3,500 Croats, and in addition there were Austrian and Prussian formations that numbered 20,000 and 35,000 men, respectively. In March 1814 outside Laon there were just 30,000 troops with Napoléon, but with Swedish troops coming to the support of the Prussians who suffered a local defeat at Craonne, the allied armies possessed a 3:1 advantage in this particular sector of operations, and this was but one sector. On other sectors there were other allied victories that ensured that any French victory or victories would be tactical and local rather than strategic and also ensured that the tide of war was taken to Paris in the last two days of this month.

Like the Thirty Years' War, the French Revolutionary and Napoleonic Wars were not singular affairs. Both were a collection of wars, some concurrent and some successive, spread over 23 years with just one short period, between March 1802 and May 1803, when there was no conflict within Europe. The initial series of conflicts, defined as the war of the first coalition, played host to fundamental change in terms of the allied invasions of France in successive years between 1792 and 1794 and then the French taking of the revolution abroad into the Netherlands and Rhineland, into northern Italy (1796–1797) and thereafter to Rome (February 1798) and Switzerland (April 1798). This initial period also saw British landings at and the capture of Toulon followed by a siege in which a certain Colonel Bonaparte for the first time came to the fore (August–December 1793). Subsequently, in 1795, there were British attempts to encourage counter-revolution initially in the form of a landing at Quiberon Bay and then the Vendée, the first incurring what amounted to comprehensive defeat and the second the crushing of the rising that in effect precluded any British landing either on the Ile d'Yeu or on the mainland. At sea what should have been an initial overwhelming Anglo-Spanish advantage never registered the one victory that might have had major repercussions, which was the action known as The Glorious First of June, 29 May–1 June 1794. Always portrayed as a British victory, one in which 26 British line-of-battleships captured 6 and sank 1 of 30 French counterparts, the victory was French because the grain convoy from North America, desperately needed in a France stalked by the prospect of harvest failure and famine, was able to reach Brest. The battle of Cape St. Vincent, 14 February 1797, in which 15 British line-of-battle ships captured 4 of 27 Spanish line-of-battle ships and forced what remained into the safety afforded by Cádiz, in effect countered Spain's defection from the first coalition and ended any real prospect of a juncture of French and Spanish naval forces that might have posed a direct threat to Britain. There were to be landings in Ireland but the resultant revolts—with the famous Vinegar Hill battle fought and lost on 12 June 1798 before the main French landings were registered on 22 August—were put down with considerable force, and in the aftermath of these there was to be the Union between Britain and Ireland (2 July 1800 effective 1 January 1801).

These first wars saw French acquisition of the Netherlands and Rhineland, but the conclusion of an Anglo-Russian alliance in December 1798 provided, with Austria, Naples, the Ottoman Empire, and Portugal entering the fray, the basis of a renewal of hostilities. These resultant conflicts gave rise to little known episodes such as the Russian campaign in northern Italy and Switzerland and the Anglo-Russian landings and campaign in the Netherlands (August–October 1799). Also, the major part of the slightly better-known Egyptian campaign came at this time. The French landed and established themselves in Egypt between May and July 1798, the capture of Malta and the battle of the Pyramids of 12 June and 21 July being the milestones of familiarity along with the British victory at the Nile. After the French had been checked in front of Acre in May–June 1799, the British secured Malta in September 1800 and Anglo-Turkish forces completed the defeat of French forces in Egypt between March and August 1801. Unfortunately for the anti-French cause, the return of Bonaparte to France in late summer 1799 resulted in the raising of new armies that undid a series of very real Austrian successes in northern Italy in two battles, at Marengo on 14 June 1800 (where Napoléon commanded) and, in the form of an overwhelming victory, at Hohenlinden outside Munich (3 December) that forced Austria from the war.

By this time there had emerged what amounted to a standoff. France had prevailed on the continent and Britain at sea and, with neither able to pose any serious or direct threat to the other, herein was the basis of a compromise— and very short-lived—peace. Nonetheless a new dimension to what was by this stage a struggle rather than a war had emerged in February 1801 in the form of the Armed Neutrality of the North, formed by Denmark, Prussia, Russia, and Sweden in an attempt to ensure maritime rights in the face of British suprem-acy at sea. The British Navy had already worsted the Dutch at Camperdown (11 October 1797) and the British response to this move was the attack on the Danish fleet sheltering under the guns at Copenhagen (2 April); the assassi-nation of the Tsar, and Russia's defection from the League, precluded the pos-sibility of a pre-emptive attack on the Russian fleet at Revel.[6] As it was, the resumption of war between Britain and France in May 1803 saw little in the way of fighting but the French undertaking major building programs in order to attempt the invasion of Britain while the British sought to create a new coali-tion amongst powers not reconciled to past defeats. Trafalgar ended the former while the latter was destroyed in what was, by any standard, one of the most impressive series of operations—Ulm, Vienna, Austerlitz, Jena-Auerstadt, and Friedland (14 June 1807)[7]—in this or indeed any war. Successively Austria, Prussia, and Russia were defeated and France emerged with client states from the Rhine to the Elbe and in a resurrected Poland while Russia undertook to enter into alliance with France.

The latter was part of a French design for a continental economic blockade of Britain, initially ordered on 21 November 1806, but overweening French ambition in 1808 drove an occupied Spain to insurrection and in 1809 Austria to war and to a very rare victory; the battle of Aspern on the Danube, 21–22 May, was Napoléon's first defeat in the field but it was one quickly reversed at Wagram, 5–6 July, by which time British ignominious failure in the form of the Walcheren expedition was beginning to unfold. The French victories in this period, 1805–1809, really represent the apogee of the French political and Na-poleonic military systems. The next six years, in the form of the Russian cam-paign of 1812 (and specifically the Berezina crossing in November), the War of Liberation (1813), the invasion of France (January–April 1814), and finally The Hundred Days (March–June 1815) represented a wasting away of a dis-eased body, and in this change, as rapid as the reversal of fortunes in the lifetime of the first coalition, one basic fact was prominent. What is so notable about Napoléon's wars was that the Emperor's capacity to win campaigns and battles was not matched by an ability to win wars and, crucially, the resultant peace. The series of treaties that France, Revolutionary or Napoleonic, sought to impose on defeated states in an attempt to ensure docility proved counter-productive. The French sought and secured political, economic, and territorial aggrandizement that meant that they could not consolidate gains by the ac-quiescence of the defeated, and it was this, the gathering of an alienated and ir-reconcilable continent, that ultimately led to French undoing.

In two matters, the final French defeat was attended by a re-ordering of Europe's affairs seldom afforded due consideration. Certainly during the French Revolutionary and Napoleonic Wars

A new age of warfare had reached its zenith, but also its end. The powers of restoration, fearful of the ultimate consequences of a people's war, returned to cabinet warfare for the rest of the century, though the Industrial Revolution set unforeseen forces free. Metternich, and in a way his successor Bismarck, held the doors firmly closed to mass democracy and all that this implied, politically, socially and militarily, almost to the end of the nineteenth century.[8]

At and after the Congress of Vienna there was a deliberate attempt to return to the Westphalian system and the exclusiveness of war, its removal from the public domain, but what was perhaps more important was that the Congress of Vienna and the resultant settlement did not constitute restoration. Napo-leonic Europe was divided with Russia ruling where France had ruled in Poland, Austria ruling where France had ruled in Italy, and Prussia ruling where France had ruled in Germany. What the three powers did was to allow various princes and other rulers who had been deposed to return but the proliferation of Ger-man states, one for every day of the year, and *Das Heilige Römische Reich deutscher Nation* were not restored. What these three powers did was not to destroy but to divide the Napoleonic legacy among themselves.[9] What the powers sought to do was to establish a genuine balance of power within Europe and to ensure that no single state, and most definitely not a resurgent France, emerged within Europe with the power to determine continental affairs.

But very seldom given much in the way of consideration in terms of the consequences of the French Revolutionary and Napoleonic Wars is the fact that the greatest and most extensive change generated by these conflicts lay out-side Europe, specifically the collapse of the Portuguese and Spanish empires in Central and South America. Suffice it to note two matters with which to con-clude this chapter. The first, very simply, is to note that these wars were world wars. The problem herein is contained in the very names of the First World War (1914–1919) and the Second World War (1939–1945), but these were only the first and second world wars of the 20th century. As noted elsewhere, the Emperor Charles V could not have attempted what he did without his being able to draw upon the wealth of the extra-European world, and even if the idea of global conflict is not afforded either a 16th or a 17th century start line then perhaps the War of Spanish Succession (1701–1714) or the War of Austrian Succession (1740–1748), but more probably the Seven Years' War (1755–1763) with the British defeat of the French in India (1757–1761), the conquest of French Canada (September 1759), and the capture of Havana (August 1762) and Manila (October 1762), would seem to possess good claim on such dubious distinction as the first world war. The French Revolutionary and Napoleonic Wars most certainly were world wars and not simply in terms of British acquisition of colonies across the world. The wars of national liberation in South and Central America and the War of 1812 were the by-products of the European struggle, and there is the little known fact that Australian troops, that is, British soldiers who had been born in Australia, were present at the burning of Washington and at Waterloo. And, second, by 1815 Britain was all but unrecognizable from the Britain of 1792. In the period of the French Revolution and Napoleonic Wars, she was to be transformed and she emerged from these wars as a state and nation that lived by trade and manufacture, and it was to be British money, shipping, and industry that were to set in place the international trading system of the 19th century.

POSTSCRIPT: SOUTH AMERICA

The first British expedition to La Plata sailed from Cape Town on 14 April 1806 and arrived at Quilmes on 25 June, Buenos Aires being occupied two days later. The local response was for a force from Montevideo to cross the estuary on 4 August and in a two-day action brought about a British surrender and evacuation on 12 August.

On 3 February 1807 a much larger British force, sent from home waters, captured Montevideo and on 27 June landed at Buenos Aires. Having fought and won a battle outside the city, the British force was then caught in a two-day battle (4–5 July) inside Buenos Aires that left it unable to prevail over local militia forces and obliged, on 12 August, to conclude an armistice that led to the evacuation of Buenos Aires, Montevideo, and the small garrison established at Colonia on the northern shore of the La Plata estuary.

What is especially interesting about these episodes is that the two operations bracketed a comprehensive British defeat in front of Constantinople in March 1807, and this Buenos Aires-Constantinople-Buenos Aires combination provides a very interesting comment on the ineffectiveness of British sea power in the immediate aftermath of Trafalgar, while the British failure in front of Constantinople stands in very sharp contrast to the Russian success first at the battle in the Dardanelles (10–11 May 1807) and then off Lemnos (19–29 June) that resulted in a blockade of Constantinople and forced the Sultan to seek an armistice (12 August) and a temporary halt in a war that was to last, intermittently, from November 1806 to May 1812.

CHAPTER 4

The Clausewitzian Context: An Aside

In this first part, there have been many ideas placed before the reader, and it is for the latter to judge the strengths and merits, or otherwise, of the arguments thus presented. But there is one more idea that is placed before the reader with which to end this particular part of this first book, and it is a corollary of the basic point that Clausewitz, the product of the Age of Reason, was basically writing about war in the European context, a context provided by the West-phalian state system, and the basic definition provided by Clausewitz was that war was the prerogative of the state.

It may have escaped attention but the basic point is that a Clausewitzian pre-decessor could not have made such a definition prior to 1618. Prior to that time war was, if not endemic in Europe, then more firmly established than is often realized and most certainly was not the monopoly of the state. Clan war-fare, wars of religion with armies raised and maintained by warring theocra-cies, cross-border marauding as well as piracy and privateering (which on all too many occasions were too difficult to separate) were well established below the level of the *état*.

The Westphalian state system, and the growth of the state in terms of pow-ers and prerogatives, saw these "other" forms of warfare curbed and assume their places in the dustbins of history, the general phenomenon of civil wars and wars of secession excepted. What happened after Clausewitz was that Eu-ropeans basically imposed their system upon the rest of the world; the establish-ment of the great colonial empires went hand-in-hand with the imposition of order, most obviously in terms of the suppression of racial, linguistic, reli-gious, and tribal conflicts and the establishment of borders that provided the basis of peace, albeit in many cases without a great deal of reference to indig-enous peoples.

Arguably, and somewhat ironically, the Westphalian system lasted until the end of empire, and what has happened over the last four decades has been a reversion to the pre-1618 situation in that in much of the under-developed world, where problems of food supply, resources, and general well-being have worsened massively, those other forms of warfare have come back if not to center stage then certainly to the wings.

Book II

War and Wars since Clausewitz: Total War and Systems

CHAPTER 1

From Total War to Total War: 1815–1918

The treaty of Vienna and the congress system that the powers put in place in 1815 initiated almost 100 years in which Europe was spared a general war. There were wars but they were singular affairs with only one war, the Russian War of 1854–1856, involving more than two great powers. There were a series of wars, specifically the wars of Italian and German unification and, as always, the wars in the Balkans, but, for the most part, the wars were few and generally of short duration and limited in terms of both objective and scale. Inevitably, in making such a definition, the caveat needs be entered, and the caveat is that in the course of the Franco-German War of July 1870–May 1871, the German states mobilized 1,183,000 men in just 18 days, and if only half of these numbers went forward to join the formations on the frontier, the fact was that such numbers—with about 840,000 men still with the colors seven months later in February 1871—were unprecedented and the German victory in this war was in no small measure the result of an initial and overwhelming superiority of numbers.[1]

The Franco-German War was to be crucial to the future both of war and of Europe in three ways. First, the German victory brought an end to some two centuries of French pre-eminence within Europe and represented profound change, not least because it was to go hand-in-hand with major population growth and industrialization that served to underline the subsequent German ascendancy within Europe. Second, the German victory invited emulation in two fields, the raising and training of properly constituted and permanently established staffs and the introduction of conscription. The realization of the importance of numbers, and the determination not to be inferior to neighbors that had adopted conscription, pointed to a major growth in the size of standing armies and reserves of all the major powers in Europe (Britain excepted) after 1871. Third, the introduction of conscription and the growth in the size of armies pointed to increased state expenditure and taxation, and the latter presented immediate problems: the conscription of sons and increased taxation could only be justified in terms of insecurity relative to neighbors, and invited direct comparison between states.

What bound these matters together was the process whereby, after 1848, there was a widespread adoption of the form—but not the substance—of democratic rule. After 1848, and specifically after 1870, there were only two republics in Europe, Switzerland and France, and these, along with Denmark and the union of Sweden and Norway, were the only genuine democracies in the sense that they were possessed of full (male) adult suffrage and parliamentary systems in which the executive was accountable to the legislature. Within the rest of Europe, the parliamentary form was adopted as the means of evading democratic substance, the incumbent conservative regimes wrapping themselves in an increasingly strident assertiveness that in most cases embraced a nationalism and racism that moved, in the course of the 19th century, to center stage in terms of respectability and widespread acceptance. The 19th century saw a marked sharpening of national, racial, and social attitudes, and this manifested itself most obviously in the redrawing of the map of the Balkans. Had the collapse of Ottoman rule in the Balkans manifested itself in the 18th rather than the 19th century then Austria and Russia would have annexed territories and absorbed these areas and their peoples within themselves, as did Russia with respect to Bessarabia and the Treaty of Bucharest of 28 May 1812. But in the period between 1815 and 1914, there were the Greek War of Independence (1821–1832), the Crimean War of 1853–1856, the Russo-Turkish War of 1877–1878, the Bulgarian-Serbian War of November 1885, and the Balkan Wars of 1912–1913 plus three Greek-Turkish wars of 1854, 1878, and 1897, and the series of conflicts that redrew the map of the Balkans, if not along ethnic lines then in a way that was to see the creation of Greece at the Treaty of London of 7 May 1832, the final recognition of the independence of Montenegro, Romania, and Serbia with the Treaty of Berlin of 13 July 1878, the establishment of a united Bulgaria in 1885 and its independence in October 1908, and the creation of an independent Albania by the Treaty of Bucharest of August 1913. Such arrangements may have left a great deal to be desired and, of course, there were matters relating to minorities living in the Austrian and Russian empires, but the fact of the matter was that the redrawing of the map of the Balkans and the creation of no fewer than six independent states would never have been countenanced for a moment in the 18th century. The 19th century saw Austria and Russia largely excluded from the Balkans by the force of local nationalisms. With Irish and Norwegian separatist movements also at work by the latter stages of the 19th century, the impact of nationalism in European affairs was fully evident before the First World War saw the destruction of Europe's two multi-national empires.

Inevitably war played its full part in the reshaping of Europe whether in the form of conflict between states or as the instrument of insurrection and rebellion, but perhaps the most significant development affecting the terms of reference of war in the first part of this period lay outside Europe, specifically the Far East where, from the 1840s onward, but specifically in 1860, Europeans demonstrated a capacity to wage total war without having to mobilize the full resources of the state in order to do so. During the event, the European powers deliberately chose not to wage war totally. In 1860, Britain and France passed up the opportunity to wage war against China totally, to the destruction of the existing Chinese regime and state, for the very good reason that they sought positions of privilege that could only be guaranteed and ensured by incumbent indigenous governments. Therefore, the Europeans exercised a certain restraint despite a superior capacity that was primarily the product of massive technological superiority over local forces. The parallel with the present time, with the United States able to seek the destruction of states designated her enemies, is very close. The United States, like the Europeans one-and-a-half centuries ago, can and certainly in 2003 did use massive and overwhelming superiority of force to destroy an enemy state, and she did not need to mobilize in the sense that this term came to be used in the two world wars of the 20th century in order to do so.

In many ways, the real force of this newfound European power manifested itself in Africa in the last years of the 19th century rather than in the Far East, and, of course, in the African context the European powers were opposed by what might be termed polities but which most certainly were not states. The process by which the Europeans subjugated Africa was amazing in terms of extent and rapidity. In 1880, European control, indeed presence, in Africa was primarily confined to coastal and isolated settlements. The only areas where there was a general European presence and control were Algeria and the southern Africa hinterland. By 1914, the only parts of Africa that were not under direct European control were Abyssinia and Liberia, and the process by which Africa was divided and conquered by Europeans was accomplished without a general war between the imperialist powers, though rivalries in certain areas and at certain specific times were nonetheless very real.[2]

What may be termed the totality of war in a sense ended with the defeat of the Old Guard at Waterloo, but in another sense it was there in place with a parallel event, the defeat of the Union Army in front of Cold Harbor in June 1864, and the fact is that at this point the American Civil War (1861–1865) is possessed of three matters worthy of consideration. First, depending on perspective, it took the Union either a very short or an inordinately long time to crush a rebellion that, in terms of disparity of resources, should never have been more than a very short, ill-judged, venture. But the fact was, in terms of federal organization, the United States barely existed outside the postal service in 1861 and it took the Lincoln administration the best part of two to three years to get a federal administrative system in place, with personnel selected by Fortune and the hazards of war, and with a coherent plan of campaign. From the very start of the war, the Union held the strategic initiative but it was not until the spring of 1864, by which time the enemy had been split by the drive down the Mississippi and was subjected to an increasingly effective blockade, that the Union armies were able to fight how they would rather than how they were obliged.

Second, one of the very curious features of the American Civil War was that it foreshadowed, almost down to the last detail, the American war against Japan, 1941–1945. Between 1941 and 1945, Japan was to the United States what the Confederacy had been exactly 80 years before; starting with the opening attacks upon U.S. military bases, the parallels between the American Civil and the Pacific Wars are striking. Both wars saw the United States opposed by enemies that relied upon allegedly superior martial qualities to overcome demographic, industrial, and positional inferiority. In both wars, the United States' superior material resources and ability to mount debilitating blockades proved decisive to the outcome. In both wars, the United States was able to use the advantages of a secure base and exterior lines of communication to bring overwhelming strength against enemies that were plagued by divided counsels, which were committed to defensive strategies involving their trying to hold widely separated positions along an extended perimeter that were not mutually supporting and could not be properly supplied for want of an adequate transportation infrastructure. In both wars, the enemies of the United States, intent upon forcing her to recognize the reality of their existence or conquests, sought to wage wars of attrition and exhaustion against a much superior enemy and, in the process, were divided and conquered. The Union drive down the Mississippi that resulted in the capture of Vicksburg in July 1863 has its parallel in the drive to the Philippines that separated Japan from the southern resources area. Both efforts, for the United States, were characterized by maneuver. The battles in eastern Tennessee and the march to the sea have as their counterpart the central Pacific offensive that, in the form of blockade and the strategic bombing offensive, took the war to the enemy homeland; both efforts, for the United States, were characterized by mass, firepower, and shock action, though on this point a certain caution needs to be exercised because the parallels are not exact. Stretching the point, one could assert that the battles in the southwest Pacific in 1942 and 1943 were equivalent to the battles in Maryland and Virginia in 1862, in that the outcome of these battles ensured that the enemies of the United States could not prevail in the wars that they had initiated; both the Confederacy and Japan had to win quickly or not at all. Moreover, in both conflicts Europe loomed large. In the American Civil War, the Confederacy looked to European intervention to ensure its victory and in the Second World War Japan tied herself to the German cause in the hope that Germany's victory would ensure the neutralization of the United States. Neither eventuality occurred, and the Confederacy and Japan were defeated in wars of very similar duration. The war of secession lasted from 12 April 1861 to 9 April 1865 or three days short of four years, and the Japanese war lasted from 8 December 1941 to 15 August 1945 or three months, three weeks, and three days short of four years.

One could add that the American strategic bombing offensive directed against Japanese cities has its parallel in the March to the Sea and the razing of Atlanta, but that particular argument may seem somewhat contrived, and, in any case, pales alongside the third point that concerns the battle of Gettysburg, in terms of its outcome. One basic fact about this battle has escaped historical attention, and it is who, or more accurately which, organization won the battle of Gettysburg. The answer, of course, is the U.S. Navy. Pickett's Charge is often acclaimed as the high-water water of the Confederacy, and the defense of the United States to the high-water mark is the responsibility of the U.S. Navy. It therefore follows that the real victor at Gettysburg was the U.S. Navy, but, of course, it never noticed.

The American Civil War foreshadowed the First World War in a number of ways. Both, involving the full demographic, economic, and moral mobilization of societies, were total war though the term itself never came into usage until 1935, when General Erich Ludendorff (1865–1937) published *Der totale Krieg*, in which he reversed the basic Clausewitzian dictum with the argument that the state, nation, and society had to be organized to wage war that would be total.[3] These two wars were also similar in terms of the conduct of war, most obviously the operations in front of Richmond in 1864–1865 that foreshadowed the trench system and deadlock of the Western Front but, perhaps more importantly though less obviously, in terms of the relationship between space, distance, and movement. On the Western Front, there was deadlock, with minimal territorial gains by either side, between November 1914 and March 1918 and even in the periods between first March and July 1918 and then August to November 1918, movement was still small, measured in miles or tens of miles but no more, and, in this respect, the Western Front does bear striking resemblance to the situation that unfolded in front of Petersburg, with the only real movement in northern Virginia—as opposed to Union formations attacking at different times in different sectors—in the very last days of the war. But outside these fronts, there was movement over hundreds, indeed thousands, of miles. The Union drives first down the Tennessee and then down the Mississippi represented movement that corresponded to operations in the Balkans in 1915 and across the Eastern Front between 1915 and 1918, German and Turkish forces ultimately reaching Baku, that is, farther to the east than German armies reached in 1942. And common to both wars were naval blockades that were crucially important in inducing economic collapse, though in both wars the final result, for the loser, was the culmination of military defeat in the field and political, industrial, and moral exhaustion and defeat. In the case of Germany and her allies in 1918, defeat and exhaustion, and resultant collapse, was in no small measure the product of the failure of the spring 1918 offensive, which had been represented as guarantor of victory. The realization of the emptiness of this promise was crucially important in terms of the breaking of morale as the tide of war turned against the Central Powers and their peoples were faced with the very real prospect of Disease and Famine, the first and third of the four horsemen, stalking their streets in the coming winter.

The points of real significance in terms of the nature and conduct of war in this period are three-fold. The first, and most immediate point of interest, is the juxtaposition that stems from the fact that in the two decades after the war of 1870–1871, the general peace of Europe was secured in large measure by an imbalance of power within Europe, by a German military superiority relative to all the other great powers, and instability within Europe returned when there was a return to balance between two opposing alliances, that is, the balance of power did not ensure peace. The second relates to the state and to the fact that the state was transformed in the course of the First World War. The rise of the state in terms of the growth of state power was directly related to the demands of total war to the extent that the state of 1914 had more in common with the state of 1815 than the state of 1918. The First World War brought about a transformation of the state in terms of the strengthening of its bureaucratic institutions and its intrusion into the lives and welfare of its citizens in three very separate areas of activity—in terms of the control, direction, and management of the economy, the provision of welfare systems in terms of public health, and the adoption of democratic substance in the form of embracing the aims and objectives with which society as a whole could identify.[4] After the retrenchment of the inter-war period—except in the dictatorships that were established in this period—the Second World War repeated the process. The role of the state in the Second World War followed the pattern established in the previous conflict, and with two results that are easily missed. For all the many imperfections of their systems, Britain and the United States proved much more efficient in the mobilization of resources than totalitarian Germany, Italy, and Japan. Indeed the latter was so incoherent in the formulation of policy and priorities that she did something that was seemingly impossible, which was to have made the Confederacy seem a model of rationality and good organization in comparison.

The third point relates to the factors that made for tactical deadlock on the Western Front, and here there are problems in terms of historical representation, for one reason. The relationship between the organization of society in order to wage war and its willingness to do so is subtle and often missed: if nothing else, it explains the indecisiveness of the Western Front in the First World War. The very words "First World War" and "The Western Front" are virtually synonymous, and automatically one thinks of trenches and the phenomenon identified as trench-lock as identical with both. Yet if one asks the question why was there deadlock on the Western Front, specifically between November 1914 and March 1918, one encounters immediate problems of interpretation and context.

The problem of interpretation is obvious: several generations of historians and military commentators have provided the answer and, unfortunately, it is the wrong answer. There is no single answer because what is termed trench-lock was not the product of any one cause but the result of the coming together of a number of factors. Two of these, whether singularly or in combination, always form the first line of alleged explanation: the superiority of defensive firepower over offensive firepower and the superiority of strategic mobility over tactical movement. Clearly, both were important. There is no disputing that offensive firepower could not neutralize a defense and any breach in the front could always be sealed by a defense that was able to move formations by rail to the threatened sector more quickly than an attacker could move by foot and hoof across the battlefield in the attempt to maintain any breach that was opened. One more matter is often cited as complementary to these two: the lack of the systems that in the Second World War were to unlock fronts. These individual systems are usually identified as the tank and aircraft, the point being that during the First World War their very limited capabilities precluded their use as the means of breakthrough. In reality, this raises the wider issue of context because the assumption that these were the means of breakthrough is contentious and the fact is that these, in terms of their absence or very limited offensive capabilities, do not explain why there was deadlock in the first place.

The second line of argument usually paraded as explanation of trench-lock is the obvious one: that terrain worked against the attack, that surprise was difficult to achieve, and the historic means of ensuring mobility, the use of an open flank, was not available. And to these can be added another. Given the rapid degradation of formations committed to offensive operations, any attack invariably reached its culminating point very quickly, as demonstrated by the returns registered in the British offensive at Amiens in August 1918. On the first day, with 456 tanks, the offensive recorded gains of seven miles; on the second day, with 145 tanks, gains of three miles; and on the third day, with 67 tanks, gains of one mile, at which point the offensive was abandoned. All these facts of life, and others, were at work and contributed to the tactical impasse of the First World War. It was very difficult to register surprise, and no enemy position could be outflanked. The Germans had the pick of the ground after November 1914, and therefore Allied armies, committed to the offensive because the war was being fought on Belgian and French soil, were faced with major difficulty, and one that worsened over time because the defense added to its power in terms of depth and firepower with every year. A rudimentary trench system in 1914 evolved by 1917 into a defensive system with three main lines of resistance, sited on reverse slopes wherever possible, and with the forward positions held lightly. The German defensive systems on the Western Front between 1914 and 1917 successively involved "a tier a year" and evolved a step ahead of the attack, at least until November 1917 at Cambrai. In this evolution, the defense acquired a depth that ensured that it could not be broken in a single offensive operation. To put the matter in reverse, successive Allied offensives were conducted a year behind requirement. With each successive year, there were tactical innovations—the hurricane bombardment in March 1915 at Neuve Chapelle, the creeping barrage in 1916 at Verdun, fire without registration in 1917 at Cambrai and, of course, novelty presented itself in the form of the introduction of the tank on the Somme in September 1916 and its first massed employment, with conspicuous lack of success, in April 1917 at Bullecourt. In addition, there was the first use of fire and mobility tactics on the part of the infantry in 1916. But, in effect, what was attempted in 1915 was what would have been needed in 1914 to overcome a defensive position, and this phenomenon repeated itself with every passing year, at least until March 1918, and therein was the irony. The German offensive that was unleashed in 1918 was again a year behind reality, not so much because of tactical consider-ations but because of the strategic reality Germany had created by herself by bringing the United States into the war against herself in April 1917.

Herein one begins to get to the real reasons for trench-lock on the West-ern Front: the identification of a mental rather than material problem at the heart of indecision. The offense, burdened as it was by problems that did not encumber the defense, could not match the latter in terms of the rate of learn-ing, at least not until the *Kaiserschlacht* of March 1918. The inauguration of new infantry and artillery techniques under the terms of the *Der Angriff im Stellungskrieg* 1918 field manual provided German armies with a means of un-locking the Allied front but did not address the problem of strategic mobil-ity, and for all its tactical success proved ruinously expensive. But leaving aside the detail of the German spring offensive, even the basic point—the faster rate of learning of the German defense compared to the Allied offense—begs one obvious question of how to overcome a defense that was too big to be defeated. At the heart of the indecisiveness of the Western Front in the First World War are two realities, and the first, simply stated, was that armies had become so large and possessed such powers of recuperation that they could not be defeated in the course of a single battle or campaign. The fact was that, militarily, deadlock in the First World War was the result of a decisive vic-tory being beyond any power because all armies were too strong to be over-whelmed in a single attack. And herein lies the second part of the reason for the deadlock of the Western Front, in terms of mental attitude and the prob-lems inherent in the conduct of operations, for the most part high commands were committed to the idea of the *Vernichtungsschlacht*, the integral and deci-sive battle of annihilation, which was incapable of realization.

In one very obvious sense, the inability to break the deadlock of the West-ern Front between November 1914 and March 1918 stemmed from a basic failure of understanding on the part of the high commands in terms of the nature of war and the nature of a campaign, specifically the latter with respect to the confusion of a campaign with a single battle. An investment of belief in "the decisive battle" served to obscure the reality that only a campaign that em-braced simultaneous and successive efforts offered any chance of victory. In a sense, that has proved elusive but historians have listed without realizing the significance of events, if there was to have been a way in which the deadlock of the Western Front was to be broken then it was to be by a series of lim-ited offensives. This was precisely what the French military envisaged in the inter-war period with its concept of the Methodical Battlefield, the seeking of victory though a series of successful set-piece battles fought on the basis of overwhelming local superiority of *matériel*, the individual efforts being short in duration and synchronized with one another, and, critically, conducted across the width of the enemy front. Herein is a point often overlooked in examinations of the German and Allied offensives of 1918 that have concentrated upon tactical matters and the detail of operations. The German military's failure in the *Kaiserschlacht* was in part the result of its attacks being conducted across little more than one-third of the immediate theater of operations and against one-sixth of the total number of Allied divisions on the Western Front. With no fewer than 61 of the 175 Allied divisions available in March 1918 held in reserve, the element of shock and paralysis that the Germans needed to induce across the Allied entirety in order to have any chance of registering strategic success could never be secured. The German attack was too narrowly concentrated to tie down the mass of Allied forces with the result that Allied forces could be redeployed to effect. The success that attended the Allied offensives in and after July 1918 was in no small part the result of their being staged across virtually the whole of the active part of the Western Front. The Allied offensives did not register success on the scale of the *Kaiserschlacht* but their greater significance lay in their relationship to one another in terms of timing and their being conducted across the entire theater of operations.

The *Kaiserschlacht* in effect anticipated the concept of the Methodical Battlefield but for two very significant differences: scope and the balance of forces. The German offensive of spring 1918 sought strategic victory as a result of a series of successive tactical successes in the course of a single campaign. But leaving aside the thorny question of whether this was a reasonable conceptual expectation—which probably it was not because it seems unlikely that decisive success could have been secured in the course of a single campaign—the point of weakness within this intention lay in the fact that this offensive was conducted at a time when there was a rough balance of forces on the Western Front, and one that tipped against the Germans in the course of their offensive because of the appearance of increasing numbers of American divisions on the battlefield. The Allied conduct of operations in the second half of 1918 conformed to the Methodical Battlefield idea, but the success that the Allies commanded at that stage probably had less to do with this concept of operations than to a series of other considerations, specifically German exhaustion as a result of the *Kaiserschlacht*, which were added to the scales at this time. If the majority of military historians and commentators identify such factors as the imbalance of firepower and mobility, the problems of ground, lack of surprise, and the absence of an open flank as the cause of tactical deadlock on the Western Front during the First World War, these other factors seldom command much attention. The changing nature of the defense, specifically the increased depth of defense in these years, is often acknowledged, but the capacity of warring states to wage war by generating resources of unprecedented scale is very seldom defined in such terms. Refuge is taken in the notion that wars between great industrialized powers are necessarily protracted and attritional and hence, in this conflict, could not produce decisive campaigns or battles. But the problem with any and all of these explanations of deadlock on the Western Front is that they are not explanations. Singularly and together they describe the battlefield rather than explain the indecisiveness of battle.

If one wishes to understand deadlock on the Western Front after November 1914, one needs to look beyond the conventional wisdom provided by most historians and commentators, and perhaps the best explanation is provided in the famous and often-quoted passage from *Tender Is The Night*, by F. Scott Fitzgerald. The explanation of deadlock is provided in a conversation between American tourists looking over the Somme battlefield in the 1920s:

"This land here cost twenty lives a foot that summer. . . . See that little stream—we could walk to it in two minutes. It took the British a month to walk to it—a whole empire walking very slowly, dying in front and pushing forward behind. And another empire walked very slowly backward a few inches a day, leaving the dead like a million bloody rugs. No Europeans will ever do that again in this generation. . . . This western-front business couldn't be done again, not for a long time. The young men think they could do it but they couldn't. They could fight the first Marne again but not this. This took religion and years of plenty and tremendous sureties and the exact relationship that existed between the classes. The Russians and Italians weren't any good on this front. You had to have a whole-souled sentimental equipment going back farther than you could remember. You had to remember Christmas, and post cards of the Crown Prince and his fiancée, and little cafes in Valance and beer gardens in *Unter den Linden*, and weddings at the *mairie*, and going to the Derby, and your grandfather's whiskers."
    "General Grant invented this kind of battle at Petersburg in 65."
    "No, he didn't—he just invented massed butchery. This kind of battle was invented by Lewis Carroll and Jules Verne and whoever wrote *Undine*,[5] and country deacons bowling and *marraines* in Marseilles and girls seduced in the back lanes of Württemberg and Westphalia. Why, this was a love-battle—there was a century of middle-class love spent here. This was the last great love battle."
    "You want to hand over this battle to D. H. Lawrence. . . ."
    "All my beautiful lovely safe world blew itself up here with a great gust of high-explosive love."

In less than half of one page, Fitzgerald noted one matter so easily missed in most histories of the First World War. Deadlock in the First World War was not the result of imbalances of firepower and movement, size of armies, conditions of ground, or technical factors affecting the conduct of operations. Deadlock was nothing to do with either the capacity of the powers to wage total war or even possession of the means to do so. It was about the willingness of states and their societies to wage total war, their willingness to continue to prosecute war despite the indecisiveness of battle, their hardening determination to fight to a finish in justification of the losses that had been incurred already, that explains the phenomenon of trench-lock. It was the willingness of societies to fight on, despite and because of the elusiveness of success on the battlefield—a social cohesion and a failure, and perhaps inability, of societies to collapse under the strain of total war that by rights should have destroyed them—that explains deadlock on the Western Front during the First World War. Trench deadlock was a military phenomenon, but primarily it was a military reflection of a political and mental phenomenon that was itself the product of decades of change and hardening social attitudes, a state ethic bound up with nationalism that precluded acceptance of failure and defeat and that ensured fighting to exhaustion and beyond.

POSTSCRIPT

And if one wants to begin to understand first 1917 and then why there was no search for peace, why this war was fought to the finish with no attempt to seek compromise, then two pieces of literature provide the basis of understanding. The journey across a wasteland in 1917 is perhaps best understandable, in terms of description rather than explanation, when referring to *Childe Roland to the Dark Tower came*, written in 1855 by Robert Browning (1812–1889).

Explanation of the driving force that made for the prosecution of war to its bitter end is perhaps best provided in the last three lines of the third verse of John McCrae (1872–1918), which are the most terrible lines in the whole of English literature:

In Flanders fields the poppies blow
Between the crosses, row on row,
That mark our place; and in the sky
The larks, still bravely singing, fly
Scarce heard amid the guns below.
We are the Dead. Short days ago
We lived, felt dawn, saw sunset glow,
Loved and were loved, and now we lie
In Flanders fields.
Take up our quarrel with the foe:
To you from failing hands we throw
The torch; be yours to hold it high.
If ye break faith with us who die
We shall not sleep, though poppies grow
In Flanders fields.

The open-ended permanent commitment to total war in order to avenge the dead: utter madness, but for want of an alternative.

CHAPTER 2

From Total War to Total War: 1931–1975

There is no doubting the accuracy of John Lukacs's observation that the two world wars form the mountain ranges that dominate the landscape of the 20th century, but one would add a rider too often forgotten. If indeed the two world wars are the mountain ranges of the 20th century, then they were separated by low-lying ground and the Great Depression of the 1930s was as important in the unfolding of the 20th century as the two world wars, most obviously in terms of the discrediting of political liberalism throughout most of Europe during the 1930s and its disastrous impact upon the economies of the colonial empires.

But these matters aside, the basic point remains, and misleadingly so. We as societies look to the two world wars, and specifically the Second World War, as the yardsticks against which other conflicts are measured. This is perhaps right in one sense and, in any case, is natural enough and inevitable. The Second World War was the greatest single event of the century and its effects were so great that it is probably impossible to escape its embrace. But that the two world wars should serve as the yardsticks against which other wars should be measured is exactly the wrong way to consider these conflicts. The more relevant way of considering the two world wars is to start from the premise that these wars were so very different in so many ways from wars that came before and since that they should be regarded as exceptions and discounted from consideration as the basis of comparison other than with and against each other.

One would suggest that there are a number of problems relating to the Second World War that render definition and analysis difficult. The first can be stated very simply, and that is conflicting national claims on credit for victory that have been compounded over time by constant and repetitive rendition on the part of film and television. One would give but three examples of this: the Soviet Union's claim that her entry into the war brought about Japan's surrender within a matter of days after nearly four years of American effort—or more accurately fumbling—in the western Pacific; the British claim on special importance not least in the Mediterranean theater where the British (and later Anglo-American) efforts in North Africa cost the German military some 14 dead a day between February 1941 and May 1943, at which rate of loss it would have taken the British some 587 years to have inflicted the military losses incurred by Germany in the Second World War;[1] and the U.S. claims on what amounts to a monopoly of credit for Germany's defeat. Looking through various websites recently, one came across *The Hundred Greatest Americans* and there was *Eisenhower: The Man Who Won World War II*. The very title is ludicrous and grossly insulting on any number of counts. Individuals do not win wars, and most certainly the Second World War was not won by an American individual or even the United States. It was a war won by the United Nations, and, in terms of the European war, the single most important contribution to victory was that of the Soviet Union just as the single most important national contribution to victory over Japan was that of the United States.

Lest this last point be disputed, two sets of figures are very revealing in terms of cost and contribution. In the course of the campaign in northwest Europe between June 1944 and May 1945, the western Allies killed some 128,000 German military personnel, which was about the size of an American or British corps and which, against a total of 5,500,000 military and civilian dead, represented 2.33 percent of all German dead and approximately 3.66 percent of all German military dead in the Second World War. Even allowing for the fact that there were massed surrenders, most obviously in the war's last days, such a toll represents a very modest contribution to victory and not its cause. In terms of Allied losses, the United States lost fewer dead, to all causes, than the Soviet Union lost second lieutenants, and of every 100 Soviet males born in 1923 and alive on 21 June 1941 just three were alive on 12 May 1945. Between these two dates, the Soviet Union lost an average of 19,014 dead a day, every day, for 1,420 days of her Great Patriotic War. Put another way, the Americans lost 2,335 military and 68 civilian dead at Pearl Harbor, which represents 182 minutes of Soviet military and civilian dead. At Tarawa, where the U.S. casualties are always represented in sobering terms, the total of 1,001 American dead represents 76 minutes of Soviet losses.

The second problem relating to this conflict that renders definition and analysis difficult is the definition itself. We consider the Second World War in very narrow terms and an occidental, or more specifically an European, perspective bestows upon it very precise dates: September 1939 and May 1945. But the Japanese official histories of the Second World War begin with September 1931 and the conquest of Manchuria. Even if one is inclined to regard July 1937 as a more reasonable start-line, one would not deny that the China Incident was nurtured in Manchuria and Jehol and the link between the two

Japanese military efforts on the Asian mainland in the period 1931–1941 and, between these efforts and the outbreak of the Pacific, war can neither be dissolved nor contradicted. In terms of significance, scale, and continuity, the claims of July 1937, certainly the claims of September 1931 less so, are possessed of a certain credibility in terms of their constituting the outbreak of the Second World War, though the obvious caveat has to be entered: either date presents very real problems in terms of explanation with reference to the Abyssinian War and the Spanish civil war. But no less important is the question of when the war ended. The surrender of the various Axis countries was complete in September 1945 but a state of war can only be ended by treaty. Officially, the German war ended in October 1955 with the last of various formal declarations by the great powers that proclaimed the end of hostilities between Germany and her enemies, notwithstanding the failure to conclude peace treaties between once-warring powers; and, with these declarations, normal diplomatic and trading relationships could be forged anew. Treaties with the other Axis countries—with Bulgaria, Finland, Hungary, Italy, and Romania—had been concluded in the various treaties of Paris of February 10, 1947 and with Japan in the Treaty of San Francisco on September 8, 1951, though India and the Soviet Union were not parties to the latter.

Such matters are straightforward, but it can be argued that the Second World War was no such thing but was two quite separate conflicts, linked across time but barely across distance, and that in reality were only two of a series of conflicts that between them resulted in the reconstitution of the international order. What we understand to be the Second World War was in reality the most destructive single part of a series of struggles that were decades in their unfolding and that together resulted in the destruction of a Euro-centric world, which, often forgotten, very largely survived the First World War. One can date the end of this process with reasonable facility. 1975 commends itself as the year when the events set in motion in eastern Asia by the Manchurian Incident can be said to have resolved themselves, at least for the moment, with the fall of Saigon, the immediate point being that the crisis that led to war in the Pacific in December 1941 was set in motion by the Japanese occupation of southern Indo-China. But 1975 was the year that also saw the end of the Portuguese empire in Africa, and with it what amounted to the end of the empire. For the first time in history, almost every part of the earth was under the jurisdiction of some form of indigenous, sovereign authority. The diffusion of power has been perhaps one of the most significant developments of the 20th century, and the Second World War played no small part in this process. It may be, therefore, that, rather than consider this conflict by its 1939–1945 conventional time frame, we should consider events in terms of a series of wars waged between 1931 and 1975 that formed the link between very different international orders.

But the Second World War, as we understand that term, demands examination on a number of counts relating to its nature and its conduct, and also in terms of what Thucydides termed the sinews of war. In terms of its nature, perhaps its most striking feature was the fact that the Westphalian system, with the state so molded as to prevent recourse to total war, was wholly set aside, and it is perhaps worth noting that after 1945 there were two very separate developments that were both set in place in an attempt to create an order that would again seek to prevent repetition. The United Nations was established in part to prevent war while in Europe the integration of national economies was in large measure put in place with the intention of ensuring that the states of western Europe could never again go to war with one another. By any standard, the evidence provided by the Second World War indicated the pressing need for such measures because, in terms of the nature of war, expressed in terms of the deliberate slaughter of captive populations, whether in Europe or in eastern and southeast Asia, the Second World War played host to scenes that previously had been assigned to the rubbish bin of history. The Soviet Union lost, in addition to the 9,000,000 soldiers killed on the battlefield or died of wounds, 6,000,000 soldiers who died in German captivity and about 12,000,000 civilians who perished from all causes; the population of Belorussia fell from 8,000,000 in 1940 to just 2,000,000 by war's end, and the greater part of these losses was inflicted not by death squads but by the German Army. Poland, with its very large Jewish population, lost about 5,400,000 of whom about one in three were non-Jewish and all but 120,000 of these deaths came after her surrender in October 1939. Yugoslavia incurred a toll of about 1,700,000 dead in her various struggles against foreign occupation and her civil wars. About 13,500,000 Chinese soldiers and civilians died between 1931 and 1945, some 2,700,000 during the course of the Japanese offensives in central and southern China in 1944. Germany and Japan lost about 5,500,000 and 2,700,000, respectively, the German total including some 2,000,000 civilians of whom about 600,000 were killed by Allied bombing and about 300,000 as a result of Nazi *Volksgemeinschaft* measures. Japan lost about 600,000 civilians, mostly as a result of the American bombing of her cities during and after March 1945.

The Allies incurred about four in five of the total dead of the Second World War, and with perhaps 63,000,000 dead from all causes—of which total perhaps two-thirds were civilian[2]—this conflict really did represent a return to darker periods of human existence, but, in certain aspects of the conduct of operations, this conflict most definitely provided matters that were new. The most obvious, of course, related to the way in which the Japanese war ended with the use of atomic weapons against two cities in August 1945, but this single episode has served to detract from what was, admittedly, both new and a failure, namely the deliberate attempt to win victory through the deliberate, sustained assault from the air on the enemy homeland. The obvious question, which provoked bitter argument in the two decades after the end of the war, was what the strategic bombing offensive achieved. Extreme positions can be discounted, but, in seeking to attempt to answer this question, one is confronted by one very awkward fact of life. It is a well known fact that German war production reached its peak in August–September 1944. What is less well known is that the peak of German distribution of war material was in October 1943. Given the fact that it was in October 1943 that American heavy bombers met defeat over Schweinfurt and R.A.F. Bomber Command had registered precious little real damage by that time, it is clear that the German distribution system was in decline even before the strategic bombing campaign began in earnest and began to inflict telling, accumulative damage on the German industrial, transportation, and social infrastructures. Much the same was true of the campaign against the Japanese home islands. The American strategic bombing campaign began in June 1944 from airfields in southern China but it was not until November 1944 that it started on any significant scale and until March 1945 it was singularly ineffective. It was only after March 1945, when B-29 Superfortresses began to become available in significant numbers and the Americans adopted low-level area bombing, that this effort began to register significant results. Yet for the most part, this effort was directed against factories already in end-run production because of a virtual halting of imports and thus was directed against surplus industrial capacity.

Moreover, the one alternative to an offensive designed to destroy the enemy's capacity to make war—the enemy's willingness to make war—also obstinately fails to provide evidence of the effectiveness of the strategic bombing offensive. Neither Germany nor Japan showed any inclination to consider ending the war because of bombing and in neither country was there any real sign of a collapse of civilian morale as a result of the Allied air offensive, though perhaps the wonder of this was not that it did not occur but that certain people had ever considered such collapse possible in the first place. The totality of war, the knowledge that the issue at stake was national survival, and the conformity imposed upon German and Japanese societies on account of their systems of government precluded the fragmentation of morale. Resistance increased in fanaticism as the war came to the German and Japanese homelands, though by the end of their respective wars, German and Japanese societies were resigned to defeat and arguably fought from habit rather than belief.

In an obvious sense, therefore, it is possible to portray the effect of the strategic bombing campaigns primarily in negative terms, more obviously in the case of Germany. German industry functioned at about 10–12 percent below theoretical production potential because of Allied bombing. The strategic bombing offensive also imposed additional costs on production, and most definitely it warped the pattern of German war production. The bombing campaign forced German concentration upon fighters at the expense of strike aircraft and upon anti-aircraft guns and communications equipment for the air defense of the homeland at the expense of vehicles, guns, and radios for the field formations. But in one other negative aspect the contribution of the strategic bomber offensive to Allied victory was immense, if impossible to quantify. The effect that this offensive had in stripping the fronts of fighter defense and ensuring that Allied armies operated under conditions of overwhelming air supremacy is widely acknowledged, but how long the war would have lasted and the cost that would have been exacted had there not been a bombing campaign that by 1945 had reduced Germany to a transportation wilderness are debatable. What is remarkable about the defeat of Germany is how quickly it was achieved once the initiative had been wrested from her grasp. In August 1943, the western Allies had yet to set foot on the continental mainland, and German forces were still in the eastern Ukraine and, in terms of longitude, remained east of Moscow. Germany retained under her control vast areas that had been conquered in a series of campaigns before these had become a war. In less than 21 months, the gains of years had been destroyed and Germany had been destroyed as a state. One wonders how long this process would have taken had the Allies not had air power that razed the German communications system.

The latter was to be crucial in what was perhaps the one dimension of military operations that truly represented something that was different. In the First World War, there was but one major Anglo-French amphibious undertaking, at the Dardanelles in the form of the landings of April and August 1915. On the German side, there was the Ösel operation of October 1917 and then a series of minor landings in the Black Sea in 1918 in the wake of Russia's collapse and departure from the war. The Ösel operation, like the bombing of Bulgarian forces in the Kosturino pass in September 1918, proved very successful but primarily because the efforts were directed against a beaten enemy that collapsed under the impact of direct assault. But these were very much exceptions. Just as the deadlock of trench warfare reflected the advantage of the defense relative to the assault, so strategic and tactical advantage lay with the defense drawing upon the resources of landmass relative to seaborne assault. Other than the Ösel operation, the only successful amphibious operations in the First World War were those mounted by the Russians in 1916 in the eastern Black Sea, behind successive Turkish front-line positions, where such conditions did not apply. But in the Second World War there were no fewer than four major landings operations on the European mainland by Allied forces that were able to establish themselves ashore and were able first to sustain themselves in the face of counter-attack and then to undertake successful offensive operations that resulted in major enemy defeat. Only in one of these four cases was an invading force subjected to major counter-attack that might have produced outright defeat but that did result in significant delay in the undertaking of major offensive operations. This was the Anglo-American landing at Anzio in January 1944 and, while the German counter-attack in the second half of February was held, it was not until May that there was a break-out from the beachhead, in part as a result of the offensive on the Gustav Line that the original landing had been partially intended to supplement and facilitate.

The landings in southern Italy in September 1943, in northwest France in June 1944, and in southern France two months later represented defeat of armies drawing upon the resources of a continent. In very large measure, defeat was the result of an inability to ensure the timely and orderly concentration of massed formations against a beachhead as a result of three matters.

First, initial defensive dispersal and strategic surprise in terms of when and where landings were effected meant that the land-based defense was always having to respond to events; second, the continuing commitment of the defense outside the beachhead in terms of lines of communications and on flanks where secondary landings might be conducted; and, third, the impact of air power. Only at Anzio did the Allies not possess major advantage in the air, and only in the Anzio campaign were the Allies unable to complete a devastation of enemy lines of communication that would have significantly slowed or prevented the gathering of enemy forces opposite the beachhead. It has been suggested that by the end of the summer 1944, by which time the greater part of France had been cleared of German forces, something like 97 percent of the French rail system had been destroyed, and this was one of two related matters that served to provide the Allied armies in Normandy with the basis of victory.

The second of these related matters was the mechanization of Anglo-American formations, and, of course, it was this aspect of military operations for which the Second World War is most obviously noted. The initial movement onto wheels, however, was motorization, and it was put in place by a German military as the means of avoiding the general mechanization of armies. It has been estimated that 85 percent of the *Wehrmacht* in 1944 was horse-drawn, and in the Second World War only the United States had the industrial base that could provide for the mechanization of armies as a whole rather than selected formations. *Blitzkrieg* was an attempt to avoid this problem, and undoubtedly the German failing in and after 1941 was the result of an inability to compete at the strategic and operational levels in large part because mechanization was too narrowly based and at the expense of the mass of the army. But without the industrial base that could provide a general mechanization that would have bestowed operational capability, the argument that it was a failure to recognize the importance of the operational concept *per se* would seem to have only limited relevance, even though this particular argument is undoubtedly correct. The success of *Blitzkrieg* from 1939 to 1942 was in very large measure the result of a German ability to bring overwhelming mass against a part of an inferior enemy force in relatively small theaters of operations. Its very success served to disguise the fact that no operational concept underpinned it, a fact that became increasingly obvious on the Eastern Front, in part because the size of the theater demanded an operational level of war, in part because of the fundamental German error of seeking victory in 1941 in the single decisive campaign or battle, and in part because the principle of tactical concentration could not produce operational victories.

In terms of explanation of events, the war in Europe invites comment on two matters. The first relates to the basis of German victory between 1939 and 1942, and in general terms this is normally represented in terms of German superiority of technique expressed to full effect in the *Blitzkrieg* concept. Leaving aside the fact that the German Army never produced a field manual with reference to a concept that was known within the German military not as *Blitzkrieg* but the *Schlacht ohne Morgen*, the real basis of German victory lay in the national ability to fight not a war but a succession of individual campaigns in every one of which Germany held major advantages in terms of possession of the strategic initiative, of geographical position (most obviously Poland in 1939 and Yugoslavia in 1941), of major military superiority over all her enemies separately considered, and, perhaps crucially, in the air. Only in 1940 in northwest Europe did Germany find herself opposed by four enemies that were the equal to her in terms of army formations and numbers, but in reality this translated into massive German advantage over individual enemies that had no common organization, plan of campaign, and, in the final analysis, strategic interest. But, and state this *sotto voce*, what provided the *Wehrmacht* with its cutting edge was not *Blitzkrieg* or any material or technical advantage but Nazism, specifically belief in the *Führer* and in racial superiority, and a sense of assured destiny—witness *The Future Belongs To Me* of *Cabaret* parentage. Arguably, and by the same token, the single most important factor in Germany's defeat was Nazism and its creed of racial superiority. There was nothing in Nazism that enabled Germany to consolidate her early victories because all that she could offer conquered peoples was slavery and death. A victorious Germany might conquer and hold down Europe, but she could not rally the continent to her support.

The second relates to the basis of mechanized success and effectiveness and usually this is identified in terms of the instantly recognizable, namely the aircraft and the tank, both of which "came of age" in this conflict. The problem of explanation with the identification of these two systems as providing the means of breakthrough is that a measure of motorization of at least part of the mass of armies was necessary to achieve the rupture of an enemy front, that is, the motorization of both infantry and artillery, but the critical development was not tanks, aircraft, or motor transport but the miniaturization of the radio, which made possible effective command and control at the point of contact. As always in such matters, it was the various bits coming together and then the knowledge of how they had to be used that was so important, and, in this respect, the previous point—the basis of German victory in terms of moral ascendancy and various points of detail—has to be considered alongside one other matter. The German military stole a priceless march on their enemies in the form of the seizure of Austria in March 1938 and Czechoslovakia in March 1939 and then, crucially, in the campaign against Poland in September–October 1939. This provided the German military with experience that set it apart from the French military. One cannot prove the point but one strongly suspects that had the German Army attempted in 1938 or 1939 what it was able to put into effect in May–June 1940 then its offensive would have stalled, but it was the experience that was gained in Poland—in such matters as the elimination of the light armored division and the knowledge of how to handle armored formations—that set it apart from a French military that (again one suspects but cannot prove) was drained by successive failures, a gathering sense of impending defeat. One has to be very careful in such matters because the French Army fought hard in May 1940 but was out-thought and out-fought, but the comprehensiveness of the collapse in June 1940 does suggest a very obvious conclusion.

The Second World War left Europe in ruins from the Bay of Biscay to the Volga from the Baltic to Sicily and eastern Asia was similarly ruined; likewise the oceans were littered with wrecks. The mighty battles that were fought were the basis of those two uneasy bedfellows, historical analysis and national mythologies, but one would suggest that there is one date in the war that really does lend itself to the latter, and to the decisive battle or turning point so beloved by self-serving hacks. The date is 7–8 December 1941 which was the point in time when two wars became joined and when the United States entered into the obligations of great power status that she had evaded in and after 1919. The Japanese carrier air strike on the U.S. Pacific Fleet was the one episode that brought together the elements that made for global war, not least in setting in motion the transformation of the United States in terms of the metropolitan homeland. In 1941, the United States was an eastern seaboard power with a continental interior and in 1945 she was a continental power that could reach across the globe. She came of age in June 1944 when her forces entered Rome, landed in Normandy and at Saipan, fought and won the naval battle in the Marianas, and for the first time bombed targets in Japan from bases in China. It was in this month, and on 6 June of all days, that the number of American heavy bombers in Britain reached 2,000, and it was in this month that the last lingering hopes of Germany and Japan that somehow they might escape total defeat were extinguished. It was a month that represented the flood tide of American success and it unfolded at the same time as the Soviet military put together the *Bagration* offensive, the first of three major undertakings that by September–October had resulted in the clearing of German forces from most of Soviet territory and that had carried the tide of war through the Balkans and central Poland, forcing Romania and Bulgaria—and Finland—from enemy ranks and taking Soviet formations to the borders of Germany and Hungary. June 1944, clearly, was one of those moments "when the world turned," but looking outside such terms of reference one wonders if perhaps the most significant single event in the war was very different: 14 August 1941. Just as one would suggest that for Britain, in terms of her 20th-century history, the Beveridge report of December 1942 was at least as important as Alamein, so the Atlantic Charter, with its promise of a United Nations, possessed massive significance not least in terms of the implication of the end of empire and the freedom of peoples who were imperial subjects, not citizens, and of territories acquired at a time of a European pre-eminence that was no more.

The Second World War produced the crisis of empire. This took different forms in different colonies. The most serious manifestations arose from those colonies and holdings that were subjected to foreign conquest; for the British, Dutch, and French their possessions in southeast Asia and, for France, in addition to Madagascar, what were to become Lebanon and Syria and throughout the Maghreb. Italy lost Eritrea and Abyssinia and then Libya, the British very temporarily their part of Somaliland. Quite obviously, the defeat of the imperial powers had obvious implications but the empires represented a mobilization and calling upon resources across the world that quite obviously demanded proper acknowledgement. In the case of India, what was to become India and Pakistan, the recognition of contribution came in the form of the promise of dominion status, that is, full independence, on March 29, 1942, but the odd point is that there was a general failure on the part of Britain and France to act on the logic of events. The French, admittedly, at the Libreville conference in January–February 1944 did hold out the promise of change, albeit undefined, for the empire and its peoples, but this was largely lost after 1945 and it was to take another series of wars, and for France one disastrous defeat, before the United Nations began to change fundamentally in nature and composition. From the late 1950s, it ceased to be in effect the means of ensuring the *status quo* and became the agency of change and national independence. On 26 June 1945 delegates from 48 independent states in the world signed the United Nations' Charter. In 50 years, the membership of the U.N. all but quadrupled.[3]

In the process of independence, armed struggle played its full part, specifically in the 15 years following the end of the Second World War, and in very large measure the script was to be provided as a result of the Second World War. The Soviet Union, when confronted by the situation of potential conflict and what became the confrontation known as the Cold War, deliberately sought to encourage revolution in what was to become known as the Third World for ideological reasons and as the means of weakening the Western world. This encouragement manifested itself at the Calcutta conference in February 1948 with the formula expounded by Andrei Zhdanov (1896–1948) at the inaugural Cominform conference in September 1947, but the real message was presented in the form of the Chinese civil war and the writings of Mao Tse-tung (1893–1976).

Mao Tse-tung wrote about revolutionary warfare at three distinct levels. To the mass of his following, Mao wrote a practical do-it-yourself guide, a Jominian checklist, governing party, military formation, and personal behavior, and in so doing he provided comment on the state of China in the inter-war period when she was the victim of a series of civil wars and Japanese aggression. His instruction to communist troops not to steal property and food and not to rape and murder was a comment on the normal behavior of soldiery in China at this time, and in so instructing his soldiers, Mao stated the basis of communist appeal: example and what was to distinguish the communists from their enemies. At a higher, intermediate level, Mao explained the stages of revolutionary warfare, starting with a phase of preparation in the lesser accessible areas, the prosecution of guerrilla warfare, and a final conventional campaign. This three-fold division of revolutionary warfare has often been defined as the kernel of Maoist warfare, but any careful consideration of Mao's more important writings would reveal that the basis of revolutionary struggle as set down by Mao Tse-tung and his associates lay in the subordination of the military aspects of war to ideological and political considerations, specifically the rendering of military effectiveness and resistance dependent upon the level of political commitment of the population. This, given the double situation—that of the communists within China and of China with respect to Japan—thus allowed an un-industrialized and primitive society, lacking modern arms and equipment, to adopt a militant political philosophy based on armed struggle. From this fundamental premise, Mao developed a military doctrine that would enable a poor country like China to adopt a political posture and form of resistance even when confronted with the militarily superior forces of a highly industrialized and technologically advanced enemy. In so doing, Mao Tse-tung set down time, space, and will as the basis of revolutionary war, and, through a dogged, unwavering adherence to principle and method, brought his party to victory in 1949 after 22 years of civil and foreign war.

The Maoist pattern of revolutionary warfare—the third level—was based on the countryside and popular support, and it sought to use time and space to overturn the advantages of technological sophistication. Time was, and remains, the equalizing factor between the rich and the poor, between the sophisticated and the backward. The extension of the state of war for as long as possible, the dragging out war to a point where it becomes politically and economically unacceptable to the enemy, was the basis for the communists' faith in ultimate victory no matter how long a war lasted. The prosecution of war over an extended area was no less important in that in a revolutionary war

its operation is according to the surface. The greater the surface and the greater the contact with the enemy's army the more that army will have to spread itself out and so much greater will be the effect of arming the people. Like a slow gradual heat it destroys the foundations of the enemy's army (because) a people's war possesses on a grand scale the peculiarity that the principle of resistance exists everywhere but is nowhere tangible.

The words may belong to Clausewitz[4] but the concept of war prosecuted over great distance in order to destroy the physical and moral resources of the enemy is Maoist, especially when the inter-dependence of time, space, and will as the determining factors in the conduct of revolutionary war was identified. Space brought time and time brought the opportunity to ensure popular endorsement because

without a political goal guerrilla warfare must fail, as it must if its political objectives do not coincide with the aspirations of the people and their sympathy, co-operation and assistance cannot be gained. . . . Because guerrilla warfare basically derives from the masses and is supported by them, it can neither exist nor flourish if it separates itself from their sympathies and co-operation. . . . The moment this war of resistance separates itself from the masses . . . is the precise moment it dissociates itself from hope of ultimate victory.

The three factors of time, space, and will, the essence of the Maoist concept of rural insurgency, whether singularly or together, provide the basis of examination of the major insurgency campaigns fought between 1945 and the mid-1960s. With the single exception of the Hukbalahap Rebellion in the Philippines between 1946 and 1954, China stands apart from all other campaigns in that it was wholly indigenous; the other campaigns that were fought in this period were directed against colonial authority. Moreover, in its final stages, the Chinese civil war was fought on a scale that eclipsed all other revolutionary wars, indeed all wars fought since 1945, but more importantly it can be argued that its outcome was decided before 1945 in that the end of the Second World War found the Nationalist regime at Chungking beyond salvation. Its endemic corruption, the lack of any radical program to address the country's many ills, its evident failure in the Japanese war, and its sheer incompetence had robbed it of credibility. Its performance over two decades had been proof of the old saying that there is no point in having power unless it is abused, and the Kuomintang had needed no instruction on that particular score. Such was the state of China in terms of the ravages inflicted upon her by the appalling combination of Kuomintang misrule and Japanese rapaciousness that the communists had been handed causes with which to build a basis of rural support without any major need for and reliance upon coercion and intimidation; the terror was to come after victory.

The Maoist concept of revolutionary warfare invited imitation, and did so even before it was brought to realization. Throughout southeast Asia, the legacy of defeat—of the European powers between 1941 and 1945 and of Japan in 1945—was the emergence of forces of national independence with which the returning Allied powers had to contend. Three major campaigns were to be fought in this area between 1945 and 1960, and if three colonial empires disappeared in the process, the course and outcome of these campaigns differed greatly. But the point was that by 1960, events elsewhere had unfolded to an end that foreshadowed the end of empire. The "Wind of Change" speech of British prime minister Harold Macmillan (1894–1986) on 3 February 1960 in Cape Town,[5] the Belgian ceding of independence to the Congo in June 1960, and the first reference by President Charles de Gaulle (1890–1970) to *Algerie Algerienne* in November 1960 foreshadowed the end of the British and French empires in Africa, and, for the most part, without further war. With reference to the latter, the situation was to be very different elsewhere, most obviously in southeast Asia where the collapse of American resolve and the South Vietnamese state and military manifested themselves in the communist victory and capture of Saigon on 30 April 1975 while with respect to Portugal's wars the army *coup* of 25 April 1974 in Lisbon that brought down the Caetano dictatorship[6] resulted in the ceding of independence to Guinea-Bissau on 10 September 1974, to Mozambique on 25 June 1975, to the Cape Verde islands on 5 July 1975 and to Angola on 11 November 1975. The *coup* itself was remarkable in terms of the military overthrowing a right-wing dictatorship that had been in place since 1932 and, after some hesitations, installing a democratic system in its place. It was no less remarkable in terms of immediate cause, namely the military's opposition to the state's involvement in wars that it, the military, believed could not be won and had to be ended; the *coup* of April 1974 in effect was recognition of defeat. Thus the Portuguese military set in motion a series of events that ensured the end of an empire, an empire that had been the first of the extra-European empires and that was in real terms the last of these empires, and, in relinquishing its overseas holdings, Portugal marked the point in time when war for empire was at an end and thus ensured the introduction of something that was different. In the future, after 11 November 1975, every war would be fought on the home soil of an indigenous sovereign state with all that that implied in terms of legitimacy and right, compromise and moderation.[7]

CHAPTER 3

When Real Hatreds Were Suspended: The Cold War, 1945–1989

The war that ended in central Germany in May 1945 is a pertinent example of the truism that wars may change problems or may transpose problems but wars never solve problems. Britain and France went to war in September 1939 in order to honor their guarantee to Poland and, in a very obvious if paradoxical sense, to ensure the peace of Europe. By spring 1945, there was nothing that either or both countries could do to help a Poland that deemed herself the Christ-nation of Europe, destined to be crucified between two thieves, while the Soviet Union had assumed the role hitherto fulfilled by Germany with reference to the balance of power within Europe and the security of those states that were not under her immediate control or influence. Conversely, for the Soviet Union, the overwhelming need for some means of security, as represented by the holding of part of Germany as a guarantee against a future, resurgent Germany bent upon *revanche*, and maintaining the countries of Eastern Europe as a defensive barrier, was set at naught by the manner in which the war ended. The insecurity that had been revealed by the invasion of 1941 had been replaced by another sense of insecurity identifiable in terms of the B-29 Superfortress, American bases and presence in east and southeast Asia and western Europe, and the atomic bomb.

It is possible to explain the Cold War in terms of great power interests that did not clash. It was because there were no areas of conflicting interest in summer 1945 that the Soviet Union and the United States were not able to agree other than on one issue, the need for Soviet entry into the Japanese war, which, at this time, American planning staffs believed would last into 1946 and which would involve major landing operations and campaigns on the Japanese home islands. In such an eventuality, a Soviet involvement in the war, and three months after the end of the European war, was essential to the United States, but a change of president and the national entry into an atomic birthright very suddenly did away with the need for Soviet participation. Together these matters formed the first paving stone on the path that led to confrontation and competition that were to go under the name of the Cold War, a term first used by the presidential adviser Bernard Baruch (1870–1965) in a speech in Columbia, South Carolina, on 16 April 1947. By that time, what was perhaps the most important single statement of options and a course of action—the (in)famous (5,363-word) Long Telegram of 22 February 1946 on the part of George Kennan (1904–2005)—was in place and, along with the article "Sources of Soviet conduct," which was published in *Foreign Affairs* in July 1947, was to lead directly to the process whereby the United States acted on the fact that there was, for western Europeans, no substitute for American power. The Anglo-French treaty of guarantee, concluded of all places at Dunkirk on 4 March 1947, came at the time when Britain, forced by U.S. pressure to float the pound with disastrous consequences, was obliged to end her financial support for Greece and Turkey, with the United States picking up the tab in the form of the enunciation of the Truman Doctrine on 12 March and the Marshall Plan on 5 June. The realization that after years of war and devastation there could be no speedy recovery of Europe without massive American financial help was behind the Marshall Aid program put into place in July 1947 though, very oddly, in the event, this four-year program gave rise to an American financial commitment of some $13 billion and this after the United States had provided aid and financial support to the value of $9 billion over the previous two years. It could be argued, therefore, that Marshall Aid was the means of lessening the American financial commitment to western Europe but, of course, what happened was a hand-to-mouth existence that was replaced by a defined and agreed program, with one immediate result. Marshall Aid saw the creation of the Organisation of Economic Co-operation and Development on the part of the European states for the purposes of administering the American program, which, along with the removal of tariffs between states, was to provide the first step in the process that was to lead to formation of the European Coal and Steel Community by the Treaty of Paris of 18 April 1951, the European Economic Union by the Treaty of Rome of 25 March 1957 and the European Union by the Maastricht Treaty of 7 February 1992.

In no small measure, the rationale for the Marshall Plan was a program that might undermine communist standing throughout western Europe and set in place arrangements that might bring an end to the somewhat chaotic state of affairs in Germany, but inevitably the economic program could not be divorced from one inescapable military reality: the western European states simply could not provide for their own defense. The Dunkirk Treaty led to negotiations between Britain, France, and the three Benelux countries, but the five states that had been routed in 1940 could not provide for the defense of western Europe. However, their search for an alliance ran in tandem with two developments.[1] The first, in the immediate aftermath of the *coup* in Prague on February 27, 1948 that brought the communists to power, was the Soviet exit from the Allied Control Commission for Berlin (20 March 1948) and then, after the imposition of a series of checks in April, the start of the Berlin blockade on 24 June 1948.[2] The second was the major deterioration of the Kuomintang's position in the Chinese civil war. January 1947 saw the final failure of American attempts to mediate between the Kuomintang and the communists and the resumption of civil war throughout Manchuria and northern China. The Kuomintang was able to hold many of the major cities and towns in these areas but their garrisons were weak and increasingly isolated, and, in October 1947, the communists were able to move into the third phase of conventional operations throughout these areas. With Shensi secured by the communists in spring 1948, the summer saw the progressive reduction of Kuomintang positions north of the Yellow River with the communist field armies routing two Nationalist army groups on the Kaifeng-Suchow line between November 1948 and January 1949 in the Battle of the Hwai Hai. With the fall of Mukden and Peking at this same time in effect marking the end of the campaigns north of the Yangtze, the river crossed by communist armies in April, after which there was the progressive collapse of the Kuomintang position throughout the south with successive capitals falling in turn—Nanking in April, Canton in October, Chungking in November, and Chengtu in December. The latter marked the point when the Nationalists abandoned the mainland and established themselves on Formosa.

With the communists in North Korea proclaiming a communist republic in September 1948, the position of the United States, and specifically that of an administration subject to presidential election in November, was somewhat fraught, but, with the election fought and won, President Harry S. Truman (1884–1972) moved with reference to European security with the negotiations that resulted in the Washington treaty of 4 April 1949 that brought 12 states— Belgium, Britain, Canada, Denmark, France, Iceland, Italy, Luxembourg, the Netherlands, Norway, Portugal, and the United States—into the North Atlantic Treaty Organisation.[3] Two days later, Truman went on record with the statement that he would not hesitate to use atomic weapons again should the need arise.

By this stage, the United States was committed to what was, in effect, the Doctrine of Containment. Kennan had been the main influence in the emergence of this policy but by 1948 his influence was on the wane. He foresaw competition, not conflict, between the United States and Soviet Union, and it was a competition that he believed the United States, by virtue of its superior resources, would win. Ironically, Marxist logic pointed in the same direction, but Kennan, by 1948–1949, favored negotiation and the peaceful resolution of various disputes if that could be arranged, but there was by this time within the Truman administration an increasingly acerbic attitude toward a Soviet Union that, in ideological terms, stood on the brink of its greatest success, the victory of the communists in China.

The forward American attitude was heaven-sent for Europe. It was a case of the European band-aid put in place with the United States paying the premiums. But the basis of American action was to be undermined all but immediately because of one fundamental U.S. error: in developing the atomic bomb, the American high command forgot to take out the patent. President Truman could make the statement he did on the basis of American monopoly and invulnerability that was tied to the fact that the United States Air Force had been established as a separate service on 18 September 1947 and, in effect, was built around strategic capability. For the United States, strategic deterrence was possible by virtue of possession of airfields around the Soviet Union, proven capability, and, in the case of Truman, credibility. The Soviet Union tested its first atomic bomb on 29 August 1949.

Strategic deterrence was to work its way through many years and different forms but in its American form it was vested initially in the U.S. Air Force and the doctrine of Massive Retaliation. Very simply, any Soviet aggression would be met from the outset by the bombing of Soviet cities, the crucial European dimension being that the assured destruction of the Soviet homeland was the counter to Soviet conventional superiority on the inner-German border in central Europe. The policy was very simple and direct, but in the second half of the 1950s two matters served as a notice of change. The first was that the American lead to thermonuclear weapons (first tested on 1 November 1952 at Eniwetok) had been followed by the Soviets within a year—12 August 1953—but on 4 October 1957 the Soviet Union launched the first satellite,[4] and this pointed to Soviet capacity to build missiles capable of striking cities in the United States. If not immediately, then the end of American invulnerability was foreshadowed, and this capability was to be crucial in the new form of deterrent, the TRIAD. The potential vulnerability of airfields and missile bases pointed the American strategic deterrent in two directions: a massive increase in size so that even the most successful of Soviet pre-emptive strikes could never account for more than a part of American strategic capability, and a diversity of delivery. In 1956, the U.S. Navy undertook its first development of a missile system that could be embarked in nuclear-powered submarines, and on 30 December 1959 commissioned into service the first such submarine, the *George Washington*. In fact, she had been laid down as the hunter-killer *Scorpion* but while under construction was cut in two and had a 130-ft. missile launch section added, and on 20 July 1960 she conducted the first test-firing of Polaris missiles.

The crucial element in calculations was that, given the difficulty of detecting and destroying even individual submarines, a submarine force which in time was to number 41 units provided the basis of an assured second strike, that is, even the most successful of Soviet attacks would leave strategic forces, and particularly the submarine force, still with the capacity to destroy the Soviet homeland. The vesting of this assured second strike capability in the submarine force meant that the target of this assured second strike would have to be Soviet cities because submarine-based missiles did not have the minute accuracy of land-based counterparts, and it also meant something else in terms of the relative standing of services within the U.S. defense establishment. The basis of the American deterrent shifted from the Air Force, which in effect lost its primary role, to the Navy.[5]

The result was somewhat strange in a number of ways. Navies invariably do badly in times of peace; their cost make them expensive and the obvious first target when economies are made, and in any case armies perform a number of tasks—at the present time such duties as peace-keeping and peace-enforcement—that navies cannot share. After 1945, the economies that were forced upon the service meant that the U.S. Navy, which at war's end had 20 fleet, 8 light fleet, and 71 escort carriers in service,[6] was reduced to some 7 fleet carriers in service.[7] In the aftermath of the Korean War, which had demonstrated the value of carrier aircraft in support of forces ashore, the U.S. Navy was to experience two parallel developments: the return of carriers in numbers to service and the Navy itself becoming the crucial part of the American strategic nuclear deterrent. The result was a considerable rise in spending and the Navy, which in effect had been reduced to third place behind the Air Force and Army, coming forward to a position that was at least abreast of the other two services.

What also happened from the mid-1950s was a massive increase in the size of strategic arsenals. The assured second strike capability rested upon both dispersal—the three different means of delivery represented by land-based missiles, submarine-based missiles, and weapons launched from aircraft—and increased numbers of weapons, and this latter growth in the course of the 1960s assumed proportions that can only be described as grotesque. Depending on the source, the United States was to acquire between 9,960 and 10,600 nuclear weapons, the Soviet Union between 7,200 and 16,000, as the two sides added to their arsenals far beyond any reasoned limit. What was available to the two superpowers was enough to destroy the world many times over, and the fact was that the search for security was never going to be realized simply by adding to the number of such weapons.

The loss of American invulnerability had one immediate and major consequence: the doctrine of Massive Retaliation was discarded. It could be argued that it had been wholly unrealistic from the time it was put into place, and one example was always used to demonstrate its dubious relevance: a Soviet landing on the Danish island of Bornholm in the Baltic would be met by all-out nuclear attack while a full-scale Soviet offensive through the Fulda Gap would be similarly met with an all-out nuclear attack. The American deterrent most certainly rested on the threat of such attack and the resultant devastation of the Soviet heartland, but the basic lack of proportionality involved in such a comparison was obvious, and not surprisingly pointed the American military in the direction of appropriate response.

But in seeking to put into place a doctrine of Flexible Response, the United States encountered immediate problems. Massive Retaliation had been an absolute guarantee of the European states, and at one stroke this would be ended.

For many Europeans, the ending of Massive Retaliation implied American flexibility and no response, and the flexibility obviously turned West Germany specifically and western Europe generally into a battlefield on which the Americans would use tactical nuclear weapons to counter Soviet conventional superiority and breakthroughs. The end of Massive Retaliation pointed the European states in the direction of their providing manpower on a scale that had been avoided over the previous decade or so. German re-armament had been authorized in the mid-1950s to cover the most obvious deficit but the basic point had been that armies were there not so much to fight as to report Soviet attack in order to facilitate nuclear strikes on the Soviet Union. From the mid-1960s, and with the American military increasingly caught in the Vietnam mire, the European armies would have to fight and would have to try to cover for the Americans. In this situation, the British and French nuclear forces assumed tacit significance. The British and French acquisition of first atomic and then nuclear weapons was obviously related to great power status, but in the 1960s these deterrent forces, while directed militarily against the Soviet Union, came to be directed politically against the United States. They were the means of ensuring that if there was flexibility then there would be response, and they were the means of ensuring that the two superpowers could not do a deal at Europe's expense. In fact, the Americans made very considerable efforts to persuade the Europeans of the wisdom and desirability of Flexible Response. The basic idea, along with TRIAD, had been set in place in 1961 but it was not until December 1967 that the Johnson administration, tiring of European procrastination, basically rolled Flexible Response into place as N.A.T.O. policy; the Europeans had no option but to fall in line, France's *force de frappe* notwithstanding.

The impact of atomic and thermonuclear weapons was profound, indeed revolutionary, and in three respects. First, from the initial acquisition of these weapons, deterrence emerged as the alternative to defense. Deterrence had always been a part of war and the conduct of states in their dealings with one another; individual national services had long been regarded as serving a deterrence role as well as existing for defense of the state. But, after 1945, the existence of such power of destruction, beside entailing massive restraint upon use and even the threat of use, imposed upon military establishments double roles, deterrence and defense, that were largely separated from and in rivalry with one another. Second, such unprecedented power of destruction, the ability to destroy whole cities and societies, inevitably meant that the avoidance of war and use of these weapons assumed a critical significance that was more important than the waging and winning of wars, and in this process deterrence and defense diverged because the means of deterrence were not those of defense and the means of defense counted for little in terms of deterrence capability.

No less importantly and third, atomic and thermo-nuclear weapons and the emergence of deterrence as the primary objective of such states as the United

States and Soviet Union carried with it implications in terms of preparation and readiness that were unprecedented, or, as N.S.C. 20/1 of August 1948 stated

to consider more definite and militant objectives toward Russia even now, in time of peace, than it was ever called upon to formulate with respect either to Germany or Japan in advance of actual hostilities with those countries.

Deterrence policies could only work under conditions of permanent readiness. Certainly deterrence policies could only work if the interests that were to be protected were properly considered—with all the moral problems thus entailed—and defined, and the party that was to be deterred made aware of that fact and the penalties likely to be exacted for transgressions. But the real basis of deterrence lay in technical capability. For deterrence to be effective, available force had to be permanently at hand, and in this fact deterrence was to lead to what was novel and perhaps the ultimate absurdity: the existence of permanent standing alliances with strategic forces on a round-the-clock footing for the purposes of not making war, indeed ensuring that war did not occur. This was, by any standard, a somewhat strange state of affairs.

The development of atomic and thermonuclear weapons affected war and military establishments at three levels: deterrence made essential the pursuit of policies aimed at avoiding strategic confrontation and with it the danger of escalation; deterrence also made essential the definition of forms of warfare below the atomic-nuclear threshold; and there was a search for forms of warfare whereby the struggle between the superpowers and their respective alliance systems could be continued "by other means." In some ways, the last of these was perhaps the most important, and for two reasons. Atomic and nuclear weapons and the resultant strategic stalemate served to continue, indeed gave added impetus to, a trend already identified in terms of 19th-century development. This was to narrow and blur still further the distinction that had existed between war and peace because, in a very real sense, strategic deadlock and ideological hostility produced struggle as the permanent factor in the relationship of the superpowers. With no real basis for either an agreed reconciliation of differences or the military victory of one side or the other, the relationship between the two superpowers became one characterized by a permanent low-grade militarization that was all the more dangerous to both states and societies because of the implication that deterrence carried with it. Deterrence involved the primacy of science and the emergence of an intellectual aristocracy that were equally dangerous since deterrence, in the long term, involved the subordination of the decision-making process to technique because the logic of deterrence was self-generating. The need to sustain the deterrent involved the subordination of the political process to that purpose, witness the American decisions to proceed with MIRV in 1967 and the Trident decisions in 1971–1972. Even allowing for the fact that these decisions were taken by individuals and were not wholly mechanistic, in a very obvious sense nuclear weapons and deterrents were and remain profoundly undemocratic.

That may seem an absurd statement but it cannot be disputed. At the level of society and the individual, there is an acceptance of responsibility for the soldier. Servicemen, individually and collectively, and the weapons that either support them or are serviced by them, belong to society; these belong to *us*. But nuclear weapons, because of their awesomeness and the frightfulness of the prospect of their employment, belong to *them*. The reasons for such a state of affairs—the recognition of responsibility for the consequences of battle and the conventional battlefield but not the nuclear battlefield—are obvious. As individuals, we cannot conceive of our own deaths, and we cannot conceive of either the total annihilation of all societies or a society with no future, but both would be the inevitable consequence of nuclear exchange. Nuclear weapons inhibit us in terms of imagination. We cannot envisage something the size of a cricket ball or baseball, weighing about 22-lbs./10-kgs., killing perhaps 100,000 people in less time than it takes a heart to beat. Our incomprehension begins because we cannot imagine 100,000 deaths, and we certainly cannot imagine 100,000 individual deaths at one instance of time, and most certainly as individuals we cannot even begin to imagine—except, perhaps, for those who survived atomic attack in 1945—what failed deterrence would involve in terms not of hundreds of thousands being killed but hundred of millions of people slowly dying of radiation sickness. Such concepts are beyond us as individuals, a reflection of Einstein's comment that the splitting of the atom had changed everything except human modes of thinking. As General George L. Butler (1939–) put it, faced with such moral problems, to think about the unthinkable, to justify the unjustifiable, to rationalize the irrational, ultimately we contrived a new and desperate theology to ease our moral anguish, and we called it deterrence.[8] Very obviously, it is easier for us as individuals to pass up responsibility for decisions involving such weapons and policies, yet as individuals we thereby pass up the power of decision to those who would actively seek control over others.

But at the level of the state and society, the impact of deterrence was undemocratic in another sense, not simply because of the self-fulfilling nature of deterrence but because of the demands that it placed upon the state and the changes it wrought as a consequence. Deterrence, and with it a state strategy for survival, necessarily involved the orchestration of all aspects of social existence as part of the process whereby the superpowers came to confront one another, and this involved a fusion of the component parts of power as instruments of state policy in a manner and to an extent that was without precedence. The inevitable consequence of nuclear weapons and deterrents was the politicization of every aspect of social existence and every aspect of life formed part of this confrontation. Aid programs, educational and training schemes, preferential terms of trade, these and many other matters formed parts of the process whereby the superpowers bid against one another for the support and allegiance of others, and, while many examples of this process could be cited, perhaps the most obvious was sport, in which respect 1936 cast a long shadow. It was not mere chance that the Soviet bloc developed so formidable a sporting reputation and achievement that, at international competitions, East Germany took as many medals as the superpowers.[9] The sporting achievement of the Soviet bloc was part of a very deliberate policy. It was part of the process of projecting a virile, clean-cut, and benevolent image. Sport was the shore-based version of the Navy's showing the flag. Holding the Olympic Games in Moscow in 1980 was endorsement of the Soviet regime and its policies, an indication of approval and respectability in exactly the same way a cricket or rugby tour of South Africa was regarded as moral endorsement of its white-minority regime and policies.

This orchestration of aspects of government within a coherent national security strategy necessarily involved the growth of state power, the latter being inevitable given the commitment of the state to the social market and welfare programs after 1945. It was also part of the process of an ever-increasing concentration of power at the upper reaches of government, the general trend of improved communications in the course of the 20th century having been an ever-greater capacity of superior authority to control and supervise rather than the encouragement of decision-making at the lower and more relevant levels of administration. Critically, however, this orchestration of the various elements of state and social existence as part of national policy involved a profound alteration in the perception of mutual exclusion of the political and military in their respective areas of competence and authority. Of course, the two were never properly exclusive, but, with means of instant communications at their disposal, restraints upon the use of force, limits on even the threat of the use of force, and strict control of the extent and severity of force when used, the elements that become essential as part of the process of crisis management and the prevention of an escalation of a local conflict to a more general war could not but erode the professional exclusiveness of the military, though the latter was under threat from two other directions.

What is undoubtedly the defining moment in deterrents was the Cuban missile crisis of October 1962, and what is very curious is that the massive increase in the size of nuclear arsenals was accompanied by the first genuine attempts by the superpowers to bring order to their nuclear waltz. The installation of direct communication in the form of the Hot Line (30 August 1963) went alongside the negotiations that yielded the Partial Test-Ban Treaty (5 August 1963) that banned tests in the atmosphere, underwater, and in outer space, but these were followed by what was a very slow and hesitant process that resulted in the Non-Proliferation Treaty of 1 July 1968 (and effective 5 March 1970) that was first proposed on 17 August 1965, the Sea-Bed Treaty of 11 February 1971, and then, on 26 May 1972, the treaties that go under the name of SALT I (the Moscow Treaty) limited anti-ballistic missile systems and set limits on the numbers of strategic missiles that the superpowers could hold.[10] SALT II (the Vienna Treaty of 18 June 1979) took the process of strategic arms limitation one step further,[11] but it was not until 31 July 1991, after nine years of very difficult negotiations and with the Cold War assigned to history,[12] that the Kremlin treaty initiated strategic arms reduction (START I).[13] Thereafter, the real problem that beset the nuclear situation was seeking to ensure that, in the aftermath of the disintegration of the Soviet Union, the Russian successor state was able to take control of weapons that had been left in breakaway states and also that non-proliferation provision remained in place.

The process of negotiation necessarily saw Britain and France pass from great powers status and the Soviet Union and the United States assume the status of superpowers—a term not in use until the 1960s—in order that they be distinguished from every other power. It is very doubtful if the Soviet Union properly entered into such status and if she did so then it was briefly, in the form of intervention in the Ogaden War of 1977–1978, before Afghanistan and domestic problems combined to rob her of any global reach she had previously enjoyed. In any event, the 1970s, so frequently written off in the United States as shameful with Vietnam, the Carter presidency, and *détente*, saw a genuine balance between the superpowers, and most certainly it is a period that demands very careful assessment not least because the Carter administration faced problems in the wake of the collapse of Bretton Woods arrangements, the dollar's problems, and unprecedented rises in the price of oil that would have confounded any incumbent administration,[14] but also because of what followed in terms of Ronald Reagan (1911–2004) and the certainties and confidence of the 1980s. And with reference to Reagan in terms of his having been the man who won the Cold War, this chapter will now close with two ideas offered on the usual basis, for what they are worth if anything.

The first, very simply, is that a confrontation that reached across five decades was not won by any individual. The pressing of the pedal by the Reagan administration certainly compounded the Soviet Union's mounting and desperate problems but the collapse of the Soviet system was the result of a combination of factors, and one would suggest one, the second point, that is hardly afforded consideration. The process of *détente* cannot be divorced from *Ostpolitik* and the arrangements that led to the Helsinki Treaty of 1 August 1975, and both opened Eastern Europe to western—and specifically to West German—money, trade, and example, and, in terms of the last of these, the person of Willy Brandt possessed obvious significance.[15] First as foreign minister (1966–1969) and then chancellor (1969–1974), Brandt, with his proven anti-Nazi credentials and record of integrity, was not a person who could be associated in any way with revisionism and *revanche*, and perhaps he should be afforded greater credit not just in terms of the rehabilitation of Germany within the international community through recognition of borders and renunciation of all territorial claims outside existing frontiers. *Ostpolitik* in effect opened Eastern Europe to forces that set aside Warsaw Pact rationale and set in place changes that served to undermine the Soviet system. Brandt's contribution in these matters was very important indeed, but has been obscured in part because of the circumstances under which he left office, in part by the discrediting of the whole *détente* process, and in part because of the logic of the 1980s. But, and, to repeat the point, it was not one man or one event that resolved these matters but the coming together of a whole series of matters, political, economic, and moral, which placed the Soviet Union in an increasingly impossible position and one fraught with irony. If the Soviet Union, its leadership, and system really were as bad as the ideological rhetoric set out then the Soviets would have resorted to force as the means of ensuring survival, and in that fact is the paradox that lies at the core of the concept of strategic nuclear deterrence.

Book III

War and Wars since Clausewitz: Naval and Air Power

CHAPTER 1

Mahan and Corbett Reconsidered: 1890–2003

Within two decades of the end of the Second World War, the British historian Stephen Wentworth Roskill (1903–1982), writing in *The Strategy of Sea Power*, set out definitions of sea power and its constituent elements.[1] Provided here is a slightly different definition of the historical role of naval power, which is

The purpose of sea power is to ensure in times of war those rights automatically commanded in times of peace, specifically the security of homeland and overseas possessions against raid and invasion and of sea-borne trade, while denying those same rights to an enemy in terms of the conduct of amphibious operations and attacks on shipping.

Such definition would not embrace what Roskill defined as sea power's constituent parts, namely fleets and warships, industrial infrastructure and bases, merchant and fishing fleets, and trained manpower, and, there was the obvious link in terms of the former in part providing navies in times of war with manpower trained in the ways of the sea. In the case of the United States and Britain, one wonders just how much of this remains in place in 2009.

The crucial point herein is that while in a general war, the offensive use of sea power in terms of assault or landing on enemy territory cannot necessarily be undertaken before and until a measure of defensive primacy has been secured, the line of demarcation between the offense and defense at sea is very different from that ashore, and battle itself is very different. The battle at sea does not possess those elements such as rivers, mountains, lines of communication, and settlement that ashore spell out the battlefield with natural lines of defense and axes of advance. The battle at sea has terms of reference supplied by latitude and longitude, daylight hours, and factors of time and distance that necessarily ally themselves with coastline and offshore hazard. The battle at sea has to be fought repeatedly over the same reaches of sea and ocean in a way that the battle on land does not, and, lest the point be doubted, reference may be made to just one war and campaign. In the course of the Second World War, the German offensive against shipping was defeated in May 1945. Various commentators have tended to focus upon the month of May 1943 as the time when the German campaign against Allied shipping was defeated, and it cannot be denied that in this month the German U-boat offensive suffered a defeat singular in significance. In this single month, the German Navy lost no fewer than 41 U-boats from all causes and this total stands in very sharp contrast to the totals of 9, 24, 35 and 87 U-boats lost to all causes in (3 September–31 December) 1939, 1940, 1941, and 1942, respectively. But the point was that the victory that was won by Allied forces in May 1943 had to be repeated until the very end of the European war, and Allied shipping had to be provided with escort and nonetheless took losses virtually to the very last day of the German war. The victory that was won in May 1943 was indeed repeated, most obviously in July–August and again in October–November 1943, and the victories that were recorded in these subsequent months were every bit as important as the victory won in May for the very simple reason that these subsequent losses were sustained by a U-boat service that had been re-organized, re-equipped, and committed afresh to the campaign in the North Atlantic. Losses in July and August 1943 were 37 and 25, respectively, and in October and November, 26 and 19, respectively.[2] In terms of the war at sea and the proper recounting of history, the crucial point is to see these subsequent Allied successes in terms of complementary victories, not episodes separate and complete in their own right. The victories that were won between May and November 1943 undoubtedly served to ensure that the initiative at sea passed finally and irreversibly into Allied hands, but the basic reality—that the defensive commitment remained until the end of the war and that the victories of 1943 had to be fought for and won every week, every month, of what remained of the war—cannot be gainsaid.

Armies win and lose wars and navies do not, and herein has been the major point of historical difference between the two services. Navies may be crucial in the prevention of defeat, witness the British Navy in the War of American Independence and the French Revolutionary and Napoleonic Wars, but leaving aside city-states and island polities, in terms of the affairs of great powers, sea power has played its part in providing the basis of victory in a number of wars but in itself has not been able to do more. In the final analysis, military forces on the ground either win and conquer or lose and suffer defeat. Sea power, by definition, had to be the basis of the European reach into the outside world, and, in terms of projection, the Spanish defeat of first the Aztec Empire and then the Inca Empire probably has no equivalent regarding the scale of the enemy and the comprehensiveness of defeat until the Japanese defeat, 1941–1945. The American projection of national power across the Pacific between 1942 and 1945, and the defeat of a great power at the end of the process, certainly possessed one element that was novel, and that was the effort was joint in terms of what in effect were three separate services. Land-based air power sought to neutralize enemy air bases; carrier air power then isolated the objective; amphibious landings then secured that objective. The process was then repeated with the Americans carrying the tide of war forward, initially very slowly—witness the advance in the Solomons from Guadalcanal in August 1942 to Bougainville in October 1943, which were tied to landings in eastern New Guinea and on western New Britain between September 1942 and January 1944—and then with gathering pace, first in the Gilbert and Ellice Islands in November 1943, then in the Marshall Islands in January–February 1944, and then the series of landings that saw the Americans move virtually the length of New Guinea between April and June 1944. Thereafter, the Americans were to fight the greatest carrier battle in history, the battle of the Philippine Sea in June 1944, then the greatest naval battle in modern history, the battle of Leyte Gulf in October 1944, before the pace of advance slowed with the United States entering into a Philippines commitment, which was to last until war's end, and which ran in tandem with the clearing of Iwo Jima (February–June 1945) and Okinawa (April–July 1945). The latter efforts also saw Allied forces impose close blockade of the Japanese home islands and carry out bombardment of targets by warships and by carrier aircraft, the continuing joint aspect of the American effort being represented by the strategic bombing campaign directed against Japanese cities, the first B-29 operation from Saipan being conducted on 24 November 1944.[3] But the point of real significance of Leyte lies in the fact that this battle was fought after the issue of victory and defeat had been decided, that it was a battle (depending on definition) that reached over seven days, between 22 and 28 October, and involved deployment that reached over three million square miles of ocean, an immediate search area of some 450,000 square miles, and a battle area of 115,000 square miles, which is about the same size as the British Isles. What is also significant about the victory that was won by the Americans in this battle was that it, along with the successful resultant landings in the northern Philippines, placed the Americans astride Japan's crucially important lines of communication with southeast Asia and, lest it be forgotten, the carrier and amphibious efforts were two parts of a three-part American naval effort, the third part (primarily by submarines in association with land-based aircraft) being directed against Japanese seaborne trade, which had all but collapsed by August 1945. To slightly change the point made in book 1, chapter 3: it was the pieces coming together, all the elements and different contributions slotting into place, which provided victory, though the basis of the victory was sea power both in terms of naval and maritime strength and capability.

One recalls reading, more than two decades ago and in a source long forgotten but that was a British joint planning staff document in 1944, the observation that, by naval standards, the last war, that is, the First World War, was a short war. The basis of such analysis, clearly, was the protracted, attritional nature of war at sea, particularly in terms of campaigns directed against enemy shipping. Very seldom can an economic war be waged directly and quickly to real effect, but any consideration of wars at sea over the last 300 years would suggest something seldom afforded much in the way of historical consideration: the relative slowness with which operations outside Europe were put together by the European navies. For example, the story of the campaigns beyond Europe during the French Revolutionary and Napoleonic Wars is seldom told and the chronology, in most history books, is mostly gaps. Without claiming in any way to provide a comprehensive summary, one would note that in this war there were three sets of naval efforts outside European waters in the Caribbean, the Indian Ocean, and the Indies. The moment one makes such a definition, one is confronted by the fact that the British first took possession of Kaapstad/Cape Town in 1795 after the French conquest of the Netherlands, January–March 1795, and the establishment of a client republic. British forces landed at and secured Simon's Town in June and then defeated Dutch formations in what seems to have been a series of skirmishes that somehow have been drawn together and given the name of the Battle of Muizenberg in August–September. The Dutch surrendered on 16 September. The British formally returned the Cape to the Dutch at the Treaty of Amiens (27 March 1802), effective in 1803, but following the renewal of war between Britain and France (16 May 1803), British forces arrived at the Cape on 24 December 1805 and on 8 January 1806 fought and defeated local Dutch forces at Blouberg. Cape Town surrendered the following day and the general Dutch surrender followed on 18 January, Britain taking formal possession of the Cape at the Treaty of Paris in May 1814.

The Cape was but one Dutch colony that incurred British attention, and British forces, in the form of troops from the East India Company, arrived off Trincomalee, southeast Ceylon, on 1 August 1795 and, after fruitless local negotiations, were landed on 18 August and secured town and harbor on 26 August. After a campaign around the coast, in the course of which the British ensured the defection of the main defensive formation that consisted of Swiss mercenaries, a general surrender, for Colombo and the whole island, was secured on 15 February 1796. But the Company's rule prompted a rebellion in 1798 that led to Ceylon passing to the crown. British possession of the island was recognized at the Treaty of Amiens in 1802.

But if the Dutch holdings at the Cape and on Ceylon were the subject of British attention during the French Revolutionary Wars, the holdings in the Caribbean and the Indies were not subjected to assault and conquest until after 1807. The British had taken Trinidad in 1797 and retained that island in 1802, and, with the resumption of war, took St. Lucia (21–23 July) and Tobago (1 July 1803). The Dutch possessions in the Guyanas, on the Demerara, Essequibo, and Berbice Rivers, were surrendered to the British in the following September with the main holdings to the east surrendered in May 1804, but it was not until January 1807 that the British took Curaçao and, in December, the Danish islands—St. Thomas, St. John, and Ste. Croix—in the Antilles. Descada and Marie Gelante were captured in the following year and Samana in eastern Hispaniola was taken in November 1808. Cayenne, the major town in French Guinea, was not captured until January 1809, but on 24 February one of the last three major French holdings in the Caribbean, Martinique, was taken, as was Santo Domingo, with Spanish co-operation and after a prolonged defense, on 7 July. In and after 1808, the British took over Madeira and other Portuguese territories other than in Brazil but this was protective custody rather than conquest. The capture of Senegal in 1809 was somewhat different, involving as it did what amounted to the elimination of the French presence in west Africa. Interestingly, it was not until 1811 that the British closed down the French trading post at Tamatave in eastern Madagascar.

Guadeloupe was the last major French possession to be taken, and in part the delay that attended the move against this island was the result of an earlier British attempt to secure Guadeloupe, 21 April–2 June 1794, which had gone wrong, in part because of the volatility of issues—specifically slavery—involved in any conquest of French and Dutch possessions. The French were able to reinforce the garrison on the island during the uneasy peace of 1802–1803,[4] and this also made for British caution but the real reasons for the slowness of proceedings stemmed from the fact that in and immediately after the resumption of war in 1803, the British naval units in the West Indies were few and heavily committed, and in any event there was the simple fact that French possession of these colonies posed no real threat to Britain. Only in terms of their serving as base and source of supply for privateers was there cause for real irritation and while, on occasion, this could be very real, it was, for the most part, minor. British forces arrived at Guadeloupe on 28 January 1810 and forced the French surrender of 6 February. The only operations after Guadeloupe were the occupation of various minor Dutch and French possessions such as Saba, St. Eustatius, and St. Martin. By the end of 1810, all European colonies in the Caribbean and the Guyanas, with the exception of those of Spain, were in British hands. In the Indian Ocean after their occupation of Réunion in July and Mauritius in November 1810, the British moved first to secure Ambon and the Molucca Islands and then, in August 1811, against the main Dutch possession of Batavia on Java. After little more than token opposition, the Dutch surrender in the Indies was completed on 17 September, the British thereafter taking possession of Java, Palembang in southern Sumatra, Makassar in southern Celebes, and Timor.[5]

In many ways this achievement was remarkable in comprehensiveness, though perhaps what is astonishing about the British acquisition of these various territories was the fact that the United States apparently made no effort against British possessions in the Caribbean after her declaration of war on Britain in June 1812 and this at a time when Britain was fully committed elsewhere. But to repeat the point made earlier, it is very difficult to credit the fact that, even allowing for a number of considerations that precluded earlier British efforts, the reduction of the more important of these French possessions—Guadeloupe, Réunion, and Mauritius—was not registered until the 17th year after the original French declaration of war on Britain in January 1793.

The reference to this one series of wars must not be regarded as necessarily typical of war at sea though it would seem to suggest the very practical limitations of sea power to which reference was made in book 1, chapter 3. Most certainly the record of British acquisitions in these wars place the extra-European events of the First World War in some sort of context. Much has always been made of the campaign in East Africa, and also the campaign in the Cameroons, which lasted into January 1916. In reality, given the fact that islands were able to escape conquest for so long, it places such episodes as East Africa and the Cameroons—where the German forces operated across hundreds of miles against enemy formations that could not form continuous fronts, could not occupy effectively, and simply possessed no margin of real superiority over an enemy possessed of choice in giving or declining battle— in perspective. But there is no doubting the basic point that the First World War was indeed, by naval standards, a short war, and in that respect the fact that Germany was brought to the point of economic and industrial collapse in just 51 months, and was brought to the point of economic and industrial collapse despite conquests that extended over the greater part of the Balkans and much of European Russia, is somewhat remarkable, and presumably explicable only in terms of the nature of industrialization and shortened lead-times with respect to the manufacturing process and end-run production.

The 20th century's two world wars provide very contrasting examples of sea power in terms of impact and importance. In the first conflict, sea power was important in terms of outcome, the famous signal sent by the British Army to the British Navy at the time of the surrender of the High Sea Fleet on 21 November 1918—"You gave us their army, we gave you their fleet"—in many ways, with due allowance for the exaggeration that must have been part of the elation of the moment, states accurately the elements of balance and contribution. The defeat of the Central Powers was a Clausewitzian trinity of the political, the economic, and the military and the latter was again a Clausewitzian trinity of the military, the naval, and the maritime. In terms of Germany's defeat at sea in the period 1916–1918, one can trace events back to the 1890s and the German decision to acquire the second largest navy in the world, the infamous Risk Theory embracing the notion that Britain either would be forced into some form of arrangement with Germany or be obliged to observe neutrality in the event of a war between the two alliance systems within Europe. The German decision had a great deal to do with the development of the steel industry in this time, a certain envy for Britain's position, and the impact of Alfred Thayer Mahan (1840–1914) and *The Influence of Sea Power upon History, 1660–1783* and *The Influence of Sea Power upon the French Revolution and Empire, 1793–1812*, published in 1890 and 1892, respectively. These provided the title deeds of imperialism and navies. The books owed more to the turn of phrase rather than serious analysis but they provided an interpretation of history that stressed the importance of financial power, trade, colonies, and sea power. In a book-reading society, the impact of these books was immense, and in a sense raised the horizon, the imperialist and naval horizon, for much of Europe and the United States.

Mahan's books and time came together. Had these two books been published in the 1870s, perhaps even the 1880s, their impact would have been minimal. They would have come to possess value as historical curiosities and no more. But in the last decade of the 19th century, the impact of the books was immense because they were published at a time of the first generations of mass literacy and at a time when empires and navies came together in terms of public perception. The popular acclaim that greeted Mahan, the indulgence shown him by European royalty, and the use that was made of Mahan's writings over the next two decades on a host of naval matters was evidence of the potency of the written word at this time, but the importance and relevance of Mahan and his writings lay in the relationship between public perception and the development of fleets in the quarter century before the outbreak of war in Europe. Clearly the development of fleets was related to the development of steel and shipbuilding industries but, in the final analysis, fleets had to be funded and navies were massively expensive. Monies had to be found, taxes levied, and the public and potentially volatile electorates had to be persuaded of the value and importance of this effort. Herein, the press, a book-reading public, imperialism, and navies were linked and related to one another. It is perhaps worth noting that in terms of the impact of Mahan's writing, it cannot simply be coincidental that in Britain the Navy League was formed in 1894.

But the German naval aspiration miscarried and for obvious reason. The building of a fleet without reference to its inferiority in terms of numbers, geographical position, and "morale stroke sense-of-history" to its British counterpart left it with no reasoned strategic purpose and indeed left it with a desire for battle that was inadvertent acknowledgement of its own strategic futility. In the First World War, the Imperial German Navy was possessed of no more than a tactical, coastal defense role until it decided upon the conduct of a *guerre de course* against shipping that was justified by the assertion, which brooked no reasoned counter-argument but was an article of faith, that Britain could be driven from the ranks of Germany's enemies before American intervention manifested itself on the battlefield. It is a process that defies ready understanding. Having embarked upon a policy that added to the ranks of her enemies, Germany then declined to seek battle in the North Sea in an attempt to break or at least wear down British naval power and came to embrace a policy that had been afforded dismissive consideration before 1914 and that necessarily would involve the most difficult of operations, namely what amounted to a stern chase of an enemy with massive margins of superiority. In fact, by spring 1917, the German *guerre de course* produced a crisis for Britain that was unprecedented.

The German recourse to an unrestricted U-boat campaign against shipping came just weeks before the February Revolution in Petrograd (March 1917) that ultimately led to Russia's departure from one war into others, which were a combination of civil wars, wars of secession, and wars of foreign intervention. Germany's action brought into the ranks of her enemies the one state, the United States, crucial to British and French survival; by 1917, France virtually had reached the bottom of her manpower barrel and by 1918 Britain would be in similar straights, unlike Germany, which in 1914 possessed an intake of manpower of military age that potentially was as large as that of Britain and France combined. The United States military contribution to the Allied cause on the Western Front between April 1917 and November 1918 was decidedly modest, but it was the certainty of American numbers, arriving in strength, that was so important in steadying the British and French under the impact of disastrous defeat in spring 1918. The final defeat of the German armies in the field, after August 1918, saw contributions on the part of all four armies—American, Belgian, British, and French—and not one, but by November 1918 there were more American troops in Belgium and France than there were British, and had the war continued into 1919 then the U.S. Army would have been the most important of the Allies and would have been obliged to provide the cutting edge of the overall Allied effort.

Sea power brought American formations to Europe, as it had formations from the British and French empires, but, in the course of the First World War, the war at sea differed very markedly from the war at sea in the Second World War. In the First World War, the German *guerre de course* was not defeated; it was checked. Shipping losses were reduced, after the peak (or trough) of April 1917, and then held at levels that represented acceptable loss. At the same time, the assorted means of destruction meant that the U-boat service did not show any appreciable increase in size between April 1917 and November 1918, the crucial point being that in 1917 the anticipation of success made unnecessary a long-term building program with the result that, in the last year of the war as the return per individual U-boat—Allied and neutral shipping losses expressed in terms of operational submarines per month—declined as convoys became increasingly widespread, so there was no appreciable growth in the size of the U-boat arm that could maintain the overall level of sinkings. In fact, in the last year of the war, new construction and losses were in balance. The quarterly returns between 1 February 1917 and 31 October 1918 tell a very interesting story:

1 February–30 April 1917:	14 commissioned and 13 lost
1 May–31 July 1917:	24 commissioned and 18 lost
1 August–31 October 1917:	41 commissioned and 23 lost
1 November 1917–31 January 1918:	14 commissioned and 26 lost
1 February–30 April 1918:	24 commissioned and 19 lost
1 May–31 July 1918:	29 commissioned and 24 lost
1 August–31 October 1918:	30 commissioned and 37 lost
Overall	176 commissioned and 160 lost

with the annual figures being 1 August–31 December 1914, 11 and 5, 1915 52 and 21, 1916 108 and 22, 1917 100 and 74, and 1 January–11 November 1918 88 and 91, it being noted that the final 1918 total of losses was exaggerated by the number of boats that were scuttled when bases in Belgium and on the Adriatic were abandoned.

In 1917–1918, the Allies survived the German U-boat campaign against shipping in large measure because of the interplay of four factors: the scale of their merchant ship-building programs, their ability to keep neutral shipping on the seas as a result of more than generous freight and insurance rates, the re-deployment of Allied shipping from the various oceans to the crucial North Atlantic run, and the very strict rationing imposed within Britain in terms of both industry and the civilian population that enabled Britain to survive in 1918 on a level of imports almost two-fifths below that of 1913, witness a decline of total imports in 1913 of 56,035,000 tons via 38,075,000 tons in 1917 to 35,593,000 tons in 1918, with subtotals of food falling from 18,136,000 tons in 1913 via 13,063,000 tons in 1917 to 11,419,000 tons in 1918; raw materials from 30,736,000 tons via 19,171,000 in 1917 and back to 19,950,000 tons in 1918, and manufactured items from 7,125,000 tons in 1913 via 5,617,000 tons in 1917 to 4,113,000 tons in 1918.

The crucial factor in the curbing but not the defeat of the U-boat *guerre de course* was the introduction of convoy in April 1917 and its subsequent extension throughout the major theaters of operation, but a certain caution needs be exercised in any consideration of this matter. Convoy was crucial in the period after April 1917 but, in the immediate crisis that faced the Allies in spring and summer 1917, convoy probably saved perhaps no more than 80 or so merchantmen, and these did not represent the margin between victory and defeat at that time. What was important in this period were the inability of the U-boat arm to maintain the level of U-boat sailings at the peak with which it began the campaign in February 1917, the loss of time on station as a result of U-boats being obliged to sail around the north of Scotland rather than move directly, through the English Channel, against the shipping lanes in the southwest approaches, and the Allied pressure brought to bear on neutrals that they returned their shipping to sea. By the last quarter of 1917 as convoy was slotted into place, these other factors remained important contributory factors in the U-boat failing, but where care is also needed is in the handling of the British Navy's claims on the subject of convoy.

The introduction of convoy was decided in April 1917, the Admiralty and its apologists claiming that the naval high command was converted to its cause, after 32 months of all but constant opposition, before the famous episode in which the prime minister appeared at the Admiralty to demand its implementation. The naval claim is exclusive in its demand on credit, but, of course, there is no doubting who would have been the target of the navy's censure had convoy miscarried. As it was, the Admiralty's claims upon credit sit ill alongside an inescapable set of facts. According to the British official history,[6] in July 1917 there were a total of 85 *River* class and earlier destroyers and

213 post-*River* class destroyers in British waters, this total not including flotilla leaders, torpedo boats, destroyers attached to submarine formations, and P-boats; the 35 U.S. destroyers on station are likewise excluded from this total. Thus there would appear to have been 298 British and 35 American destroyers in British waters.

The breakdown of commands indicates that 95 destroyers were with the Grand Fleet (plus 9 under repair), 25 (plus 3) were at Harwich, 27 (plus 9) were with the Dover command, 40 (plus 10) were with east coast commands, 23 (plus 4) were with Portsmouth command, 42 (plus 5) with Devonport command, 14 (plus 2) with Buncrana command, and 24 (plus 3) with Queenstown command. That would give a total of 290 in service and 45 under repair for an overall total of 335 destroyers, the American destroyers being discounted from totals.

Whatever the number, and the differences seem impossible to reconcile, it would seem to place the 19 British and 16 American destroyers, plus 13 other units, assigned convoy duty in some sort of perspective, as indeed does one other set of figures given again in this source. The listings for July 1917 indicate that Portsmouth had 1 British destroyer working the Atlantic convoy route, Devonport 10, Buncrana 3, and Queenstown 8. "Patrol of trade routes, submarine hunting, escort of transports and supply ships," was 10 for Portsmouth, 16 for Devonport, 5 for Buncrana, and 10 for Queenstown. In other words, and three months after the Admiralty (allegedly) was converted to the cause of convoy without in any way being influenced by the prime minister, its arrangement in four of the major commands that would be obliged to handle convoys provided for 22 destroyers assigned convoy duties compared to the 41 assigned other duties, which included failed submarine hunting. Even allowing for the fact that the institution of convoy was in its early days and that previous arrangements could not be undone quickly, such a state of affairs, three months after this greatest naval crisis of the war and the Admiralty's (allegedly) independent conversion to the cause of convoy, does seem to be in need of proper professional explanation.

But what does defy explanation is that at war's end, there was one major study undertaken that sought to examine the U-boat campaign and to draw appropriate lessons. This study examined shipping losses, convoy, escort numbers, and the relationship between ship numbers, escort numbers, and losses, and were put together in one paper, *The Elements of Convoy Defence in Submarine Warfare*, with two appendages, *Escort Supplement* and *Evasion Supplement*.[7] Perhaps predictably for an organization so concerned with such vitally important matters as the *Royal Oak* court martial, the papers were filed away, forgotten, and not found until 1943, by which time the basic lessons enunciated in these papers had been relearned the hard way.

With reference to the Second World War, the paucity of battle goes alongside two very different results, namely the defeat of the U-boat *guerre de course* against shipping and the devastation of the Japanese merchant marine. Within the European context, the naval war was clearly secondary, perhaps even tertiary, in importance, but sea power nonetheless provided the basis whereby there was to be useful Anglo-American contribution to victory in 1944–1945. The main part of this effort came after May 1943. There is no doubt that this month possessed singular importance. This was the worst single month of the war to date for the U-boats and their operations were halted and they were recalled on the 24th, two years to the day after the battlecruiser *Hood* had been sunk in the Denmark Strait. The dramatic quality of events in this month arises because crippling losses were inflicted on the U-boat service within two months of the worst month of the war in terms of Allied convoy losses and because of the apparently decisive intervention in the battle of land-based air power. The bare facts, however, are misleading. The events of May 1943 conformed to a trend many months in the making to which the losses of March 1943 were very much the exception. If the impact of V.L.R. Liberators in May 1943 was exaggerated by German operational errors and subsequently overstated by historians, the fact was that land-based aircraft were beginning to inflict significant losses on the U-boats some months before May 1943. More obviously, the Allied success in May 1943 was but one part of victory and it had to be complemented by the successes of July–August and October–November 1943, which, if lacking the obvious and singular importance of May 1943, were in some ways even more profound than that of the earlier month. These were victories that were won over a U-boat service that had been re-organized and partially re-equipped and was deliberately committed in order to try to win back the initiative after the May debacle. It was the combination of these losses that broke the U-boat effort, and it was their being repeated after November for the remainder of the war, with the result that there was no resurgent U-boat threat, which spelled Allied victory in the Battle of the Atlantic. The latter was not won and lost in a single month any more than the events of this month were sudden and divorced from previous events.

In the Pacific, there are any number of considerations and episodes deserving of proper examination, but suffice to note two matters. The first is the comprehensiveness of Japan's defeat in a war that she initiated. To repeat a point made previously, states as mismatched as Japan and the United States seldom fight one another, and even more seldom do they wage wars initiated by the weaker side, but Japan resorted to a war that quite obviously she never understood, involving as it did separate naval and maritime dimensions. The second is the seven-stage plan of attrition, penned by Commander Akiyama Saneyuki (1868–1918), which had been the Japanese naval plan of action prior to the battle of Tsushima in May 1905. The first two stages would involve torpedo attacks by destroyers and torpedo boats south of the Strait before, with the third phase, the main action would be joined. The following phases would see night torpedo attacks while the fifth phase would witness the resumed action between the major formations the following morning. The final phases would see pursuit in the direction of Vladivostok and the driving of Russian units into the minefields that had been laid on 15 April in the approaches to the Russian harbor. Inevitably, and in accordance with von Moltke's dictum that no plan ever survives the first contact of battle, the initial phases did not materialize, and the Russian formations evaded detection and hence contact until well into the Strait, but thereafter the battle unfolded very much according to plan, and to an end, in terms of Japanese national and service interests, which proved a formula for disaster.

Akiyama's concept, with its concentration on battle and Japan's inevitable victory in decisive battle, became the basis of subsequent Japanese naval planning for war, specifically a war in the Pacific against the United States, and indeed the war plan with which Japan went to war in 1941 was a case of Akiyama re-incarnated. The idea of American task forces being subjected to attrition by submarines and shore-based aircraft and then to massed torpedo attacks by destroyers at night before action was joined by the battle divisions was no more than the Akiyama idea re-cast in order to take account of different geography and theater of operation, albeit one that differed in one fundamental way from the 1905 original. The Akiyama concept related to the conduct of battle but, in 1941, the Japanese Navy's concern was with the conduct of a war, yet by some strange and mystical process, somewhat akin to transubstantiation, what had been a plan for battle became a campaign plan and thence a war plan and the distinction between war and a war, between a war and a campaign, and between a campaign and a battle was lost, while the ultimate irony of the 1941 plan can too easily be missed. The route between battle plan, campaign plan, and war plan necessarily must be a two-way and not one-way street, but the basic point was that in 1941 the objective of the war plan was to fight and win one battle.

The Akiyama concept was the basis of victory and when tied with the other factors at work in the inter-war period—the ideas of the sacred mission, the divinity of the Emperor, and the trust vested by the gods in *Yamato*—it, the Akiyama screed, which might have become the basis for the asking of questions, became the answer. It is in that sense that, despite Akiyama and its contents, the concept conformed to the notion of good servant, bad master, and the formula for national and service disaster. And, state it *sotto voce*, what is really remarkable about this whole process is that the Imperial Navy spent the inter-war period preparing for the battle fleet action, and, on the one occasion when it was able to fight that battle, it failed lamentably and was outfought by a navy about which one simple fact provides comment. Both in 1943 and in 1944, the United States Navy commissioned into service a tonnage that was equivalent of the Imperial Japanese Navy prior to the outbreak of the Pacific war, and it did so with no diminution of quality and with an ability to conduct carrier air, amphibious assault, and anti-submarine operations on a scale that denied the Japanese any means of effective response. On the first score in February 1945, a U.S. carrier force conducted a series of operations over the Japanese home islands with a total of five task groups that numbered 11 fleet and 5 light fleet carriers, 8 battleships and 1 battlecruiser, 5 heavy and 9 light cruisers, and 77 destroyers. Of the total of 116 warships, just the carriers *Enterprise* and *Saratoga* and the heavy cruisers *Indianapolis* and

San Francisco were in service on "the day that will live in infamy," and, with U.S. submarine losses being discounted from the reckoning, between November 24, 1943, when the escort carrier *Liscome Bay* was torpedoed off the Gilberts by the submarine I-175, and October 24, 1944, when the *Princeton* was lost off the northern Philippines as a result of attack by a land-based aircraft, Japanese shells, torpedoes, and bombs failed to account for a single U.S. Navy fleet unit other than the *Fletcher*-class destroyer *Brownson*, which was lost on December 26, 1943 off Cape Gloucester, New Britain, to air attack. In other words, the whole of the American effort that resulted in the breaking of the outer perimeter defense in the central Pacific, the carrier rampages into the western Pacific that resulted in the shipping massacres at Truk (17–18 February) and Koror (30–31 March),[8] the landings at Hollandia and Aitape that took the tide of war from one end of New Guinea to the other in two months, and that finally led to overwhelming victory in the Philippine Sea (19–20 June) and thence to the approaches to the Philippines, cost the United States just one destroyer, plus the destroyer escort *Shelton*, which was sunk off Morotai on 3 October by the submarine Ro. 41. Such immunity to losses was the mark of American superiority in the Pacific war by the final phase of this war after November 1943.

The Japanese war ended with the U.S. Navy having developed into the greatest navy in the world and so powerful that it was unchallengeable, and possessed in the form of its carrier aircraft its own air force and, in the form of the Marine Corps, its own army, yet within four years it had been reduced to the status of *minor inter pares* relative to the U.S. Army and the newly formed Air Force. Yet within little more than a decade, its fortunes had been transformed, and on two very different levels: the Korean war, 1950–1953, provided the need for naval air and gunnery support for army formations ashore and hence led to the return of many carriers to service, while the New Look at the end of the decade provided the U.S. Navy with the key role—the secure second strike—in terms of strategic deterrence. As noted elsewhere, navies, historically, have always done badly in times of peace, and most certainly in the immediate aftermath of the Second World War the U.S. Navy conformed to historical example, but thereafter it assumed a status that, if not on par with its position in 1943–1945, certainly ensured that it was not the poor relation compared to its sister services. It was a status that it enjoyed into the 1990s but, by that time, four kindred matters were at work in ensuring change and diminished status. The end of the Cold War and the demise of the Soviet Union in real terms spelled the end of the strategic deterrence role and left the U.S. Navy surplus to requirements in terms of not being faced with a blue-water opponent; the emergence of the U.S. Air Force with a newfound capability that placed it ahead of the other two services; the increased importance of military formations in terms of the wars in which the United States found herself regarding manpower-intensive commitments for which navies had no part; and the long-term problems of building requirements, industrial and shipyard contraction, and an increasingly difficult manpower situation not so much in terms of recruitment but retention given increased sea-time per warship as the latter's numbers declined.

Only off southeast Asia was the United States involved in major naval operations after 1965 and a considerable part of that effort was brown water. There were a number of other operations, most obviously the series of events that led to the suicide bombing of the Marine compound in Beirut on 23 October 1983 and the loss of carrier aircraft on 4 December 1983 over the Beqaa valley to Syrian missiles, the crippling of the frigate *Stark* by an Iraqi Mirage F-1 on 4 May 1987 and the destruction of an Iranian civilian airliner over the Persian Gulf on 3 July 1988 by the U.S. cruiser *Vincennes*, and the three actions involving Libya, namely the operation of 24 March 1986, the raids on Tripoli and Benghazi on 15 April 1986, and the shooting down of two Libyan Mig-21s by F-14 Tomcats on 4 January 1989 in the very last days of the Reagan administration. But these were episodes and not ongoing commitments that were part of a war or wars, and for a generation after 1975, the U.S. Navy was spared a war. It faced down the Soviet naval challenge in this time, but very significantly it did so as the navies of allies more or less disappeared from the scene. The end of empire and the sheer cost of replacing carriers meant that in the second half of the 1960s, the British Navy accepted reduction to secondary, even tertiary, status, and certainly by the mid-1990s the decline of the British and French navies was such that together they mustered fewer warships than the Japanese maritime self-defense force though, of course, the latter did not have carriers and nuclear submarines. For the British Navy, the Suez episode (October–November 1956), the confrontation with Indonesia (January 1963–August 1966), and finally the war in the South Atlantic (April–June 1982) represented its swansong, though in the case of the latter this conflict was described, acerbically but with some accuracy, as a fight between two bald men about a comb; as it was, this was perhaps the only conflict since 1945 in which naval power, or perhaps in the Argentine case an absence of naval power, was important and indeed crucial to outcome. That being stated, perhaps three matters seldom acknowledged need definition, namely the (never properly acknowledged) aid and support provided by the Americans and French to the British effort, the fact that the last Argentine missile fired at British warships was a Gabrielle, and the fact that in the aftermath of the Argentine landing in the Falklands and the resultant *furore*, an official from the Foreign Ministry had to go to the presidential palace in order to explain to General Leopoldo Galtieri (1926–2003) what the Security Council of the United Nations was—a state of affairs that would suggest that there was a great deal more to Argentine failure and defeat in this episode than mere sea power. As it was, this conflict can be represented as the last of the imperial wars just as it could be represented as the first war of the post-imperial order, perhaps the first war of the 21st century[9]—but such matters represent entirely different stories.

CHAPTER 2

Air Power and Two World Wars

The great problem confronting any attempt to set out an objective assessment of air power is that from the first flight the protagonists of air power have set out claims that, depending on perspective, were either highly ambitious or grotesquely exaggerated, but in a sense produced a situation that amounted to the closing of a vicious circle. Successive failures on the part of air power to register the results that were claimed and predicted were proof to the skeptical and the proponents alike of the rightness of their very different arguments, to the skeptical that air power could never achieve the results that were claimed and to the proponents that air power could achieve the results that were claimed if it were afforded the priorities and investment that were *sine qua non* of its endeavor.

The story of air power inevitably starts with the first controlled flights by a heavier-than-air machine by the Wright brothers at Kitty Hawk, North Carolina, on 17 December 1903 and the crossing of the English Channel by Louis Blériot (1872–1936) on 25 July 1909. But the first flight across the English Channel was on 7 June 1785 by Jean Blanchard (1753–1809) and John Jeffries (1744–1819) in a hydrogen balloon that was equipped with human-powered tiller and wings, and this came less than two years after the first manned flights in balloons and just eight days before the first fatalities in flight.[1] The first airship, complete with steam-powered engine, was developed in 1852 but it was not until the development of the internal combustion engine (1896) that the airship became a practicality. The first airship thus powered, developed by a Brazilian in France, flew on 18 September 1898, and for the next two decades, the balloon, airship, and then the aircraft/seaplane rested uneasily alongside one another, occasionally partners but usually rivals in terms of role, funding, and priorities. The aircraft first saw service in the Italian-Turkish war of 1911–1912 but obviously it was in the First World War that the new dimension of war manifested itself from the outset. August 1914 saw German airships fly over London and German aircraft bomb Paris and a number of British ports while the same month saw British aircraft report the German outflanking movement at Mons and German aircraft report the unsupported Russian advance on Tannenberg; the following month saw French aircraft report the gap between German armies advancing on the Marne. September 1914 also saw the first use of a seaplane in war and the bombing of a warship, at Tsingtao, and the first British air raid on Germany, the targets being Zeppelin sheds at Cologne and Düsseldorf while, on Christmas Day, the British conducted a raid involving seven seaplanes from three carriers on the sheds at Cuxhaven. January 1915 saw the start of what was the first strategic bombing campaign in history with the bombing of Great Yarmouth by German Zeppelins, and if June 1915 saw the first bombing (and destruction) of a Zeppelin, the summer saw the start of a systematic German attempt to secure air superiority over the Western Front through the introduction of formation operations. By June 1916, the French and British, by adopting similar tactics and by virtue of their superior numbers, had fought for and won air superiority over Verdun and the Somme, respectively. By April 1917, the Germans had recovered air superiority, and this in a single month when the British lost half of their aircrew and when life expectancy fell to 11 days. The Germans introduced specialist ground-attack aircraft and used them to considerable effect at Cambrai in November 1917 and in the *Kaiserschlacht* offensive of March 1918, but the fact was that by 1918 disparity of numbers ensured marked Allied superiority. In the offensive in front of Amiens in August 1918, the British for the first time supplied advancing troops by air, while, as noted elsewhere, the following month saw what was arguably the first defeat of ground formations by air power at Kosturino. A certain care needs to be exercised on this latter point. The British and Greek offensive east of Doiran had been badly defeated but this was part of a deception effort and the main French and Serbian attacks were successful. The Bulgarian formations around Doiran were ordered to withdraw and did so, but clearly were demoralized by doing so, and were then caught by aircraft in the Ruppell Pass and scattered. The exact relationship between the attack and the defeat is difficult to define. Clearly the attack was more than a *coup de grâce* but whether it was the cause of a defeat that was obviously in the making is a moot point. Be that as it may, this episode unfolded on the very same day as British aircraft are credited with having turned the Turkish retreat from its positions around Megiddo into a rout, so it may be that the result and date (September 21, 1918) was correct but the place was wrong.

In the course of the First World War the bomber was of secondary, perhaps even tertiary, importance, and bombing was more important in terms of psychological impact than damage caused. The airship did possess a certain value, specifically in terms of reconnaissance at sea, and certainly there was one episode that merits reference; in the course of a mission that was to take supplies to German formations in East Africa but was abandoned when she was over Khartoum, the German airship L. 59, with an overall length of 743 feet, five engines and a 51-ton payload, flew 4,223 miles to and from Jamboli (present-day Yambol) in Bulgaria between 21 and 25 November 1917. In real terms, this was the first inter-continental flight. It involved a distance and speed that were unprecedented and by an airship that was more than three times longer than a Boeing 747.[2] In this respect, the airship proved to have a greater durability than seemed likely at the time. Range and lift gave the airship almost two decades of life after the end of the First World War and ended with the destruction of the *Hindenburg* on 6 May 1937 at Lakehurst Naval Air Station in New Jersey,[3] but the fact was that in the course of the First World War, the inferiority and vulnerability of the airship to the heavier-than-air machine, which came complete with machine guns and two-way radio, increased significantly. By war's end, the reconnaissance value of the airship was limited while the increased size and lift capability of the latest aircraft meant that its strategic role was in the process of being usurped by such newcomers as the Handley-Page O/400. Had the war continued into 1919 then this bomber would undoubtedly been in the forefront of a major Allied offensive directed against German industrial targets.

Should there have been such an offensive then it would have been led by the Royal Air Force, which was the only independent air service in the world and was thus endowed with a commitment to strategic bombing as the basis of its *raison d'être*. In strategic terms, the First World War saw Britain cease to be an island—though the evidence of 1940 points to a very different conclusion. But the primary role of air power in the First World War was tactical and involved reconnaissance, spotting for artillery, ground-attack, and the battle for air supremacy. With reference to the first two tasks, the introduction of two-way radios and automatic cameras were essential for timely reporting while the latter two tasks necessarily spelled the end of the knight of the air; individuals, such as Albert Ball (1896–1917), Georges Guynemer (1894–1917), Manfred von Richthofen (1892–1918), and Werner Voss (1897–1917), though raised to the status of national heroes, were replaced by formations and mass.

The impact of air power in terms of deciding the outcome of the First World War was minimal, but in the immediate post-war world there emerged a number of individuals who were to dominate the air power debate over the next decade. Probably the most important of these, though not the most high-profile, was Sir Hugh Trenchard (1873–1956), who, as head of the Royal Air Force between 1919 and 1930, was primarily responsible for the survival of an independent air service whose very *raison d'être* was strategic bombing. Trenchard was head of a service beset by economies and massive reduction but that in the 1920s was responsible for the conduct of not one but two campaigns, in Iraq and British Somaliland, that saw the employment of aircraft and poison gas as means of ensuring the pacification of rebellious peoples and territories. Less well known is the fact that Trenchard expressed the view that the Royal Air Force could and should be used in the event of domestic disturbances, specifically of socialist or trade union persuasion. Far better known as the advocates of air power were Guilo Douhet (1869–1930), Alexander de Seversky (1894–1974), and the notorious Billy Mitchell (1879–1936). Douhet's *Il Dominio dell' Aria/Command of the Air*, perhaps the most famous and influential of all air power publications, appeared in 1921, the same year as the surrendered German battleship *Ostfriesland* was sunk in trials off Cape Henry, Virginia, which, in all truth, proved nothing other than that if enough aircraft and bombs were directed against an unmanned battleship then they would ultimately sink her, though there was an irony about these proceedings; the *Ostfriesland* was sunk primarily as a result of near-misses rather than direct hits.[4] Another five years were to elapse before the crash of the airship *Shenandoah* and the subsequent court-martial of Mitchell,[5] but in fact none of these four army officers were the first to put forward a strategic bombing concept; that was the prerogative of a naval officer, Nakajima Chikuhei (1884–1949), who left the Imperial Japanese Navy in 1917 in order to found the aircraft company that was to bear his name.

Throughout the inter-war period, the claims and capabilities of air forces were a matter of personal persuasion and states proved very reluctant to embrace an unproven doctrine and arguments that were as much articles of faith as reasoned. The obvious uncertainties of the future clearly precluded uncritical acceptance of air power advocates, and indeed for much of this period air arms for all major powers were third in the military pecking order. By the 1930s, however, major change was in place on several counts. The aircraft emerged as the flying machine ahead of its rival airships, seaplanes, and flying boats, and with the monoplane came the first of two developments that were to profoundly alter the balance of advantage between the bomber and fighter. For much of the inter-war period, there was a general view that, as the British three-time prime minister Stanley Baldwin (1867–1947) stated (in November 1932), along with a whole series of qualifications, "the bomber will always get through," and the first development of monoplanes, in the form of bombers, seemed to provide confirmation of this dictum; the bombers of the mid-1930s were considerably superior in speed to biplane fighters. But from the mid-1930s, the monoplane began to enter general service, and while U.S. carriers still had biplanes even in 1941, the balance of advantage reversed itself. Monoplane fighters could out-perform bombers in terms of speed, altitude, rate of climb, and maneuverability, and to this came the added second development of radar. This was to provide the defense with a capacity to fight a defensive battle in depth and indeed the Second World War was to witness successive failures of strategic bombing efforts between 1939 and 1944 in very large measure because of these two developments that, together, ensured that the bomber did not always get through.

The failures of these strategic bombing campaigns were the result of the coming together of a number of factors, obviously with certain of these peculiar to individual campaigns. With reference to the failure of the German offensive against Britain in 1940–1941, three matters may be cited as crucial in determining outcome: a rough balance of numbers in terms of fighter aircraft of the two sides and the limited range of German fighters; the problems inherent in seeking to change the *Luftwaffe* from what was in effect a single-purpose (close-support) air force to a general air force in the middle of the campaign; and in the aftermath of the defeat of France a general lack of understanding on the part of the *Luftwaffe* high command of what a strategic bombing campaign would entail. To these matters should be added a German conduct of operations that left something to be desired, most obviously in comparison to a British air force that had one very simple task. To these must be added one other point, and that was that the German effort was too short and indeed was scaled down, as a result of commitments in the Balkans, in the east, and at sea, at the very time when it might have achieved results. In effect, the German campaign ended in May 1941 when for the first time the bombing of British ports and industries was causing major disruption of patterns of production and distribution.

Mutatis mutandis, these same factors were at work in ensuring the failure of British strategic bombing between 1940 and 1944. Very quickly in the war, the British high command was obliged to abandon daylight bombing because of the losses incurred by bombers to an alert defense, and only slowly came to the realization that claims of major success in night attacks were no more than self-deception. It was only at the end of 1941 that the British high command grasped that inaccuracy of navigation and aiming were such as to preclude a deliberate campaign—the raid of 1–2 October 1941 directed against Karlsruhe and Stuttgart resulted in R.A.F. Bomber Command dropping bombs on no fewer than 29 German cities—and that indiscriminate area bombardment had to be adopted and for obvious reason: if the bombers could not find selected targets but might only be able to find cities then cities had to be targeted. The result was the area bombing directive of 15 February 1942 and a campaign that over the next two years manifestly failed in its objectives and was curtailed in spring 1944 in readiness for preparations for operations in support of the Normandy invasion, and this after Bomber Command had been literally beaten to its knees in the course of the Battle of Berlin. Between 18 November 1943 and 31 March 1944 R.A.F. Bomber Command lost more aircraft—1,047 with a further 1,682 damaged—than it possessed at any single time during the campaign, and in the last disastrous operation of this particular offensive, against Nuremberg on 30–31 March it lost 108 of the 1,009 aircraft sent against this and other related targets. By the end of March 1944, R.A.F. Bomber Command had been brought to the edge of defeat and had manifestly failed to bring about the collapse of Germany that its commander, Air Marshal Sir Arthur Harris (1892–1984), had claimed on 7 December 1943 it could achieve by 1 April 1944.

By this time, however, there was one major change in place that was to ensure a different future. In the first three months of 1944, the United States

Army Air Force fought for and secured air superiority in German skies, courtesy of the P-51 Mustang fighter that for the first time escorted heavy bombers of the 8th Air Force against German targets—the port and U-boat facilities at Bremen, Hamburg, and Kiel—on 13 December 1943. The P-51 was able to out-fight German fighters over Berlin, and in thus fighting for and winning the battle for air supremacy the Mustang might have paved the way for the successful prosecution of a strategic bombing campaign but for the Normandy commitment. It was not until September 1944 that the greater part of the heavy bomber effort was re-directed, back to German targets, and by that time the strategic bombing effort and its resultant success was basically irrelevant, for two reasons. In September 1944, German industry entered end-run production and the collapse of German industry and hence Germany herself in spring 1945 was assured. Moreover, the defeat of Germany *per se* was assured by that time on a very different count. Soviet armies in the east and Allied armies in the west by August–September 1944 had brought the tide of war to Germany's borders, and they were by this stage possessed of such superiority of numbers and capability that the conquest of Germany in the coming months was assured, though it did take a little longer than had been anticipated. The strategic bombing campaign — and in truth there were separate British and American efforts that did not complement one another — at very best contributed to the defeat of Germany but was not the agency of that defeat. The bombing effort completed the laying waste of the German canal, road, and rail systems and resulted in the physical isolation of the Ruhr but this was achieved a matter of days before the juncture on 1 April at Lippstadt of the 9th and 1st U.S. Armies completing the physical encirclement of the Ruhr.

The strategic bombing offensive most certainly had results that were more than a little useful to the Allies and on three very different counts, to which brief reference has been made elsewhere. First, it forced the German high command to commit ever more of its fighters to home defense and thus resulted in a major reduction of *Luftwaffe* tactical presence and capability; after July 1943 Allied armies fought under conditions of increasing air superiority and effectiveness. Second, it distorted the pattern of German production, most notably in terms of aircraft production. While one-quarter of artillery and ammunition resources, one-third of optical output, and half of Germany's electro-technical production was directed to home-based anti-aircraft defense in 1944, German aircraft production rose to 39,807 aircraft in 1944 from totals of 15,556 in 1942 and 25,527 in 1943. In the process, however, German offensive power declined in real terms as the fighter share of output rose from 40.2 percent in 1942 to 53.7 percent in 1943 to 77.7 percent in 1944, yet even this over-concentration of productive effort was insufficient to allow any significant increase in the *Luftwaffe's* front-line fighter strength during 1944, and most certainly not on the scale needed to allow the *Luftwaffe* to regain air superiority. Third, the strategic bombing offensive could not prevent German industry from achieving unprecedented levels of production in 1944, and German war production reached its peak in the third quarter of

1944 when the index of production stood at 308 relative to a base of 100 in January–February 1942, but the fact remains that even in 1944, German industry worked at some 10 to 12 percent under capacity and costs were between 6 and 8 percent above what should have been normal because of the Allied bombing campaign.

Examination of the Second World War in terms of the strategic bombing campaign against Germany necessarily must be accompanied by an examination of the strategic bombing campaign directed against Japan, though in truth it must be noted, if only *en passant*, that this was the second of two strategic bombing campaigns in the Japanese war. The first was the series of campaigns staged between 1939 and 1941 by the Japanese with reference to China, and these, whether singularly or together, represent the first strategic bombing campaigns in history and the first deliberate attempt to break Chinese morale and resistance by an indiscriminate campaign of area bombing. This was an offensive forced upon the Japanese for want of any alternative. Japan lacked both the political and the military means to bring her special undeclared war in China to a successful conclusion, and accordingly adopted the strategic bombing option as the only means by which she could take the tide of war into the Kuomintang heartland. Very interestingly, the initial effort, in 1938–1939, foreshadowed the various problems that the German, British, and United States air forces were to encounter after 1940 most obviously in terms of unrealistic levels of expectation, inadequate numbers of bombers, and lack of fighter escorts. Indeed the Japanese efforts would have foundered but for the timely entry into service of first the A5M Claude and then the A6M Zero-sen that were more than a match for Chinese fighters and provided a degree of cover and support for the bombers. But, of course, the Japanese effort proved unavailing and for reasons that, at least in retrospect, are obvious; the Japanese never understood the force of any nationalism other than their own, and simply had no means of inducing regime change or breaking morale as the means of securing their national objectives with reference to China and east Asia. Chinese cities such as Chungking, which were highly vulnerable to bombing given the narrowness of the valleys in which they found themselves, were razed and public offices and private citizens alike were obliged to seek safety in burrowed safe havens in the surrounding hills, but there was no deflection from the basic calculation that governed Kuomintang considerations: to await Japan's defeat in a wider war in which she would ultimately find herself and that would ensure China's liberation *en passant*.

The second of the two strategic bombing campaigns in the Japanese war was the American effort directed against targets in the home islands. The initial U.S. effort began in June 1944 from airfields in China but this was abandoned in part because of the Japanese offensive that resulted in the overrunning of these bases and in part because the American landings in the Marianas brought possession of bases that were secure and more easily supplied from the United States than airfields in India and China. XXI Bomber Command conducted its first mission against Japan on 24 November 1944 but the campaign that was waged over the winter months manifestly failed to record results on two counts: the number of bombers that were available for operations were too few to conduct a campaign on a scale that had any chance of registering significant results, and the bombing effort that was staged was tied to a doctrine of daylight precision-bombing that was inherently flawed. Lack of fighter escort, a Japanese defensive effort that peaked in January 1945, and the problems of high-level missions in the Gulf Stream combined to defeat the initial American effort and to ensure that future operations were very different. After two raids, initially against Hankow on 18 December 1944 and against Tokyo on 25 February 1945, the American high command adopted the policy of night area bombing from low altitudes in an attempt to limit losses and cause the maximum possible general devastation of Japanese cities.

Thus in March 1945 began the second phase of the strategic bombing campaign and one in which some 41.6 percent of Japan's six largest cities was destroyed, the first raid being the (in)famous Tokyo Raid of 9/10 March that resulted in the leveling of 16 square miles of the city and killed or wounded 124,711 people and left 1,008,005 homeless.[6] With these raids curtailed by the requirements of the Okinawa campaign and the mining of Japanese home waters, a total of 18 major raids, staged over a 14-week period, resulted in the destruction of some 42.46 percent of Japan's six largest cities: thereafter the final phase of the war, between 17–18 June and 14 August, witnessed the destruction of 48.13 percent of 57 other major Japanese cities, 8 of which incurred 75 percent or more and 22 between 50 and 75 percent destruction of their total area.[7] In the course of these operations the Americans registered success that had proved so elusive in the European context, for three reasons. First, by the second and third quarters of 1945 the American formations in the Marianas had come into possession of the numbers needed to sustain a major offensive. The Tokyo raid of 23/24 May with 562 B-29 bombers was the largest single Superfortress raid of the war while the largest single effort, by 627 Superfortresses, was the raids on Hachioji, Mito, Nagaoka, and Toyama on 1/2 August.[8] Second, the peculiarity of Japanese cities in terms of smallness, massive concentration of population, lack of parks and open spaces, and buildings of wooden construction meant that Japanese cities were vulnerable in a way that European cities were not,[9] and area bombing, with its destruction by fire of whole areas, necessarily inflicted major damage on Japanese industry that was small-scale, local, and widely distributed; something like 42 percent of Japan's industrial capacity was destroyed in the course of these operations. Third, the concentration of the U.S. effort was directed against a Japanese enemy that had no experience on which to draw in terms of preparing its population for what lay ahead and making ready the resources needed to combat incendiary raids. In effect, Germany had some four years' notice of what awaited her in this respect whereas the Japanese had a matter of weeks, at best months, and were wholly unprepared for an effort that killed, injured, or rendered homeless an estimated 22,000,000 people and resulted in major absenteeism throughout industry.[10]

The American effort by war's end took the form of the strategic bombing campaign, which by this time was properly provided in terms of fight escort, and operations by carrier formations, but in one sense the effort was largely irrelevant because, by this time, Japanese industry, already in end-run production, was operating at something like a third of its peak wartime production. Japan, in real terms, had been defeated before the use of atomic bombs against Hiroshima and Nagasaki, and arguably the recourse to such weaponry and means of attack in a sense lessened the achievement of the air forces in this campaign. Had the war finished with either the invasion and conquest of Japan or the country's surrender in direct response to the Allied demand for Japan's surrender (the Potsdam declaration of 26 July 1945) then the achievement of the strategic air campaign would have been obvious and could not be gainsaid, but the manner in which the war ended in a very perverse way lessened the value and importance of the strategic bombing campaign. One final point does need noting though: with a disastrously bad harvest in the offing and the virtual collapse of all seaborne trade by August 1945, Japan faced the certainty of mass starvation, and perhaps as many as seven million deaths, had the war continued into 1946. The strategic bombing campaign, while it registered in eight months the destruction and results that had taken five years to achieve in Europe, was crucially important in the Allied victory, not least in taking the tide of war directly to a population that was then confronted by the reality of national defeat. But, as always in such matters, it was the coming together of the different strands—naval, amphibious, maritime, and air—that produced the fabric of victory, though, in the aftermath of victory, claims did tend to be exclusive most obviously with reference to the establishment of an independent air force in the United States complete with its strategic deterrence role. Be that as it may, one basic point that arises primarily from any study of the strategic bombing offensive directed against Germany would seem worthy of consideration, and it is, very simply, its anti—Clausewitzian dimension in that the offensive came to dominate policy rather than the other way around and, in so doing, marked a recurrent theme in war: technology has a way of becoming an end in itself, to be pursued for its own sake rather than as a means to an end.

CHAPTER 3

Douhet Reconsidered: (1) Inside-Out Warfare and 1991

The first two chapters in book 2 have made reference to air power and indeed the second chapter, relating to the Second World War, devoted some attention to air power and the strategic bombing offensives directed against Germany and Japan. Air power, in the form of the U.S. Air Force and the strategic deterrence role, was cited in the following third chapter. But it is probably not inaccurate to assert that air power *per se* did not come of age until the Arab-Israeli War of June 1967.

This war represented massive failure on the part of the Arab nations, first in failing to realize that war would be the inevitable consequence of their various actions and second in terms of being comprehensively out-thought and out-fought. With reference to the latter, the failure was in very large measure the result of a double-failure, to appreciate Israeli capability and to understand the nature of the Israeli plan of campaign, which, with an overwhelming pre-emptive air assault directed against Egyptian airfields and aircraft, most certainly possessed aspects of novelty in terms of air supremacy being the *sine qua non* of Israeli offensive operations on the ground. The Israeli attack on 5 June, initially directed against eight airfields, registered surprise and broke the back of the only formation that possessed the numbers and capability to contest Israeli intent, the Egyptian Air Force losing more than 200 of its total of some 431 aircraft on this first day of operations, the Israeli Air Force losing 19 of its 260 aircraft in the process.

On the afternoon of this first day, Israeli air attention switched to the other fronts and with 53 Syrian and 28 Jordanian aircraft destroyed, the Israeli Air Force secured supremacy on these fronts before re-concentration of attention and effort over the Sinai where the initial ground offensive had begun. The

Israeli effort again was directed against the main enemy—the Egyptian Army—and against its main defensive positions in the Khân Yunis-Rafah and Abu Aweigîla areas in the certain knowledge that once these were broken the Egyptian overall situation would be beyond redemption. In fact the deployment, with two armored divisions held back and five infantry divisions forward, proved disastrous. Because of Israeli air supremacy, the armor could not advance in order to support the infantry formations with the result that the various formations were subjected to defeat in detail. As it was, the Egyptian decision on the second day to order all formations and units to withdraw behind the Suez Canal merely compounded the twin process of demoralization and disintegration. With the campaign in the Sinai unfolding successfully, the Israelis were able to switch forces and attention to the other two fronts. The West Bank, and specifically Jenin and Nablus and, crucially, Jerusalem, were secured with little difficulty though the inability to use aircraft, tanks, and heavy artillery in these areas meant that something like half of Israeli fatalities, and more than four-fifths of all killed and wounded, were sustained on this front. In the north, the main Israeli effort unfolded on 9 June, after a U.N. cease-fire had been agreed, and by the time it became effective on the following day the Israelis had cleared the Syrian Heights of its six resident brigades and secured El Qunaytirah.[1]

In the desert, where there are no hiding places for formations, air power was critical, and Israeli possession of the advantage won in the first minutes of this war was never to be relinquished over the next 40 years. Certainly in the War of 6–24 October 1973 Israeli air power was initially checked, primarily because the Egyptian use of Guideline and SAM-3 Goa missiles to harass Israeli aircraft at high and medium altitudes and SAM-6 Gainful shoulder-fired missiles and the ZSU 23-4 and ZSU 57-2 to meet low-level air attack. This combination proved very effective in the opening days of the war but primarily in the denial of air space to the Israeli Air Force rather than numbers of aircraft destroyed. Initially, the Israeli Air Force had no answer to the problems that an integrated air defense system presented and was unable to support ground forces. The fact that it began to attack strategic targets in Syria on the 8th was partial acknowledgement of its having been neutralized tactically in the first two days of the war, but by the 8th it had begun to equip itself with chaff and decoy flares and by the following week the Americans had delivered advanced E.C.M. equipment and AGM-62 Walleye and Shrike missiles. Thus supplied, the Israeli Air Force was thereby equipped to re-appear over the battlefield in its anointed role. It flew 1,419 sorties on the Sinai front and destroyed 43 SAM batteries between 18 and 22 October, but in fact the decision of the war had been reached in what had been, more or less, its absence.[2]

Interestingly, the 1967 and 1973 wars coincided with the war in southeast Asia in which air power was crucial in ensuring the American military against defeat but that proved unable to provide victory. The point that the Vietnamese war was not America's to win but in the final analysis could only be decided by the

Vietnamese themselves cannot be gainsaid, but the basic argument reference the limits of air power cannot be disputed, though this was not recognized with respect to Operation *Rolling Thunder* at the time and there is no disguising the fact that the bombing campaign came to represent a massive political liability in terms of both international and American domestic opinion. Most certainly the bombing of the north was turned against itself by a very astute communist leadership. The American promise to halt bombing if the North Vietnamese came to the conference table was countered by the North Vietnamese promise to come to the conference table if the Americans stopped the bombing, and the American high command was thus foisted on its own petard—and this leaves aside the fact that the North Vietnamese agenda for a peace conference was very different indeed from what Washington had planned. But all these events, in the Middle East and southeast Asia, came some 20 years before the following, in the form of an overhead vu-foil, opened a presentation given by the Chairman of the Joint Chiefs of Staff, General Colin Powell, on 15 August 1990 (with emphasis as per the original):

> *IRAQ AIR CAMPAIGN*
> *INSTANT THUNDER*
>
> WHAT IT IS: A **FOCUSED, INTENSE** AIR CAMPAIGN DESIGNED TO IN-
> CAPACITATE IRAQI LEADERSHIP AND DESTROY KEY IRAQI
> MILITARY CAPABILITY, IN A **SHORT** PERIOD OF TIME.
>
> AND IT IS
>
> DESIGNED TO LEAVE BASIC IRAQI INFRASTRUCTURE
> INTACT
>
> WHAT IT IS NOT: A GRADUATED LONG TERM CAMPAIGN DESIGNED
> TO PROVIDE ESCALATION OPTIONS TO COUNTER IRAQI
> MOVES

It was, by any standard, a rather remarkable statement of intent, not least that of not conducting large-scale operations against major industrial and economic targets. It was an intention that was realized by recourse to alternative means of attack. For example, rather than seek to destroy power stations as the means of closing down the Iraqi grid, the Americans used cruise missiles with extended grappling hooks and flew these through pylons with the result that the latter were uprooted and the grid system reduced in output to about 12 percent of pre-war capacity, the cost and length of time needed to replace pylons being little compared to the rebuilding of power stations. But the real point is what had happened in the intervening two decades that made *Instant Thunder* and this sort of operation practical propositions.

The answer is that the various events of the late 1960s and early 1970s went alongside developments that were to transform the conduct of operations, specifically with reference to technological developments that produced aircraft and weapons of unprecedented capability. These were tied to doctrinal changes

that, with a cause-effect relationship with these developments, were to produce, over time, fundamental change, indeed changes that were so fundamental as to genuinely constitute a revolution in military affairs.

Between 1945 and 1975, a whole range of weaponry entered service for the first
time but, for the most part, these various developments represented qualitative
improvements over existing weaponry. The North Vietnamese T-54/55 tanks that
completed the conquest of the south in April 1975 clearly derived from Second
World War parentage. The majority of American carriers and destroyers that
served off southeast Asia remained ships that first entered service during the Second World War. Only in terms of aircraft and missiles were there development of
the kind that represented quantum change in the conduct of war, witness such
systems as the P.1127 VTOL Harrier, designed between 1957 and 1959, and
the AIM-54/AAM-N-11 Phoenix air-to-air missile that began life in 1960 and
that, in prototype form in 1965 as the XAIM-47, destroyed a target aircraft at a
launch range of 127 miles. Such systems did represent something that was
new, but the elements of novelty that were apparent in southeast Asia primarily
concerned jet aircraft and the helicopter, the Vietnam War being the first in
which both were used on an extensive scale. The Korean War had seen the employment of both, and the Algerian War saw the employment of the helicopter
on a major scale, but the intervening decade between this conflict and the Vietnam War had seen developments that had transformed both the jet aircraft and
the helicopter in terms of performance. When the U.S. Navy's F-4B Phantom
fighter was tested in 1961—it flew for the first time in May 1958—it was found to
be superior to all existing fighters in American service by very wide margins in
virtually every aspect of performance, while improvements of engines, couplings,
rotors, and streamlining by the second half of the 1950s had produced the
power, lift, speed, and mechanical reliability that enabled the helicopter to perform a number of different tactical roles over the battlefield.[3] The increased importance of aircraft and helicopters in the conduct of war was made evident in
the course of the Vietnam War. In a way that was unique at the time, the Vietnam War was synonymous with the B-52 Stratofortress, the Phantom and F-105
Thunderchief, the UH-1 Huey, the AH-1G Cobra and the CH-47 Chinook.[4]

The year 1973 that saw the completion of the withdrawal of American combat formations from southeast Asia and the turning of American military attention to the increasingly vexatious problem of how a war inside Europe was to
be fought, the commitment in southeast Asia having largely prevented the small
print of Flexible Response being added. In this matter, the Vietnam War pointed
the U.S. military in two related directions. As early as 1966 in South Vietnam, the
1st Cavalry Division, complete with its equipment and supplies, was able to undertake sustained operations over several provinces over a four-month period,
while in 1968 the same formation, in the course of Operation *Liberty Canyon* and
at one day's notice, was redeployed over a distance of 570 miles in the course of
two weeks. It was able to assign its leading brigades to other divisions before
being re-formed with the arrival of divisional headquarters and being committed immediately to operations. Such mobility was obviously unprecedented, and
it is small wonder that, in the aftermath of the Vietnam War, American military

attention should have turned to the use and implications of air mobility to square the circle within the European theater of operations. Moreover, the Vietnam War also brought home to the American military the practicality of the concentration of firepower by air. The combination of command helicopters, fighter-bomber and AH-1G Cobra strikes, scout helicopters for the marking of B-52 missions, and the use of such aircraft as the AC-130H and C-130 Hercules and the Chinook in the support role enabled the Americans to concentrate overwhelming firepower in the course of their operations. In terms of the conventional battle, the potential importance of concentrated and properly coordinated airborne firepower was self-evident, especially when tied to the development of such weapons as TOW missiles for the anti-tank role. Thus, at the very time when the Soviets were seeking to enhance an existing conventional superiority and capability by improvement of the firepower, mobility, and supply of massed armored formations, the Vietnam War opened American eyes to a very different combination of fire and movement in the form of air mobility.[5]

The programs in hand within the United States in late 1973 are bewildering in their diversity and numbers, and ranged from the new Trident submarines and a missile program that was to yield the D-5 to the Army's M1A1 Abrams tank and M2 Bradley armored personnel carrier, while for the Air Force there was the B-1 Lancer bomber, a refurnished F-111-F bomber, and a host of missiles[6] that, when allied to parallel developments in communications, E.C.M., and surveillance equipment, represented potentially a major change in the conduct of battle specifically in terms of a range of new fighter aircraft coming into service. The F-14 Tomcat first flew in December 1970 and the F-15 Eagle in July 1972, while the F-16 Fighting Falcon was to make its maiden flight in January 1974.[7] The significance of the F-15 Eagle and F-16 Falcon lay in the fact that, given the development of the F-100 engine, they were the first aircraft to possess thrust-to-weight ratios of more than one, and both incorporated "fly-by-wire" and electro-optical "heads-up display" technology. They were to the Phantom what that aircraft had been to all other aircraft when it had entered service. The new aircraft could out-maneuver any other fighter in service with ease, while "heads-up display" allowed a pilot to engage an enemy without switching attention between the sky and instrument panel: "fly-by-wire" technology allowed aircraft to be deliberately designed or loaded to be unstable but handle correctly and conferred a tolerance to damage denied aircraft with conventional hydraulic control systems. Subsequent advances in the micro-miniaturization of computers and software produced aircraft increasingly capable of flying themselves. For example, when the F-15A Eagle entered service in November 1974 it was equipped with 60,000 avionic software codes but its successor, the F-15E, by 1990, carried 40 times as many. The extent of the qualitative advantage thus conferred on this new generation of American fighters can be gauged by the claim that the F-14 Tomcat, equipped with multiple target "track-while-scan" and "look-down/shoot-down" capability, could track a maximum of 22 targets and engage 6 simultaneously. The U.S. Navy's calculation was that the new aircraft would be able to deal with minimum odds of 4:1 in combat with Soviet land-based fighters, and the corollary needed little in the way of elaboration. With the

new fighters coming into service in the foreseeable future, the Americans possessed a confidence in their ability to fight and win the battle for air supremacy
in the N.A.T.O. theater of operations.

Leaving aside the fact that this American confidence went alongside what
would have been a certain European skepticism but for the fact that the European N.A.T.O. members were trying to hold their collective breath at this time,
these various developments, alongside the formation of the Training and
Doctrine Command (TRADOC) in 1973, pointed in the direction of AirLand
Battle. This was essentially an army doctrine that envisaged the use of the Air
Force to win the battle for supremacy over Europe and of highly mobile groups,
very heavy in terms of firepower, to move against Soviet formations in depth.
A radical departure from orthodoxy lay in the abandonment of the linear defense, the dispersal of force in the face of enemy superiority, and the bringing
of massed firepower against flanks of an advancing enemy, and this went alongside a determination to ensure, by operations directed against lines of communication forward from the Soviet Union into central-western Germany, that
second-echelon Soviet forces could not be brought forward into the combat
zone. To Europeans, such intent seemed neither here nor there given the very
strong likelihood of first-echelon Soviet forces being able to win the initial battle. There was little point in preventing second-echelon formations coming
forward if the first-echelon battle had been lost. But the Americans in effect held
the power of decision, and if the Europeans did keep faith, as indeed they did,
AirLand Battle came to sit alongside Flexible Response regarding the European
theater, but, of course, this doctrine had general applicability. The Carter Doctrine, enunciated January 23, 1980, pointed to a major arms program designed
to provide the United States with the means of intervention throughout the
world, and specifically in an increasingly volatile Middle East.

There were two parallel developments in what was to be a both tortuous and
protracted process whereby AirLand Battle emerged onto center stage, primarily between 1978 and 1982 but was not complete until 1986 when the final
FM-100-5 became established orthodoxy. The first was the process whereby
blessed with academic and joint service backing, the Maneuver Warfare school
emerged complete with a formidable array of arguments, seemingly endless definitions and acronyms, and a vocabulary that appeared to have been devised in
order to confuse rather than enlighten. The second was that even though
TRADOC and its personnel were careful in seeking to establish a working relationship with the Air Force and primarily on the basis of equality, AirLand Battle in effect meant a subordination of the Air Force to the requirements of army
formations on the ground, and most certainly a commitment to AirLand Battle in
effect precluded any other major Air Force combat role. But the new aircraft and
weaponry made possible an Air Force search in quite another direction. With
the strategic deterrence role in third or fourth place in the Air Force pecking
order, the new aircraft and weaponry re-opened the strategic option, away from
the tactical—away from the enemy military and the battlefield—and back to the

enemy state and system. In a very obvious sense, this new developments meant that Nakajima, Douhet, Seversky, Mitchell, and Harris, and others, were back in the frame.

The strategic bombing cause came to be associated with two individuals within the U.S. Air Force, the first being a certain Colonel John Ashley Warden III (1943–) who, throughout his career, was a figure to whom controversy attached itself at all too frequent intervals; he was regarded within the Air Force as something of a maverick, a loose cannon. But in August 1990, he headed the Checkmate organization in the air staff in the Pentagon, which was one of six divisions within a team of some 80 officers concerned with the development of war-fighting concepts. Warden was an individual who sought to marry Clause-witzian centers of gravity to strategic bombing, and this he did in terms of the development of the idea of the Five Circles, which saw society as rings within rings. On the outside was the military and inside the protection thus afforded would be the population of the state, then the infrastructure, specifically communications physical and otherwise, then key production, and, finally, at the core, the leadership of a country. To Warden, the crucial point was to identify the centers of gravity—the points of potentially critical vulnerability—within each circle, and he sub-divided each circle or ring into five further parts based on the same structure until the true centers of gravity were revealed. To Warden, the outer four rings should be attacked only as the means of exposing the leadership ring, and this belief emerged as he felt his way toward concepts that were to be labeled "Inside-out Warfare" and "Bombing for Effect," and which aimed at strategic paralysis of the enemy state (i.e., system warfare) rather than the destruction of the enemy field forces (i.e., military warfare). The whole notion of "Inside-out Warfare" embraced the idea that historically wars had been fought from the outside-in, that is armies had to fight their way through an enemy defensive system, past armies in the field, in order to reach the crucial areas of state and society, of government and the economy, but in the future, air forces, committed to a decapitation strategy, could defeat a state without having to destroy the enemy field forces. In effect, the Warden concepts were akin to the removal of an apple's core, without first having to peel and cut the apple into pieces. These various ideas, which were committed to paper in *The Air Campaign: Planning for Combat* and published in 1988, were not well received within the Air Force, which in the 1980s was primarily concerned with its responsibilities under the AirLand Battle label that had been finally agreed upon with the Army in 1984.

Warden was inside the Pentagon at the time of the Iraqi invasion, conquest, and occupation of Kuwait in August 1990, and it was he who came to the fore in early August 1990 when the United States was confronted by a situation in which she faced the crisis thus created without any plan of campaign for a war with Iraq and without even a plan of mobilization and movement of forces to the theater. Warden came forward with the *Instant Thunder* proposal, which in its initial form proposed an attack conducted in overwhelming force that would isolate and incapacitate the Saddam Hussein regime and in effect destroy Iraqi offensive and defensive capabilities, and, as its name implies, would be very different from what had been attempted in southeast Asia two decades previously. When proposed, the Warden ideas were very attractive and for obvious reason—they provided offensive options at a time when the United States seemed to have none—but two matters served to produce a plan of campaign that was very different from what Warden had proposed. The second of these, the long-term matter, was the simple fact that in August 1990 the promise of victory was part of a package that envisaged the offensive effort being directed against no fewer than 84 centers of gravity. Over the months that followed, this was expanded to the extent that by 15 January 1991 the number of targets that were attacked and had been afforded strategic centers of gravity status had risen to 481.[8] Leaving aside the problem created by physics and language in terms of each and every object having only one center of gravity, the basis of the August 1990 claims, given the proliferation of targets over the next six months, is somewhat hard to discern. But, and the first matter that was the immediate concern, the Warden thesis, while it did impress certain individuals in the American high command with the power of decision, came to be part of a wider air power formula that envisaged a campaign with both strategic and tactical dimensions but that would be primarily the latter, directed against Iraqi military forces in Kuwait.

As the air power options slipped into place Warden, *non grata* with certain individuals in positions of authority at this time, was moved to one side and the second individual, Major David Deptula (1952–), in effect was charged with turning the strategic proposal and outline into a detailed operational plan. Deptula had been in the doctrine section within the air staff some two months before Warden arrived, and quite independently had been thinking along very similar lines to Warden. When both were in the staff, Warden in effect became Deptula's mentor, and after Deptula left for a position on the staff of the Air Secretary he was to become the main author of the 1990 "Global Reach—Global Power. Reshaping for the Future" paper that envisaged major changes for the Air Force, specifically in terms of the acquisition of an ability to "inflict strategic and operational paralysis on any adversary by striking key nodes in his war-making potential." In August 1990, Warden and Deptula worked together on the Checkmate papers, and after one visit to theater after which Warden returned to Washington, Deptula assumed responsibility for the preparation of that part of the plan of campaign directed against cause rather than symptom, against the Iraqi state and leadership rather than the Iraqi military formations within Kuwait. In so doing, Deptula sought to set in place what would be a very deliberate attempt to wage "Inside-out Warfare" though in the event this particular effort was overshadowed, both in terms of scale of effort and public portrayal of events, by the tactical option.[9]

The final plan of campaign, and indeed the course and outcome of the air campaign, lend themselves to a number of interpretations and conclusions, and one would suggest that three of the latter—a trinity no less—might be in order. The first point very simply is that air power was the basis of the victory that was won in this campaign. In the immediate aftermath of the campaign, there were attempts by certain military personnel to claim that the army did a job in four days that the air forces failed to complete in 38, but this was wholly mendacious and was related to inter-service standing not least in terms of such matters as funding and status. As part of the planning, the army staffs tried to insist that the tactical part of the effort should aim at the destruction of half the Iraqi armor, artillery, and armored personnel carriers in theater prior to the start of a ground offensive, but while such proportions proved beyond the air effort the fact was that losses of between 30 and 40 percent effectively wore down Iraqi strength, and with a corollary that was wholly unanticipated. The waging of an air offensive over a month, with full coverage on television and radio, left Iraqi troops in the front line only too aware that their turn would come, and there was a progressive demoralization within the Iraqi Army formations in Kuwait that manifested itself in widespread desertion. The simple fact was that the air offensive provided the basis of victory. The victory had to be completed by the forces on the ground, most obviously in terms of the clearing of Kuwait and the advance to Kuwait City, but the fact was that the ground offensive did not begin until the victory had been won and outcome assured, and at minimal cost to ground formations.

The second conclusion that might be drawn from this campaign is that for the first occasion in five decades the idea of the *Vernichtungsschlacht*, or the single battle of annihilation, has been restored to the military vocabulary. The idea was all but totally discredited in the course of the 20th century and this suggestion that the technological developments of the last two decades may have restored such battles to the military repertoire would seem to border on the absurd. Certainly the suggestion is flawed in one respect. The concept of the decisive battle historically has concerned itself with a narrowly military phenomenon, namely the destruction of enemy field formations, yet at the present time the idea of a defeat that did not embrace state, society, and military would seem to be wholly unrealistic. The nature of the state in the late 20th century renders the idea of a victory with only a military dimension—against an army in the field—quixotic. But, perversely, any consideration of the 1991 campaign must provoke two thoughts: that the decrease in the size of armies and the difficulties of reconstitution that have been constants since 1945 must expose an army to the danger of defeat in a single battle, and that in 1991 what was nominally the fourth largest military establishment in the world was effectively destroyed in a single campaign. Arguably such a defeat as the one sustained by the Iraqi military in 1991—a comprehensive defeat incurred within a single campaign that lasted little more than a month—was something that had not occurred since 1940 and the defeat of France, and the parallels between the two events are quite close, even if one of the most important differences was that the aspect of single-nation advantage of 1940 was no more by 1991. Both France in 1940 and Iraq in 1991 shared a lack of strategic depth despite considerable area, massive inferiority in the air, less than adequate understanding of the balance between the offense and defense as it existed at the times in question, communications systems that were simply overwhelmed, and possessed of, perhaps more accurately trapped by, experience of outdated forms of warfare that actually contributed to defeat. The defeat of

France in 1940, however, is very much the exception in warfare in the 20th century and is the only case of a great power being defeated in the course of a single campaign. 1940 excepted, however much great powers sought the decisive battle in two world wars, the *Vernichtungsschlacht* was incapable of realization. On the evidence of the 1991 campaign, it could be argued, and seriously, that a *Vernichtungsschlacht* can now be fought and won by air power, and perhaps even by air power alone.

The third conclusion that might be drawn from this campaign is the extension of the second, that not simply was it the case that the *Vernichtungsschlacht* can now be fought and won but that this campaign foreshadowed the return of the element of decisiveness in war. So many of the 20th century's wars were protracted, exhaustive, or lacked any element of decisiveness, but the 1991 conflict could be said to have returned the element of decisiveness to war and for one reason—the defeat of the fourth or fifth largest military in the world in a little more than a month must represent speed and decisiveness—but for one fact of life: the Americans may have won the campaign that was fought but did not win the war, in large measure because those with the power of decision within the American high command did not know the difference between a war and a campaign.

How and why this came about is not the subject of this examination of warfare, but the fact was that the American high command was not prepared to prosecute to its logical end a war against a regime that it had consistently supported during its war with Iran and that Washington had not condemned, regarding the use of chemical weapons against the Kurdish village of Halabja on 16 March 1988 and then repeatedly against Iranian formations over the next six months. In this refusal to move against the regime in Baghdad—which in effect meant that the greater part of the American and coalition effort in 1991 was directed against the symptom rather than the cause—there were obviously various factors at work, presumably the most immediate being a desire not to undertake any form of action that might strengthen Iran, and this extended to the refusal to sanction one of Warden's proposals, which was to halt the bombing of Iraqi Army formations and to ensure their immediate surrender and then their being moved to Baghdad in order to overthrow the regime. The point of this refusal to move in February–March 1991 was two-fold. The Baghdad regime was left free to suppress revolts that the United States had encouraged, an estimated 240,000 Marsh Arabs being killed in the process by formations loyal to the regime. More importantly, at least in terms of war, warfare, and the situation in the Middle East, the resultant American long-term commitment in theater, which was similar to the French after 1919, with each passing year left with the commitment to prove and enforce the victory that had been won. By 1995, the Hussein regime had secured full control over its territory and even if over-flights could not be prevented the Americans were left with a massively expensive commitment to no purpose.

A number of other matters might be presented as points of significance regarding this campaign. This campaign witnessed the arrival of the 24-hour battle and possibly foreshadowed campaigns irrespective of seasons, and it demonstrated an unprecedented reach inland of naval units with respect to direct fire. The 1991 campaign was the first in which Space provided a dimension of war, and this conflict was the first in which there was real-time coverage by the media. With reference to the air campaign, it could be argued that this was the first occasion in history when ground elements operated in support of air (and naval) power, in which air power was the primary agency of destruction, and was illustrative of a trend to use air power either primarily or alone in the conduct of war. The 1991 conflict was the first occasion in war when a state of reasonable size and depth was subjected to attack across its entire area in an initial offensive operation, and, in accordance with the vu-foil content, this campaign witnessed the conclusive defeat of a state without the necessity of having to complete the wholesale destruction of its industrial infrastructure, society, and armed forces. It was a campaign notable for the fact that one party deliberately exercised a measure of restraint in leaving certain enemy command and control facilities in service in order to better read the battle that was in the process of unfolding. These points may be disputed as might others, witness that the campaign saw the comprehensive defeat of a nation that was quite separate from the defeat and destruction of its armed forces and was the first conflict in which mobility presented itself on the battlefield before the battle of destruction on the ground had been fought. But there is one last point that seems to have eluded many commentators, namely that this conflict was perhaps the first occasion when it was not necessary to fight for air supremacy. The battle for air superiority was decided by the scale of the initial attack and the technological and operational qualitative advantage that the U.S. air formations possessed over the Iraqi air defense system. There was no need to fight a battle for supremacy—and for the Iraqis there was no point in even trying to dispute coalition air supremacy—because of initial, overwhelming advantages of coalition forces, and in this respect one comment is perhaps interesting though by the nature of things must remain un-attributable, but when asked when the American command knew that the campaign had been won, the response was after ten minutes. Thus, perhaps, we may have in this campaign, the shortest conflict in history, real time.[10]

CHAPTER 4

Douhet Reconsidered: (2) Doctrine and the Kosovo Campaign, 1999

One of the features of certain of the more recent wars has been the prominence of air power in the conduct of operations, and in the previous chapter was set out the idea of the 1967 campaign representing the coming of age of air power. Also in that chapter was set out, by implication rather than direct statement, the idea that the 1967 and 1973 campaigns were fundamentally different from the campaign fought in 1991. The latter represented the first "inside-out" campaign directed at least in part against an enemy system whereas the 1967 and 1973 campaigns were conventional in being tactical and directed against enemy military forces in the field. But perhaps the 1999 campaign with respect to Serbia and Kosovo rather than either the 1991 or 2003 Iraqi campaigns, or the N.A.T.O. operations in the Bosnian conflict in 1995, was "The Air Campaign." It was an undertaking that was not attended by major offensive operations by military formations, as was the case in both 1991 and 2003, but it was a conflict that has commanded much controversy, not a little of it directed along lines set down by the observation

The almost universal belief among air warfare professionals that a more aggressive effort starting on the opening night, in consonance with a more doctrinally pristine strategy, would have yielded the same result more quickly may have been correct as far as it went, but that conviction was based solely on faith in the intrinsic power of the air weapon, not on any evidence directly related to the case in hand.[1]

Perhaps no single individual embodies the first part of that statement better than Lieutenant-General Michael C. Short, commander of the 16th Air Force during the campaign, and this analysis of the 1991 campaign will be presented not on the basis of detailed examination of events but by consideration of the claims Short presented in his Copenhagen and Oslo papers in 2001 and in the interview he gave on the website.

In his analysis of this campaign, Short developed four main lines of argument. First, he argued that the 1999 air offensive represented a wholly misdirected and largely irrelevant undertaking on two counts, that it was gradualist and that he was not allowed to use all available force from the outset and that the effort initially and primarily was directed against Serbian military formations in the field rather than the Milošević regime. Second, Short asserted that there was no declared end-state, a point of criticism that he continued to make even in 2001 as evidence of his correctness; his point was that in 2001 N.A.T.O. forces were still in Kosovo with no end in sight. Third, Short was dismissive in that he deemed the result of the N.A.T.O. effort as "victory by happenstance" rather than victory by design. Fourth, and last, he asserted that the nature and deliberations of the coalition worked against proper and timely decisions regarding the conduct of operations. This, one would suggest, represents a fair and objective summary of the views expressed by General Short, the gist of his arguments being that what was a 78-day offensive really represented a great deal of effort wasted primarily on two counts, first, that its framework was provided by political considerations of very dubious worth and that were not operationally valid, and, second, that the offensive was primarily directed against Serbian ground forces in Kosovo rather than regime targets in Belgrade, that is, against symptom rather than cause.

Such views invite two initial comments, first, that with these views the general placed himself in the line established from Nakajima and Douhet via Mitchell and Harris to Warden, an unbroken line of argument that insists that air power alone could produce the desired result in war. It would seem that he embraced a belief in the efficacy of air power—represented by aircraft and weaponry of unprecedented capability—in terms of effect upon an enemy's will and capability, but it would appear that such views would seem to embrace a knowledge and correct anticipation of every aspect of the enemy's organization, capability, and intent.[2]

That, in turn, invites the obvious conclusion, the second comment, which, with just a little bit of help from history, may be summarized with four observations: first, that wars invariably assume courses and outcomes different from that intended by their authors; second (and to return to Clausewitz's dictum):

the greatest and most important act of judgement that a statesman or general is called upon to exercise is to correctly understand the nature of the war in which he is engaged and not to take it, or attempt to make of it, something it is not and cannot be;

third, it is easy to conquer, it is hard to occupy; and fourth, no plan ever survives the first contact of battle. In fact, any examination of this campaign would suggest that for every complicated human problem there is a simple solution that invariably is neat, plausible, and wrong, and that men are seldom at their best in dealing with insoluble problems.[3] To these may be added Sarrail's comment cited earlier and, being concerned with the workings of a coalition, does possess a certain relevance with respect to General Short and 1999.

The most important of the four views expressed by Short concern not how the campaign was conducted but his view of "The coalition of the willing." Short was very emphatic on this point. He was derisive of the fact that what was on line in 1999 was a coalition in which the power of veto was exercised by any and all member states. As the general put it:

Does everyone have a vote, or is it like it was in the Gulf, where we put together a coalition of the willing? Someone sets the rules, and everyone who was willing to follow those rules became part of the coalition. That is the way I prefer it, quite frankly. If I were ever to fight again, I would fight in a coalition of the willing where we all agree on how we will do this beforehand.

Short, in this one paragraph, in his frustration, seems to have forgotten that coalitions are not created and organized to suit the dictates and prerequisites of an individual state or a commander. The drawing of the lessons of history is possessed of obvious dangers but two would seem to be the desirability of the coalition rather than the single nation and, that in 9 cases in 10, one fights as one finds the war rather than by script. By the very nature of things, one fights as one must rather than as one would. The ability to fight in a manner and to ends that accord with one's own terms of reference has proved very difficult indeed, and perhaps may be confined only to the latter stages of a war fought over a protracted period and then, of course, only by one side.

As it was, one would note that in dealing with the question of the coalition, Short was very emphatic in one matter. As he noted:

N.A.T.O. had a chain of command in place in Naples for fifty years that was supposed to run this war. Instead, thirty days before the war started General Clark shuffled aside that N.A.T.O. chain of command and set up a U.S.-only chain of command—a joint task force with only Americans throughout the process. That was how the war was run. Essentially General Clark was saying (to all of the other N.A.T.O. members) that only the Americans were capable of doing this thing for the rest of you should get out of the way: it is OK for you to drop bombs but we will make all the choices and decisions. That is incredibly arrogant and not the right way to do business.

One would not quarrel with the sentiment herein, but one would note the obvious: European N.A.T.O. over the decades has become dependent upon U.S. leadership and capability, incredible though that might seem regarding central Europe in 1999. But one would note two matters, and the first is that, for a number of European N.A.T.O. states, the 1999 campaign represented their first military commitment since 1945. Second, one would note the German reluctance to be involved in this campaign. In the event, of course, *Bündnisfähigkeit* prevailed, and Germany could not escape the obligations and responsibilities of membership of N.A.T.O., but reference to one matter might be in order. In 2003, both France and Germany refused to be involved in the American campaign against Iraq; one suspects that most of Europe heaved a quiet sigh of relief that these two countries on this occasion turned their backs on involvement in a military campaign.

One wonders if Short's comments about the nature and composition of the chain of command invite the observation that presumably he would not have objected to an all air force chain of command or a chain of command that thought like he did in terms of the use of air power. As it was, in his Internet interview, Short expressed the view that in the event of N.A.T.O. going to war and in light of the primacy of the United States within the alliance "then we need to have more than one of nineteen votes"—a comment that suggests misunderstanding the nature of a coalition. So the United States needs "to have more than one of nineteen votes"—and if she does she will have no allies.

But lest the point be missed, Short was basically protesting the fact that a number of states objected to proposed operations and that their objections, which were political rather than operational, prevailed. One does find this aspect of Short's objections to be somewhat surprising. War is not necessarily a purely military phenomenon. The essential characteristic of war is political. Combat and fighting, obviously, are primarily military, but war, in essence, is a political manifestation of armed conflict, and Short's objection to the use of the power of veto by various states on grounds other than military does seem somewhat incongruous; political considerations dictate targets and methods of attack, and such matters are not the call of a commander serving heads of states or government. One has utmost sympathy for Short on two counts in this matter, namely the fact that it took up to two weeks to get target approval within the American high command and that if and when approval was then forthcoming the other N.A.T.O. members could then have their say. Such a situation must have been most difficult and frustrating, but one would suggest, at least in terms of the power of veto, such a situation was very right and proper.

What is at issue here is the crucial point that is so often confused—the different levels of war involving states, combat involving services, and fighting that involves formations and units—and this confusion goes hand-in-hand with a parallel set of confusion, namely between the nature of the war and the conduct of the campaign. This point is made because so many accounts of this and the 1991 and 1999 conflicts do not seem able to distinguish between on the one side the nature and the conduct of operations and on the other side a war and a campaign.

Written elsewhere is the comment

What was fought in 1991 was not a war but a campaign, and western problems in dealing with Iraq since February 1991 have stemmed from the fact that those members of the Western political and military leadership with the power of decision in 1991 never understood the distinction. The Gulf War, which began on 2 August 1990 with the Iraqi invasion of Kuwait, ended on 9 September 1996 when, with the Iraqi re-conquest of the northern provinces, the United States found herself in a position similar to that of France in summer 1925 after her two-year occupation of the Ruhr—no longer able to confirm an earlier victory with every passing year. For the American-led coalition, the campaign of 1991 was won, the war of 1990–1996 was lost. . . . in very large measure because neither Bush nor Powell understood the difference between a war and a campaign.[4]

In considering the 1999 campaign—note campaign rather than a war—one would repeat the basic argument and for the very good reason that General Short, as a true disciple of Douhet and Mitchell, would seem to be convinced that air power has blurred the distinction between the nature and the conduct of war. There is, throughout the general's pronouncements on the subject, the basic point that air forces, or more accurately the U.S. Air Force, possesses weaponry of unprecedented accuracy and destructive power, and there would seem to be two attendant conclusions. The first would seem to be the efficacy of such power and its use against an enemy state unchanged and unchanging other than the damage inflicted upon it by one's own offensive action, the second that, properly used, this air power, this unprecedented destructive power, can in itself produce the desired result, witness the Short view concerning the correct use of air power

on the first day or the first night of the war . . . an attack with incredible speed and incredible violence . . . that (the enemy) could never have imagined . . . (and which will) shock him into inaction until he is paralysed so that you can get ahead of him inside his decision-loop and force him to accept your terms.

This is the first part of Short's two-part argument that, in 1999, air power was not used properly, that he was not allowed to use all available force from the outset and that he was ordered to concentrate the air effort against Serbian forces in Kosovo rather than against the Milošcvić regime in Belgrade. One would confine oneself to two comments on these arguments. First, the 1999 effort worked and it did produce the desired result. The Short line of argument really affords this fact minimal and grudging admission, and it is very quickly passed over, but the fact was that the N.A.T.O. effort in 1999 worked. One would willingly acknowledge, however, that air power was but one factor, probably the most important single factor in that success. Conflicts are seldom if ever decided by single factors and one would note that in 1999 air power was complemented by evidence of N.A.T.O. solidarity and commitment despite the differences, by the German contribution within the N.A.T.O. effort and by the contribution of the new N.A.T.O. members, and by diplomacy and other instruments of power. With reference to the latter, one would suggest that the importance of the visit of the Russian special envoy and former prime minister Viktor Chernomyrdin (1938–) to Belgrade in June 1999 should not be demeaned. General Short's view was that the Chernomyrdin talks "probably had some influence," but this utterance sells short the efforts of the Russian. President Slobodan Milošević (1941–2006) took the decision to accept N.A.T.O.'s terms on 3 June and as a direct result of the Chernomyrdin exchange when he was confronted, for the first time, by the double realization that there would be no Russian help or intervention and that N.A.T.O. was not prepared to be seen to have failed. This discussion with Chernomyrdin marked the point where various matters began to come together to shape Milošević's decisions, and however important air power *per se* undoubtedly was both in terms of what it had done and what it threatened to do if the war continued, it was the coming together of various matters—alliance solidarity, Serbia's diplomatic and political isolation, the fact that Serbia was incurring major damage and popular support for a war in Kosovo had been all but extinguished, and the threat of future N.A.T.O. action that could only end in Serbia's complete and comprehensive defeat—that brought about Milošević's decision to cut losses at this time.[5]

Second, in 1991 the victory that was won by air power nonetheless had to be completed by a ground offensive. As noted in the previous chapter, some U.S. Army accounts of 1991 set out the claim that ground forces had to win a victory that had eluded the Air Force, and one can be suitably dismissive of such claims. But the point was that a ground campaign was necessary and if ground action did not begin until the campaign had been won, it was nonetheless necessary as part of the effort that resulted in overall victory. The contrast with 1999 needs no elaboration but perhaps one observation is in order. The air dimension, clearly, was the most important of the various parts, but it was the instrument of policy and not policy *per se* and, in June 1999, air power came in three packages: its performance over the last three months, the certainty of increasing destructiveness if the campaign continued, and the long-term threat of air power in conjunction with a ground offensive.

One would conclude with reference to four matters placed before the reader. First, the 1999 result was what General Short termed "victory by happenstance" as opposed to "victory by design." This statement implies that the only real victories are those by design? One can think of any number of campaigns in history in which campaigns and battles have unfolded in ways very different from what was intended, but one would suggest that the victories that were ultimately won were no less real than had they been wholly intended.

Second, this first point does raise another matter that Short himself paraded ostentatiously, namely:

On this particular day General (Wesley K.) Clark was giving Admiral (James O.) Ellis (Jr.)[6] and I guidance on how he thought business ought to be done. At the end of giving us that guidance he said: "Mike and Jim, I hope this will work." Admiral Ellis thought about that and he said, "General Clark, hope is not a course of action." A pretty insightful comment for a Navy Admiral! But he was dead right.

What General Clark stated was that he hoped the plan that he was proposing would work, and in the final analysis that is all an individual commander can do. The basis of a plan must be rational calculation, but there can never be any guarantee that either a plan can be implemented or if put into effect it will deliver the desired result. In the final analysis, a plan can never be more than the basis of hope.

Third, the centers of gravity fixation within American planning staffs would seem to represent a disservice. It smacks of there being a simple solution—as long as it can be properly and correctly identified—and represents a pertinent example of good servant, bad master and it has now become the latter. And fourth, and last, the notion of an attainable end-state. General Short was very critical indeed of the leadership, specifically in terms of entering "this conflict with no idea of what the end-state would be." The idea of an end-state in the Balkans would almost seem a contradiction of terms, but the whole idea of a predictable end-state implies a level of anticipation and correctness that flies in the face of von Moltke's dictum that no plan survives the first contact with the enemy.

What is very disturbing about these arguments is the element of certainty, the grip of commander on truths that seem to have eluded everyone else, and this exists at so many different levels. There is the firm, indeed unshakeable, belief that an end-state can be defined and secured, that war itself can be controlled, and that air power has the means to realize objectives. The latter is perhaps the most pernicious of the various arguments enunciated by General Short because it would suggest that the conduct of operations by an advanced and sophisticated air force with massive technological superiority over an enemy can in itself determine the terms of reference and the nature of war. Suffice it to note that at very best such an argument is dubious, at worse false and potentially disastrous in terms of holding out to an electorate the promise of certain victory that cannot be realized, witness the present campaigns in Afghanistan and Iraq that have now lasted longer than the Second World War in Europe. And with reference to the Iraqi conflict, that war apparently was at an end in March 2003 while, with reference to the events of 11 September 2001 more than eight years after the event, and after billions of dollars that have been spent, Osama Bin Laden (1957–) remains at large.

The greatest and most important act of judgement that a statesman or general is called upon to exercise is to correctly understand the nature of the war in which he is engaged and not to take it, or attempt to make of it, something it is not and cannot be.

—Carl von Clausewitz, *On War*.
—Book I. *On the Nature of War*.
—Chapter I. *What is War?*

This episode that culminated with the meeting of Chernomyrdin and Milošević and the latter's decision to seek an arrangement that would meet N.A.T.O. demands has commanded a great deal of attention.[7] These various sources list a number of factors that made for Milošević's decision of 3 June, and that these divided into two parts, an initial series of miscalculations and the final calculation that nothing was to be gained, and potentially there was much to lose by continuing to resist N.A.T.O. demands. With reference to the first matter, the basic point would seem to be that Milošević calculated that he could outlast any bombing effort and on three counts, first, that N.A.T.O. would be confronted with considerable anti-war protest movements that would hamper and perhaps curtail its operations; second, that the failure of the Desert Fox campaign in December 1998 suggested that Serbia would be able to survive the worst that N.A.T.O. might do; and, third, that a bombing campaign would consolidate Serbian popular support for the regime. With reference to the latter, it should be noted that there was a very real popular resentment at the terms presented at Rambouillet in February that most Serbs thought to be thoroughly unreasonable. It may very well have been the case that such opposition precluded any real possibility of Milošević accepting or even negotiating with N.A.T.O. regarding the Rambouillet terms.

With reference to the second matter, there would seem to be a number of related considerations at work. There was the awareness that the air campaign to date had inflicted increasingly serious damage on Serbia and that public support for the regime was declining. This went hand-in-hand with a growing awareness that refusal to accept N.A.T.O. terms could only result in an intensification of the campaign that would result in increased damage to Serbia and specifically to the regime itself. There was also an awareness that N.A.T.O. was preparing for a future effort that would involve major ground operations that would most likely result in disastrous, total defeat. In addition to these points, there was the awareness, for the first time, that Russia could not provide Serbia with any form of military help or assistance, that former members of the Warsaw Pact had denied Russia rights of transit through their air space, and China was not in any position to provide support. By this time, it was clear that N.A.T.O. was united in its collective determination to see the matter through to its end, that the alliance was not going to divide, and would not allow itself to be seen to have failed. All these matters appear to have come together in the form of a calculation on the part of Milošević that he had nothing to gain and much to risk by holding out any longer.

There is no point in seeking to define which of these was the one that finally prompted the decision to settle but clearly Russia's inability to provide succor, when combined with the fact that a settlement would be conducted under U.N. and not N.A.T.O. auspices, was very important, but the fact was that it was the coming together of various calculations, not a single one, that was important, and with reference to the air campaign one comment might be in order:

It was not what we bombed but that we bombed. The coalition did not crumble, the Russians did not bail Belgrade out, China was unable to affect the war. At some point [it was made clear] to Milošević that he was not going to be able to wait out the bombing, that N.A.T.O. was not going to go away, that Serbia was going to be progressively dismantled. He chose to try to get the best negotiated settlement he could. To say that it was this or that target that was important is to engage in [pointless] mirror-image speculation.[8]

and the important point would seem to be the cumulative effect of air operations, and, as a corollary to this, the point that an all-out offensive from the start might well have proved self-defeating.

Book IV

War and Wars since the End of the Cold War

CHAPTER 1

The End of the Cold War

In terms of war and wars, the 20th century was dominated by two world wars and the confrontation between the United States and Soviet Union, but arguably the collapse of a Euro-centric world order, the emergence of three non-European states among the most powerful states in the world, and the shift of industrial and financial power away from Europe and indeed away from North America into the Pacific rim represent massive changes, but these go alongside other changes no less significant. The Green Revolution, the medical revolution, and major population growth in developing countries have been no less important than the other changes that were the by-product of war and confrontation, and, of course, there remain the technological revolution and the changes wrought by global warming and climate change. All these matters were the product of the 20th century and their consequences reach into the new millennium, but in terms of war perhaps the most important change stems from the fact that the Westphalian state system came to be set in place across the world and directly as a consequence of European primacy, but since the end of empire, and specifically since the end of the Cold War, war itself has undergone fundamental change. The Cold War was akin to European colonialism in that both froze hatreds, and their passing has seen thaw and the re-assertion of those hatreds. With their return there has been a proliferation of conflicts that have resulted in a re-writing of the terms of reference of war *per se*.

Perhaps the most important of these various changes relates to the collapse of the Soviet system that brought an end to a period of stability within Europe but did not bring peace. The process of Soviet disintegration spawned a series of conflicts that added to those already being fought around the world. It has been estimated that in 2004 there were more than 60 wars being fought around the world and perhaps the most serious of these were the ones that flowed from the collapse of the Soviet Union and Yugoslavia, and possibly the most serious consequence of the collapse of the Soviet Union may well be the removal of one of the major obstacles to nuclear proliferation. The little-known Indo-Pakistani crisis of May 1990, which was only defused because of the American ability to confront both parties with the reality and likely consequences of their own actions but which many Washington insiders regarded at the time as the most dangerous international crisis since Cuba, represents a salutary warning of the dangers that will attend crises between regional powers that have strategic weapons in their arsenals, most obviously in the Middle East, on the Indian sub-continent, and on and around the Korean peninsula. Herein may be the real tragedy of the last 50 years, that the Cold War was merely the period of nuclear initiation, that proliferation cannot be contained, and that the rest of the world will follow the example of powers that were irresponsible enough to vest their security in the threat of annihilation.

But more immediately, at the other end of the spectrum, future conflicts, or more accurately many future conflicts, are certain to follow the basic fault line of 20th-century history. Much, arguably most, of 20th-century strife concerned itself with the struggle of identity. At the start of the 20th century, virtually the whole of humanity outside the western hemisphere belonged to some nine European empires,[1] either as citizens or subjects. The First World War was fought about, or at least the treaties that ended that conflict tried to base themselves upon, the principle of national self-determination within Europe. The Second World War and its aftermath saw that same principle extend itself to colonial empires. The passing of time that has placed independence from colonial rule at the distance of at least two generations has seen the search for identity take on new dimensions, the search for a new frontiersmanship at the expense of previously-existing national and state characteristics as different groups have sought to establish and confirm their individual and separate singularity, whether within or across existing boundaries.

In various parts of the world, this breakdown of consensus and re-assertion of traditional loyalties and identities previously held in check by some form of *ancien regime* has been accompanied by a savagery and ferocity that suggests a new barbarism. In different parts of Africa, a relapse into tribalism has been accompanied by a re-primitivization of warfare in terms of weaponry and practice, and international disinterestedness. In such places as Bosnia-Herzegovina, knowledge of appalling atrocities proved to be the basis of inaction on the part of the international community, and the latter's final involvement in this particular crisis was disgraceful in terms of its tardiness; such international disinterestedness in events in Rwanda and the Congo would never have happened in the period of the Cold War. It is possible to see in such developments as the passing of the *apartheid* regime in South Africa and the repatriation of Hutu refugees and attempts of reconciliation in Rwanda as the base for a certain cautious, very guarded, optimism. But it is possible to see in parallel and more frequent events of recent years, specifically the upsurge in armed conflict, as merely the first stage in a process that lends itself to portrayal in apocalyptical terms, not least because in many cases the recourse to violence and conflict has been attended by economic considerations. So many of the conflicts in western Africa would seem to be related to control of resources, which have become increasingly scarce—and hence valuable—as a result of major population increases, climate change, and the worsening of terms of trade for developing countries.

At the present time, some 80 percent of humanity has access to about 20 percent of the world's resources. The vast majority of the world's population—which experienced a three-fold increase between 1945 and 1995—does not have access or has only very limited access to proper shelter and decent clothing, while a quarter of humanity does not have access to clean water. One in five people in developing countries, some 840,000,000 souls, suffers serious hunger, and if 200,000,000 children between the ages of 7 and 11 years are obliged to work for most of the hours of daylight, 3 in 10 of all adults that form the world's employable population lack work and the means to sustain themselves and their dependents. Given continued population growth in developing countries, in part the result of the continued importance of the family in terms of generating income and security, this situation can only worsen, yet Third World states are wholly incapable of generating wealth and employment that can meet increased demand while the end of colonial rule, and the operations of multi-national companies, have passed the added burden of rising costs to these states without any commensurate balance; the end of the Cold War in effect spelled the end of major aid packages. The resultant problems may be summarized by the increasingly desperate situation in which Kenya has found itself over the last two decades. In 1989, the total number of children in state secondary education numbered but 30,000, and such numbers were wholly inadequate in terms of the human base for future economic expansion, and specifically future economic expansion commensurate with population increase. By 2005, the population of Kenya, which had been about 5,500,000 in 1952 and about 8,500,000 at the time of independence in 1962, had risen to 34,300,000, but *per capita* income was just $540 per annum, that is, for the vast majority of Kenyans less than £1 a day, while life expectancy was 48 years for males and 46 for females, which was less than in the last years of colonial rule.[2]

Most certainly in many developing countries, corruption compounds all problems, but even the most competent and honest of regimes would be pressed to deal with the mounting problems of developing countries. These matters form, however, the background to the emergence of a series of conflicts that are wrongly termed civil wars but that are not about the existing state and society but are wars of secession, specifically turf wars that have been fought with reference to ownership or control of resources. In this respect, the fate of Sierra Leone reference its civil war between 1992 and 2001 is salutary. More than a third of the population of the country died or became refugees in a war that came to be concerned primarily about control of the diamond trade, and a country that certainly had its fair share of resources was reduced to the poorest in the world. Interestingly, this war was ultimately ended as a result of foreign intervention and the imposition of peace and disarmament terms under the auspices of the United Nations,[3] but other countries have not been so fortunate. There was no intervention in Rwanda and indeed foreign troops were withdrawn as a prelude to massacres that were simply ignored by Western governments, and this despite the fact that, prior to their being evacuated, besieged foreign troops had been begged by Hutus to shoot them rather than leave them to be hacked to pieces, and worse, by marauding Tutsi gangs.[4] The Rwanda war was part of a wider conflict that engulfed Burundi, the Congo, and Uganda, and that claimed perhaps as many as 4,000,000 lives in what was undoubtedly the most costly conflict since 1949. The scale of these conflicts, the deaths and devastation, may be worse in Africa than elsewhere, but the appalling manner in which killing has taken place has not been an African monopoly; some methods of killing employed by the Provisional Irish Republican Army in Northern Ireland beggar belief.

Lurking over the horizon are food and fuel crises. In October 1994, an article in the *International Herald Tribune* posed the question of whether China could survive beyond the year 2034, by which time China would require the total surplus food production of the world. The question was meaningless. The food crisis, given the depletion of the resources of the sea and the passing of so much arable land in the United States from production as a result of spreading urbanization, is going to explode long before 2034, and, in any case, the China crisis will present itself before that time. Merely to maintain present levels of employment and prosperity, Chinese development will have to see increased diversification of light engineering and consumer production, and by or about 2012 the resultant energy requirement will be equal to the present level of world surplus energy capacity. All other considerations being equal, China's requirements can be met at least in the short-term, but seemingly only at the expense of a major increase in energy prices at a time when alternative food sources must be developed, and none need reminding of the disastrous consequences of the 1974 and 1978 oil price increases for developing countries. Whether the United States and Europe will accept continuing trade arrangements that favor China and that alone would provide her with the means of paying for these needs is quite another matter.[5]

In light of these developing crises of food, fuel, and employment, it seems unlikely that Western-style democracy will have much to offer the greater part of humanity in years to come, and this leaves aside the fact that what we in the West understand to be the basis of liberal democracy—the rule of law, consent, compromise, the concept of opposition, and the denial of the right of any individual issue to justify systemic resistance—are not well founded in developing countries. Indeed, even in the Western world, such values are under an attack unprecedented in the last 50 years. Yet the real point is that the Western capitalist system, which has imposed itself upon the world, since the time of Locke and Smith has been based upon a double premise in terms of the stability of expansion and an acceptance of labor dislocation as the short-term cost inherent in long-term growth and advancing prosperity. We have been as-sured that "technology makes possible the limitless accumulation of wealth"[6] but one remains less than convinced—not merely on account of the deprivation in such countries as Bangladesh where per capita income totals $6 per week and two-thirds of all children suffer from malnourishment—but because both ele-ments of the double premise that have underpinned the capitalist system would seem to be dead.

Leaving aside the fact that we have no guarantee that the trough is infinite, that at the end of such a process as the limitless accumulation of wealth one would not be forced back on the definitive reality of food resources as the basis of real wealth, and with one obvious consequence: the real social problem that is likely to emerge is the reality of permanent labor dislocation. The impact of the Infor-mation Revolution has been to reduce the wealth-producing base within soci-ety in real terms, while the pattern of education and social development of the last 50 years means that those who fall outside this base are unlikely ever to re-gain a position within it and that the greater part of society will remain outside it. The long-term implications of an ever-greater concentration of wealth in rel-atively fewer hands and the existence of political expectation created in a pre-vious age can hardly be missed.

Moreover, the tendency toward a global leveling of income over the last three decades promises no relief for Western societies, quite the reverse since it has partially involved the loss of traditional manufacturing industries. But it also carries massively disruptive implications for developing countries because the same manifestations of social divisiveness so apparent in Western societies relative to persistently high levels of unemployment and growing income inequality within national economies have attended their development. The ten-dency toward a leveling of income has not been more evenly spread in devel-oping countries any more than it has been evenly spread in Western society, but it has taken place even at a time when the terms of trade, specifically in terms of earnings from food and primary products, have worsened massively for these countries.[7] No process of industrialization has ever taken place without massive upheaval and social strife. The shift of industry into the Third World represents a movement into areas that are generally unstable, and industrial-ization is likely only to aggravate this instability because the immediate impact is certain to depress living standards. The living conditions of the majority of the population of South Korea have been said to equate to those of Victorian Britain, and realistically conditions cannot be expected to be better in other countries. Having undercut Western industries and even Japan, South Korea has been presented with their problems in its turn, and all the Pacific-rim Tiger Economies face the long-term problems associated with industrialization—the breakdown of the nuclear family and under- or lack of insurance—that form the downside of their impressive economic performances of the last three decades. In addition, the events of July–August 1997 with respect to the enforced devaluation of the currencies of southeast Asia demonstrated the weaknesses and vulnerabilities of the Tiger Economies despite and in some ways as a result of economic growth. Dependence on foreign capital, trade deficits, engrained corruption, and the burden of change fell upon those least able to bear it. And none of this takes any account of the impact of ecological degradation, climatic changes and continuing desiccation, the perversity of existing borders, and enforced mass movement of populations. In terms of the search for identity, one can only presume that the changes presently in hand cannot work in favor of permanence and accord. Herein may be repetition. Rationalism, in the form of the primacy of the Left, did not survive its postwar success, and after five decades in which the idea of the centrally planned economy did not prove wanting in terms of the creation of wealth and ensuring decent living standards, economic liberalism, *laissez faire* capitalism, may not survive its victory in the Cold War.

If, at one end of the spectrum, the future of warfare were to be dominated by advanced technology, it would appear very likely that at the other end some form of guerrilla warfare remains undiminished in potency and relevance. The Soviet Union may have passed from the scene and with its passing, and the subsequent loss of patronage and support for revolutionary struggle, other forms of political struggle may emerge as alternatives to revolutionary warfare. But the balance of probability must be that revolutionary warfare remains undiminished in its relevance given the poverty that will continue to embrace so much of humanity. Indeed it is possible to see revolutionary warfare having enhanced relevance as a result of considerations of rising cost affecting the ability of states to conduct protracted war. But if such a situation is predictable enough in terms of developing countries, the relevance of armed struggle within advanced Western societies may well have been enhanced as a result of one of the less notable aspects of the Information Revolution, namely the erosion of the basis of social consensus as it has evolved over time. Satellite television will ensure the importing of outside values, perhaps anti-values would be a better word in some cases, while the movement away from mass programming to individual payment of television cannot have any effect other than to weaken the degree of social cohesion that broadcasting provided for most societies between 1950 and 1990. The days when everyone watched the same few programs or read the same few newspapers is over, and with it, perhaps, the basis of social consensus, not least because of television's capacity to import the expectations of other societies and its gearing of advertising to levels of wealth deliberately denied a permanent part of society that is outside the economic and political system. The emergence of a permanent underclass—with all the associated problems of family breakdown, poor health and worse living conditions in inner city areas,[8] racial tensions, and inadequacy of educational facilities[9]—that consists of individuals stranded at the bottom of the qualifications league and therefore wholly unappealing to any potential employer has already resulted in depressed city centers, a rise of drug-related criminal violence in these same areas, and a mass refusal to participate in the political system—a deliberate self-disenfranchisement on the part of an alienated part of society that has equipped itself with its own *mores* and culture.

While western Europe has yet to experience anything like the 18th Street phenomenon in the United States, the example of the current struggle in Algeria—which dates from 1992 with its progressive weakening of the state in direct relationship to its manifest inability to protect its citizens from such organizations as the *Groupe Islamique Armé* and its successor organizations and the increase of racketeering, prostitution, drug dealing, and revenge killings in the urban areas—points to the dangers presented by urban-based militants even in a society where the state and the military possess the determination to sustain themselves.[10] The possible implication of such developments for advanced Western states, specifically those states where there has been a deliberate repudiation of the concept of society on the part of governments[11] intent on the shedding of powers and responsibilities that have been gathered for most of this century, are self-evident, though not necessarily for reasons that are self-obvious. The last 30 years have witnessed Western societies grapple with intractable economic problems, and the persistence of a depression that has existed for two decades without formal acknowledgement. In one very obvious sense, politics in this time, perhaps politics in any time, has concerned itself with the management of illusions, and illusions of prosperity have been maintained by deliberately divisive social policies and the marginalization of impact through the deliberate infliction of the cost of these problems upon the powerless underclass. In Britain, this burden has fallen upon the unemployed and in the United States the black community, and in the latter case this has had the impact of maintaining racial segregation and setting aside most of the achievements registered in the Civil Rights movement of the 1960s; the black share of national wealth in 1994 was smaller than it was in 1968. Between 1967 and 1986, the percentage of the working population involved in manufacturing in the United States fell by a third, but the massaging of the employment figures was disguised by the enforced movement of the otherwise unemployed into the lowest paid ranks of the service industries. One is reminded of the cartoon depicting an American senator, at a dinner, claiming responsibility for the creation of so many million new jobs, and in the background a waiter thinking to himself that he had three of them. The cartoon would be amusing but for its uncomfortable brush with truth; as it is, in 1997 Britain had more actors than miners.[12]

In any event, the state, and despite a massive increase in its powers of surveillance, has been weakened over the last three decades, but in ways that extend beyond a failing police control over deprived inner city areas. The real weakening of the state exists in the erosion of power, authority, and will, specifically in terms of the direct management and control of the economy and the use of power in an anticipatory manner.[13] But anticipatory demands are increasing and, because of the impact of television and the Information Revolution, the time available to meet such demands has lessened. In Western society, we may be witness to the enfeebled politics of increasing poverty. Elsewhere weakened authoritarianism may well become the norm, the latter being accompanied in many parts of the world by the spin-off from the many conflicts that have erupted over the last decade. A permanent low-grade militarization of society in many developing countries[14] and the development of the politics of grievance in advanced Western societies may well be the constants of political life in the future. Arguably, already in the West, we have seen both. The militias in the United States have never entered into the power and status they sought but they and the emergence of what has been dubbed sub-political activity—protest and the rise of the politics of grievance—would seem to be permanent, irreducible features of national life, and armed militancy may well follow in their wake. Most certainly militancy has underpinned religious fundamentalism—whether Christian, Hindu, Islamic, or Jewish—in the last decade in a response to the stresses of modern society, most obviously in dealing with non-believers.

Such could be the basis of struggle in the years to come: increasingly polarized societies, the rise of the politics of anxiety and the emergence of what has been described as "the anxious classes," increasingly dismissive attitudes on the part of those who own and work the means of wealth toward the underclass, be it foreign or domestic; a growing portion of society permanently alienated from prevailing institutions and values, and a resultant increase of un- and anti-political protest; and over the last 20 years perhaps as much as one-fifth of adults of working age have been marginalized in the advanced Western societies; increasing poverty and desperation; a weakening state the tax basis of which has been severely impaired not least because of the massive shift of balance between productive and non-productive elements of society.[15] And a technology that may well provide the militantly disaffected with unprecedented means of disruption—the revolutionary hacker, given the extensive use of the Internet bulletin board by various militant organizations from Mexico to Northern Ireland for propaganda and the critical preparation phase—cannot be long delayed, if, indeed, the phenomenon has not manifested itself. The claim that two capable hackers and a billion dollars could paralyze the United States certainly cannot be dismissed lightly, and presumably has been entertained over the last decade by various revolutionary groups.[16] The Virtual Nation is with us, and quite possibly military operations as we presently understand that term are upon the point of passing into history because other, more efficient forms of warfare are or will be to hand. Among the more powerful states, information and economic warfare present the attraction of use of superiority, minimal casualties, and maximum returns in the form of control of resources without commensurate responsibilities.

For lesser states and societies, the lesson of Operation Desert Storm in 1991, and perhaps even more relevantly of Mogadishu, must be to wage war in cities where enemy—that is, in general Western but specifically American—advantages would be at a discount. The lesson of the Gulf campaigns must be never to fight the United States in the field but by other means, specifically at short range with "hug-and-hold" and herein the example of Groznyy[17] and the U.S. Marine Corps' experience in Exercise *Urban Warrior* and in autumn 1996 in Exercise *Sea Dragon* must be salutary. Perhaps, and as with everything that has been placed before the reader in this chapter, perhaps not, and we must be conscious of the fact that historically similar such prognostications have not been borne out by events that were even-handed in their effects. The 1590s was a period of acute uncertainties and severe economic disruption and privation, of severe disorder and unrest, and if the first half of the 17th century more than amply justified the worst fears, the second half more than exceeded hopes. The scenario that has been recounted in these pages tends toward the apocalyptic, and perhaps unrealistically so, but we would ponder on four points with respect to the future of war and the changing nature of political argument, and another matter does impinge upon deliberations. Every generation has its Cassandra and its Jeremiah and Lamentations, but at some stage or another they will be proved right by events, though there will be no prizes for correctly predicting the end of the world.

First, at the conventional level, one ponders the implications of the 1991 Iraq, 2001 Afghanistan, and 2003 Iraq campaigns in terms of the new technology having restored the power of decision to war that was denied by deterrence and the Cold War. One wonders whether this will affect the willingness of states to engage in war with an anticipation of success that did not previously exist. Second, in terms of the conduct of future war, one wonders about the impact of new weapons systems that will come into service in the next two decades. Automated and networked tanks, robotic infantry—six-legged automatons capable of lifting weights of one ton—and laser weapons already exist and are certain to enter service and in the next generation will change both the battlefield and the basic structure of armies as a result of the reduction of "teeth" and the increase of "tail" and to accommodate the networking of formations. Radiators are certain to blur the distinction between the conventional and the strategic. New camouflage suits that can make individual soldiers all but disappear and netting that can render tanks undetectable even by infra-red surveillance point to the "empty battlefield" being superseded by either the automated or the invisible battlefield, perhaps both. One prefers not to think of the real alternative battlefield that might become reality with the deployment and use of genetic weapons—the Biotech Revolution—presently in the process of being developed. Third, one wonders, too, the future in terms of a world directorate that still consists primarily of Western countries that owed their claims on positions of privilege to rights that are no longer unique, and one wonders, in the long term, of the constancy of links between the United States and western Europe. One wonders what the impact of the U.N. Agenda for Change might be in terms of a commitment to permanent revolution at the very time when Western countries must decide whether the United Nations exists as the instrument of change or as the means of trying to preserve the existing *status quo*. Fourth, and last, at the level of society and civil war one wonders if one stands on the brink of a new brutalization of attitudes,[18] a public indifference to violence—an unconcern on the part of those with money and over-familiarity on the part of those without— and a collapse of the shared values that have provided the basis of social existence.

Lest this be considered overdrawn, the massive changes of political argument and civic culture that have taken place in the last generation hardly provide cause for re-assurance. The global market, and particularly the global money market in which an estimated 95 percent of finance is speculative and adds nothing to the production of real wealth, has proved profoundly disruptive of employment patterns and social security expenditure. If the immediate impact has been registered in terms of lack of training programs and wage freezes for the lowest-paid members of society, the longer-term impact upon conventional political wisdoms is certain to be very divisive. When the fragmentation of existing political orders, and the accompanying widespread public perception of corruption, complacency, and incompetence on the part of government is added to the scales, the fact that so many aspects of state policy have been rendered irreconcilable by forces over which the state has no control points to the fact that a basic redefinition of the state, society, and civic culture is in hand.

In addition, one must note that the democratic process has never been under such strain than at the present. In the course of the 1990s, Britain, Canada, France, Italy, Japan, and the United States, and India, saw the repudiation of governing parties by electorates on a scale and with a degree of comprehensiveness without precedence. It may be that electoral volatility of unprecedented dimensions will become a permanent feature of political existence, but it is difficult to believe that fundamental change, a process of fragmentation and re-alignment, could be accomplished without violence. One cannot be unaware of a comment that may well summarize the next decades: new orders will emerge from chaos but there must be chaos first.[19] What is certain is that global integration is changing both states and business and what they attempt to do, and consequently neither the conventional economic wisdoms of the Left and the Right nor the traditional political agenda of existing parties can be expected to provide solutions to problems or the basis of identity for the disadvantaged. What is equally certain is that the destruction of the broad consensus that favored equity and social justice, which underpinned the modern industrial state in the decades following the end of the Second World War in 1945, was deliberate, with nothing put into its place other than privilege and what we will see in Western society will be "the quiet, and perhaps not so quiet, war between the comfortable and the underclass,"[20] and that this will come down the aisle in the company of similar forms of strife—racial, tribal, regional, religious, and political—established in the Third World.

POSTSCRIPT: NOTHING IS EVER NEW—SO WHAT OF GLOBALIZATION AND THE INTERNET?

The changing patterns of industry and trade of recent years invites the following observation:

The need of a constantly expanding market . . . extends over the whole surface of the globe . . . and through its exploitation of the world market has given a cosmopolitan character to production and consumption in every country. . . . It has drawn from under the feet of industry the national ground on which it stood. All old-established national industries have been destroyed or are daily being destroyed. They are destroyed by new industries . . . that no longer depend on indigenous resources but resources drawn from every quarter of the globe. In place of old wants, satisfied by domestic production, we find new wants, requiring for their satisfaction the products of distant countries. . . . Instead of old local and national exclusiveness and self-sufficiency, we have diversity and universal inter-dependence of nations. And the process does not merely involve *materiel*: intellectual creation is common property and from national and local literatures has arisen a new world literature.

One would suggest a very perceptive summary of the impact of globalization and, with the last three lines, the nature and impact of the Information Revolution and Internet.

The comments were provided by Karl Marx and Friedrich Engels in the first section of *The Manifesto of the Communist Party*, published in 1848.

CHAPTER 2

The Developing Countries
and the Re-emergence
of Other Wars

The first two books have concerned themselves primarily with war since the time of Clausewitz and in a double context, (book 1) an examination of war in the Age of Reason and the French Revolutionary and Napoleonic wars that were the basis of Clausewitz's subsequent analysis of war and (book 2) an examination of subsequent wars. In so doing, these two books have incorporated a basic premise that perhaps the greatest single problem relating to Clausewitz and *On War* lies in the legacy of singularity whereas war is not singular in nature but exists in different forms, and to repeat the point made some pages ago: the Clausewitzian definitions could not have been applied to the situation that prevailed in Europe prior to 1618. Prior to the Thirty Years' War, war in Europe was if not endemic then firmly established and at different levels, and most certainly was not the sole prerogative of the *état*. Cross-border raiding, clan warfare, military operations by trading companies against rivals, and the operations of militias of various persuasions were in place and possessed of a certain respectability and durability.

The 18th century witnessed the triumph of the Westphalian concept of the state, and the 19th century saw the European pattern of war imposed throughout Africa and Asia. The Westphalian system of states and war thus became established throughout the world, but the aftermath of the Second World War provided both the apogee of the state and the breakdown of restraints in terms of the nature and conduct of war. In a very obvious sense, the European colonial system saw the suspension of rivalries and enmities that have returned with the end of empire: the diversity of conflict that had existed before 1618 has returned since 1975 with the result that war has lost any singular character that it may have possessed between times. War, at the present time, is endowed with different forms, and the very diversity of forms makes for difficulty of comprehension for societies and peoples still largely conditioned by the conventional Clausewitzian norms.

The problem with such definition lies in the simplicity of definition and the fact is that History is the story of continuity and change that together shape events, and the latter defies simplicity of explanation and interpretation. For example, the argument that there has been a return to the diversity of war since 1975 can be contested and for obvious reason; the argument that the Westphalian system eliminated other forms of conflict can be disputed, and rightly so. There was no general peace outside Europe between 1648 and 1945 and the process by which the various colonial empires were established was not peaceful. It has been suggested, for example, that there were hundreds if not thousands of polities in Africa prior to European conquest, partition, and control, and that these ranged from what were roughly the equivalent of states with demarcated territory, monarch and system, via demi-states, which were loose confederations of peoples with shared identity but lacking permanent institutions and many of which were minor kingdoms, to the acephalous village systems that were not necessarily settled but could be nomadic or shifting.[1] Conflict and the shifting of boundaries and populations were common and widespread, and too often forgotten is the fact that the process of European conquest of Africa pre-dated the arrangements made at Berlin by much more than half a century. This process of conquest, when it began in earnest after the defeat of France in the war of 1870–1871, was relatively quick and for the most part was not massively expensive in terms of battlefield dead, but there were nonetheless many wars of conquests and many subsequent campaigns in which rebellion was suppressed and a certain order imposed. Moreover, the selection of 1975 as the date representing the point of change is at best contentious, most obviously with reference to the wars of national liberation that were fought in the three decades after the end of the Second World War.

At every point along the path that has led us from the time of the Westphalian treaties, there is evidence that suggests that the basic premise and arguments set down in these pages may be challenged and, indeed, they are perhaps flawed, but very respectfully it is suggested here that warfare in the last four decades has indeed re-assumed a diversity that was very largely lost in the century of so between the death of Clausewitz and the birth of the United Nations. Why this should be so, and the nature of the conflicts that have come back to center stage in recent years, are not easily defined but very clearly there was no single cause. The very number and diversity of conflicts over the last decade or so point to very different origins and causation at work though perhaps it would be in order to make one basic point: the end of empire, in the form of independent statehood, provided the stage-setting for the re-appearance of pre-colonial conflicts in many Third World countries.

The end of empire saw the passing of independence to indigenous sovereign states, but many of these were artificial in terms of boundaries and peoples and most certainly many Third World countries lacked genuine identity in terms of shared perception. What we have seen in many of these countries (of which Rwanda is just one example) has been a reversion to local identity—in many parts of Africa tribal—that had been held in check by colonial rule. As noted elsewhere, European imperialism in Africa froze hatreds, and with the passing of decades from colonial rule those hatreds have very slowly thawed. Ethnic diversity has returned in many Third World countries and at the expense of the emergence of genuine national identities. But, of course, two obvious correctives need to be entered. On the reverse side of the coin, shared identity has not necessarily been a factor making for stability and order, witness Somalia, and this process was not confined to Africa. India, Indonesia, Iraq, and Pakistan are just four countries in Asia that have their share of certain of these problems.

In this same time, the state itself in many Third World countries has been severely weakened as a result of developments beyond its terms of reference. The worsening terms of trade for virtually all primary producers as a result of the import of Western inflation and technology, the ending of not ungenerous aid packages in the aftermath of the end of the Cold War, and the repatriation of profits by multi-national companies on scales that would never have been tolerated in previous times, plus obligations in such matters as defense, which were previously discharged by colonial authorities, have combined to leave the Third World state ever less able to put into effect programs that its peoples demand and expect. When such matters as massive population growth, the movement of peoples within countries and particularly to marginal urban areas in numbers and on a scale that was unthinkable 40 years ago, the emergence of major groupings of young peoples left destitute outside the system with neither jobs nor land, and major environmental degradation are added to the scales, one can see the basis of crises and conflicts, and it is possible to see in such matters the basis of proliferation in terms of the number of wars of recent years that may well constitute something that is new, though in setting forth this argument the citing of two caveats would seem to be in order.

The first represents the need to note one major weakness of this argument, namely that it is very much an impersonal, hands-off interpretation of events that seeks to explain in terms of the inter-play of major forces. Undoubtedly major factors and influences have been at work in many Third World countries and conflicts, but in numerous cases personal factors also have been at work. Individuals have been more than mere instruments of forces more important and powerful than themselves. The origins of the civil wars in Liberia, for example, had a very great deal to do with the brutal and increasingly incompetent regime of President Samuel Doe (1951–1990) and the start of military operations against the regime on the part of first Charles Taylor

(1948–) and then Prince Yormie Johnson (1959–). The paradox was that after Doe's abduction and (filmed) murder by Johnson, the civil war played host to fragmentation, with a proliferation in the number of presidential claim-ants and would-be replacements, to a violent factionalism that was very largely tribally-based and that was increasingly concerned with the control of re-sources, specifically the proceeds of the diamond, timber, and rubber trades. Moreover, this spreading and proliferation of conflict within Liberia was not limited to that country because it spilled into Sierra Leone and in no small measure was responsible for instigating a parallel civil war in that country. But be that as it may, the basic point remains, individuals must not be dismissed out of hand, as mere representation of external forces, and most certainly in many parts of the Third World, and particularly in those parts of Africa where primitive religions are in place, demonology is and for the foreseeable future will remain a very powerful factor in the political process and in the conduct of war.

The second caveat is to note the obvious that such developments are not wholly new and without precedence, and not simply with reference to rever-sion to tribalism. For example, any examination of the origins of the *Taliban* militia in Afghanistan would necessarily note its embrace of Islamic funda-mentalist principles, which, arguably, does represent something that is novel, but in terms of origins in a struggle against foreign occupation and control, the *Taliban* specifically embraced (local) Pushtun nationalist and specifically Sunni roots, and most certainly in facing a Soviet enemy the knowledge of past resistance to outsiders could not have been too distant from an Afghan national and historical consciousness.

Clearly in certain cases—and not just with reference to the January 1842 campaign and the annihilation of the British formations in Kabul—there are links across the ages that would contradict representation of post-1975 devel-opments as new. But the representation of this diffusion in terms of prolifera-tion of conflict below the Clausewitzian level of the state invites classification under six main headings, the first of which would be the classification of rural struggle under a conventional label, and one would cite as an example the proliferation of organizations that established themselves in the Colombian countryside after *La Violencia* (1948–1958), the most (in)famous being the *Fuerzas Armada Revolucionarias de Colombia* (F.A.R.C.) and the *Autodefensas Unidas de Colombia* (A.U.C.). Most of these groupings took to the country-side not as a result of Maoist or revolutionary persuasion but because of the way in which the struggle for power in Bogota unfolded, but this movement into the countryside was subsequently overlaid by revolutionary impetus in the wake of the defeats of the 1960s/throughout Latin America. In Peru, the *Sendero Luminoso* remains established, unreduced, and unreduce-able, but seemingly as distant from success as it was more than three decades ago, while in Colombia the revolutionary and vigilante counter-revolutionary groups that emerged in the 1970s both came to be associated with kidnapping and ransoming, cocaine trafficking, and protection rackets that are not normally regarded as legitimate military or revolutionary activities.

The second classification relates to those militia that very deliberately embraced rural-based resistance as the means of advancing revolutionary objectives, specifically in response to the revolutionary failures—and particularly the collapse of the Guevara *foco* concept—in the 1960s. Such organizations range from such exceeding unlikely, such as the communist *Ejército Revolucionario del Pueblo* (E.R.P.) in Argentina that sought to establish a Guevarist base area in the mountains with results that would seem to have been eminently predictable, to the *Frente Farabundo Martí para la Liberación Nacional* (the F.M.L.N.) in El Salvador. The 1970s in El Salvador saw a proliferation and then a re-alignment of left-wing revolutionary militias, the *Frente* being an amalgam of five major left-wing factions formed in October 1980. In the 1980s came a low key and modestly successful campaign, and on 1 January 1992 a peace accord that resulted in the end to a 12-year war and the revolutionaries return to the political fold, the *Frente* subsequently emerging as one of the two largest political parties in the country.

The third classification relates to those revolutionary groupings that, in very large measure as a direct result of revolutionary failure in the Latin American countryside in the late 1960s, very deliberately took the tide of armed struggle to the cities. The first such groups appeared in Venezuela and Brazil, and it was the Brazilian Carlos Marighella (1911–1969) who assumed genuine international stature on account of his urban guerrilla warfare manuals,[2] but the most important groups to emerge were in Argentina and in Uruguay. But in none of these four countries did revolutionary endeavor come anywhere near registering success and, indeed, as certain critics predicted, was wholly counter-productive in terms of paving the way for military *coups* that came complete with their own very definite way of dealing with opposition. In Uruguay, armed resistance to a repressive regime manifested itself after June 1968 most obviously in kidnapping, and peak effectiveness was in 1970–1971, but after the military coup of July 1973, the *Movimiento de Liberación Nacional Tupamaros* and other left-wing groups were all but suppressed. Some sought refuge in Colombia or Nicaragua but in real terms these represented a spent force, a brutal military regime remaining in place until 1986. In Argentina a fragmented society with divisions that reached back decades provided the background to a campaign on the part of the communist *Ejército Revolucionario del Pueblo* (E.R.P.) that began in 1969 but which really began to get under way after November 1973. The removal of the Peronist regime in the military coup of 24 March 1976 paved the way for the infamous Dirty War in which some 30,000 prisoners disappeared while in military custody, and the incumbent military dictatorship was only consigned to history in December 1983 in the aftermath of its humiliating failure in the Falklands campaign (April–June 1982).

The status afforded the South American urban groups at this time owed itself in part to the nature of operations, most obviously in terms of public relations give-aways, and to the revolutionary tide in Western society, most obviously in western Europe and North America, in the first half of the 1970s. But there was also one other factor at work, and that was that the South American urban endeavor came at the very time when *Fatah* had emerged on the international stage complete in its own right and as a direct result of the failure of Arab states in the war of June 1967 that left the Palestinians with no alternative but to fend for themselves, and with one codicil: the position of overwhelming Israeli military advantage in theater left the Palestinians with no real alternative to the conduct of operations outside the Middle East. In effect, the 1967 Arab-Israeli war internationalized the Palestinian/Israeli problem, and brought various elements of revolutionary endeavor—South American, American, European, and Palestinian—together, and the fourth classification relates to this development in the fact that the ongoing Arab-Israeli dispute has given rise to a succession (or bewildering array) of Palestinian resistance movements. The Israeli attack on Lebanon in 1982 had the effect of compounding the effects of civil war (1975–1990) in terms of the unraveling of the Lebanese state that resulted in a proliferation of militias of various persuasions. Various communities in Lebanon—Druze, Sunni, Shi-a, different Christian groupings, and left-wing political parties—all created militias for themselves as civil war gripped the country but in the event it was one Shi-a group, *Hezbollah*, that began to emerge as the most powerful single militia in the wake of the Israeli invasion of 1982. It emerged with ministers in a reconstituted Lebanese state and, after the Israeli offensive of 2006, it gained Sunni and Christian support on account of its being the only Lebanese military organization capable of offering some form of military resistance to Israeli aggression. To the south, in the Gaza Strip, *Hamas* emerged after 1987 and the start of the *First Intifada* (1887–1993) for exactly the same reason though in the event there was double irony. *Hamas* was financed in the early years by Israeli military intelligence as a means of compromising the authority of Yasser Arafat (1929–2004)[3] and *Fatah*, and when *Hamas* won the general election in January 2006, Western countries, so committed to ensuring fully-fledged democracies for such peoples as the Palestinians, refused to recognize its victory.

The fifth classification relates to various organizations and to conflicts that, for the purposes of simplicity, may be defined in religious, cultural, and ethnic terms, and foremost among these would be the *Liberation Tigers of Tamil Eelam* in Sri Lanka, the *Taliban* in Afghanistan, and *al-Qa'ida*. The *Tamil Tigers* emerged in the aftermath of the 1983 disturbances and after 1987 conducted a revolutionary struggle, with suicide bombings prominent in the repertoire, that sought to achieve a separatist national identity and independence. The *Taliban* and *al-Qa'ida* were among the various *Mujahedeen* militias that emerged in Afghanistan in response to the Soviet take-over of December 1979, and most certainly their emergence to center stage was in no small part the result of the support that the various anti-Soviet organizations received from the United States. Indeed, one of the persistent stories to emerge from this time is that the filming of the murder of Soviet prisoners by Islamic militias has its origins in American practice, which was to provide *Taliban* and other groups with cameras in order to film murders so that financial remuneration was forthcoming.[4] *Al-Qa'ida* was formed in August 1988, after the Soviet defeat was assured, and it and the wider *Mujahedeen* achievement would seem to have been partly the inspiration of various Islamic movements ranging from the Maghreb via Egypt, Saudi Arabia and Pakistan to Indonesia and the Philippines, and which have as their *raison d'être* a concept of struggle based on religious and cultural difference.

The sixth and last classification represents a return, in part, to the previous reference to the conflicts in Liberia and Sierra Leone. These two neighboring West African states played the role of unwilling hosts to civil strife that lasted a more than a decade and which resulted in Sierra Leone (March 1991–January 2002) being reduced to the status of poorest country in the world. The war left Sierra Leone with a legacy of illegal activity, in the diamond trade, that means even today perhaps as much as 30 to 40 percent of annual state revenue is lost while corruption, in terms of individual pilfering of state funds, is of a level that even neighboring countries have noticed.[5] In Liberia much the same situation applied, the point of these two sets of conflicts being that, whatever their origins and causes, they very quickly became "turf wars" in no small measure were tribally based, and in these respects were conflicts with which the Africa of pre-colonial times would have been immediately familiar. Here in these lines is not the place to repeat arguments listed earlier but perhaps in order would be a comment in terms of potential conflicts that exist with reference to environmental degradation—the advance of the desert and the move of Moslem northerners into the central provinces—in Nigeria, to Kenya with specific reference to the unraveling of the paternalist Kenyatta state in the period of the Moi and Kibaki presidencies,[6] and to South Africa with reference to problems of over-population, urban poverty, a dispossessed under-class, and increasingly widespread corruption, plus a loosening sense of national unity as the primary architect of the great changes set in place in the last two decades, Nelson Mandela (1918–), passes from the scene.

The proliferation of conflict over the last two or three decades has no single cause or momentum, but this short examination of these proceedings needs be closed and with reference to two related matters seldom afforded much in the way of consideration. In the aftermath of the end of empire, there has been a proliferation of conflicts that have proved largely intractable and beyond solution, and this development has been compounded by the fact that with the end of the Cold War, Western states have displayed a remarkable lack of interest and willingness to involve themselves in any attempt to limit or curtail conflicts and to re-write the terms of reference of these areas, peoples, and conflicts. In no small measure, the sheer number of conflicts account, at least in part, for this distancing from conflicts because the United Nations or groups of Western counties simply cannot deal with the number and diversity of the conflicts that have come onto center stage over the last two decades. Moreover, even if there was a willingness to become involved in these conflicts then the means to do so are at best uncertain, and in two very obvious respects. The financial cost of peace-keeping and peace-enforcement operations, plus the cost of diverse training of regular professional organizations to meet demand, provide cause for hesitation but perhaps more significant is the fact that the real cost lies in manpower numbers, and that conscripts do not necessarily meet the demands and requirements of these types of commitment.

The capacity of Western states to intervene directly in Third World countries and their wars is perhaps more limited than may appear at first sight, but this fact of life goes alongside a related matter, namely a general contraction of interest in and knowledge of Third World countries on the part of Western society. Many of these conflicts reach back into history and most certainly are but little understood in the Western world, and one would suggest, and not facetiously, that there was in Europe in 1929 or 1949 a better basic, working knowledge of Africa than at the present time, one lifetime later, and this makes due acknowledgement of the efforts of such institutions as the School of Oriental and African Studies in between times.[7] For example, one would suggest that the recent (and continuing) conflicts in the Congo, Burundi, Rwanda, and Uganda and in what was Somalia would have been better understood in terms of origins, causes, and courses by societies with levels of knowledge and interest that have receded with the end of empire, and, to provide a second example, the fact that the resident colonial administration in the inter-war period did not raise local forces in British Somaliland because of the patchwork of local rivalries and loyalties within the colony but sought to ensure security against external attack and to maintain public order by British formations and one Bantu battalion raised in Nyasaland, represents a state of affairs that may provide some limited or introductory insight into the problems that beset the Horn of Africa at the present time—but it also represents a basis of working knowledge that most certainly was known prior to 1939 but which has been largely and long forgotten.[8] As it was, the conflicts in the Congo, with a death toll that has perhaps reached 4,000,000 and which thus makes these conflicts the most costly conflicts since 1949, elicited virtually no response from Western countries, a state of affairs that contrasts very sharply with fact that the Belgian crown, after holding the Congo for more than two decades as a personal fiefdom in which time its treatment of the native population was singularly appalling with a fall of population of some 3,000,000 in this period, in 1908 was relieved of the Congo by the Belgian state as a direct result of international protests. This argument can be reversed upon itself in the sense that misrule extended over the best part of two decades before protest made its appearance and the death tolls really do not compare, specifically when set against relative population totals for 1885–1907 compared to 1998–2008,[9] but the fact remains that Belgian royal rule was set aside by a popular demand, and a parallel demand never manifested itself a century later at a time when the Information Revolution brought such matters as the Rwanda massacres to homes across the world. To summarize, in terms of Developing World conflicts there has been on the part of Western states a decline of commitment and interest in terms of the end of the Cold War and globalization, a decline of capacity to intervene in terms of available forces and capability, and a decline of interest and knowledge on the part of present-day society compared to previous generations.

In setting out this summary of these other wars and their assorted organizations, one obvious point needs to be made. There is clear diversity in terms of basis of support, objectives, and modes of operation, but the elements of diversity and novelty go alongside elements of continuity, and most certainly there are various links between different conflicts and different times, but which cannot be identified in these few pages. For example, any consideration of urban guerrilla warfare should examine the example of such organizations as the Irish Republican Army and the war against Britain (January 1919–July/December 1921), the Jewish terrorist group *Irun Zvai Leumi*,[10] which was responsible for the bombing of the King David Hotel in Jerusalem (22 July 1946) as part of its anti-British campaign, the E.O.K.A. organization and its campaign between 1952 and 1959 in Cyprus,[11] and the F.L.N. in Algeria,[12] which tried to carry the tide of war to metropolitan France in the wake of its having been checked and brought to the verge of defeat in North Africa (by the end of 1957) and that sought to mobilize both international and French domestic opinion in an attempt to secure by political means the victory that it could not win by military means. What may thus seem at the present time to be the diversity of organizations, and the diversity of their appeal and support, is not wholly new and it is possible to reach back in time in order to see similar patterns in place in an age of massive certainty, or growing uncertainty, before 1975. Certain differences exist on one particular score, namely the emergence of organizations that reach across national boundaries and that embrace religious and cultural rather than secular values and standards. Most certainly there is a second element of difference in the form of opportunity and access provided by the Information Revolution and modern means of travel, but what must also be noted are the elements of similarity, not just difference, between modern resistance movements and their predecessors.

Book V

On the Nature
and Conduct of War

CHAPTER 1

The Nature of War, the Conduct of War, and Basic Definitions

War is a state of armed conflict between recognizable political entities. Such a definition would thus exclude various conflicts and their authors from consideration, most obviously organizations and individuals involved in conflict but over matters other than the political. In various countries, there are organizations that have marked out for themselves areas of access and areas of interest, and these, and their resources and peoples, are indeed the basis of conflict but distinct from war *per se*. Difference in this matter lies in one matter perhaps best summarized in terms of the dissimilarity between hijacking and piracy, though this distinction has been largely obscured as a result of ill-informed newspaper and television reporting. Piracy is basically concerned with finance and individual profit whereas hijacking, in most cases, has been usually identified in political terms, however tenuously on occasion.

The problem presented by such definition, however, is obvious. There have been and are a number of conflicts in which distinctions have been blurred. An obvious example would be the campaign in Northern Ireland that really was a Thirty Years' War, or thereabouts (1969–1998). But most certainly for a very considerable part of this conflict, and specifically at street level, the issue was less about whether or not Northern Ireland should be part of the United Kingdom and more about control of local populations in terms of social standing, protection rackets, and general criminal activity on the part of various paramilitary forces. It is possible to argue, and with some conviction, that whatever ostensible political aim was embraced, individual commitment and involvement was very largely personal rather than political, and that in many cases this personal commitment was somewhat unstable. The balance of probability would suggest that such circumstances have been at work in a number of recent and concurrent conflicts, and that what may be defined as armed conflict below the threshold of war in various countries, such as those in Sierra Leone and the Congo, possessed similar pedigree as the recent troubles in Northern Ireland.

Perhaps the greatest single problem relating to Clausewitz and *On War* lies in the legacy of singularity, but war most definitely is not. Wars may be fought between opposing coalitions or directly between individual states though the latter is unusual, and wars, to use the terms that came to be used in the course of the 20th century, could be and are total or limited. With reference to the latter, wars may be waged in pursuit of conquest and annexation or for other reasons, such as status and primacy and without acquisition, witness the Austro-Prussian war of 1866. Moreover, wars could be one part of a wider conflict, albeit a conflict waged by means other than armed force, for example the Korean War as part of the Cold War confrontation. Moreover, there are, as there always has been, the ultimate in contradiction of terms, civil wars, wars fought within a state and society relating to issues of identity and form, and wars of secession. And, of course, there are wars that would seem to embrace all and every possible option, witness the Vietnam War between 1959 and 1975, which was a civil war between northern and southern Annamites, a number of conflicts involving different groups and regions within southeast Asia in general and South Vietnam in particular, a war about status and leadership in southeast Asia, and a war with a background formed by the Cold War. Likewise, the conflicts in the Balkans in the last decade of the 20th century verily have a background provided by many hundreds of years of ethnic, cultural, and religious rivalries and conflict. The events in Bosnia-Herzegovina and Kosovo since 1994 may be said to have immediate roots in the events of 1941–1945 but in reality reach back well before the Ottoman conquest of the Balkans after 1354, to the time of the incursions of various peoples into the Haemus in the sixth and seventh centuries, and to a pattern of rivalry, enmity, and all but constant war that was established thereafter and that was to last the best part of four centuries.

War exists at different levels, and the business of war as understood in Western countries over the last three centuries is very different from war as manifest throughout the world at the present time. In Western countries, where the Westphalian legacy remains in place and where there is a general consensus with regard to states, borders, and national identities, war remains the prerogative of the state and the only legitimate alternative to the state prerogative remains clearly defined as civil wars and wars of secession.[1] In this context, war and the military remain the instruments of policy, state policy, and the basic definitions that have been in place over the years remain unchanged and unchanging; states wage war, services fight, and individuals see combat, and, in the conduct of war, strategy provides signposts along operational paths, which themselves consist of tactical paving stones. With reference to the latter, the operational path is two-way not one-way in the sense that the operational may lead to the tactical just as the tactical may lead to the operational, and the inter-dependence of the strategic, the operational, and the tactical is absolute not least in terms that all are and must be related to the administratively possible. And, of course, all must be governed by political terms of reference.

In a very obvious sense, this is very Clausewitzian, but to repeat the basic premise of this screed: the Clausewitzian definitions belong to a period that was by definition somewhat unusual in the sense that war in the Age of Reason witnessed the elimination of all forms of conflict other than wars waged by states. The 19th century saw the European pattern of war imposed throughout Africa and Asia, the Westphalian system of states and war established throughout the world, but the aftermath of the Second World War has provided both the apogee of the state and the breakdown of restraints in terms of the nature and conduct of war. As noted elsewhere, the European colonial system saw the freezing of hatreds that have returned with the end of empire. The diversity of conflict that had existed before 1618 has returned since 1975 with the result that war has lost any singular character that it may have possessed between those dates. War, at the present time, is endowed with different forms, and the very diversity of forms makes for difficulty of comprehension at this present time for societies and peoples still largely conditioned by the conventional Clausewitzian norms.

If one were to seek to provide just one historical example of such diversity and lack of singular character, and their attendant problems, then it would be the example of 19th-century cabinet war, and its implied assumption that war could be controlled and controlled by the state. But the example of the Third Republic, proclaimed in September 1870 in the midst of France's national defeat in war with the German states, would suggest that wars most definitely possess their own logic, that wars indeed assume courses and outcomes not intended by their authors. The Third Republic represented a return to popular will as the basis of armed struggle, a reversion to the example of 1792–1793, but was unsuccessful primarily because of German possession of overwhelming advantages of numbers, *matériel*, and position. But the consequence was that, after the collapse of the French Second Empire, the logic of war pointed to German acquisition of Alsace-Lorraine, which was the German public and Prussian military demand, and with this acquisition the long-term enmity of France was assured. Such eventualities were quite contrary to what had been the original Prussian-German anticipation, expectation, and intent.

The example of the Franco-German War of July 1870–May 1871, and specifically the example of German public demand with reference to Alsace-Lorraine, possess singular relevance at the present time in terms of the mass state, that is, democracies, and the immediacy of conflict, but also in another matter, less well understood. The defeat of France resulted in the collapse of state authority not once but twice, and the second resulted in the formation of the Paris Commune and what was a very nasty but short civil war. It may well be that, at the present time and into the foreseeable future, the pattern may repeat itself in the sense that the defeat of states may well release forces that make for civil conflict and with it the elimination of the middle ground and forces of moderation, witness Afghanistan since 2001 and perhaps more obviously

Iraq between 2003 and 2008. But that latter point aside, for a democracy it is hard to mobilize and for obvious reason; societies are not inclined to undertake major military commitment without overwhelming—and seemingly just—cause and are not inclined to undertake major military commitment without complete and utter exhaustion of alternative means. But, one would suggest, once the commitment has been accepted it is harder to disengage, and even harder to disengage without complete and comprehensive victory. By the very nature of things, democracies and total war walk hand-in-hand and in a way that other societies, whether cabinet-directed or overt dictatorships, do not. The requirements and demands that war imposes on society in terms of curtailment of rights and civil liberties, control and direction of industry, the demands of taxation, and, perhaps most important of all, the demands upon manpower, inevitably mean an exhaustion of limitation, which democracies necessarily have difficulty in waging limited war for obvious reason. If the war that is to be fought is one that is worth fighting then it is a war that must be won, and won by the employment of all means necessary, but a war that is not worth winning is a war that is not worth fighting in the first place. The problem, obviously, is one of correct discernment prior to commitment, and every state has waged the wrong war or the right war at the wrong time and has lost a conflict that, by any rational standard, it should have won with ease. The most obvious recent example of such loss remains the United States and its war in support of South Vietnam, though as noted elsewhere it needs to be stated that the Vietnam War was not one that could have been won by the United States. The war could only be decided by the Vietnamese, but the war was nonetheless one that the United States could and did lose and primarily because her leadership never understood the nature of the war and the enemy.[2]

War, or perhaps more accurately conflict, thus exists at different levels and in different forms, and the criteria applicable to one form do not necessarily transpose themselves to another. There remains, for example, war at the level of the state, and in the last decade the conflicts in Yugoslavia, Afghanistan, Iraq, and in the Caucasus are but four examples of state conflicts involving the world's major powers and their deliberate waging of limited war, which may well prove a pointer to future intent. There is conflict at the level of the state in numerous civil wars that are being waged around the world at the present time. There are other forms of conflict, most obviously various turf wars about control of local resources, continuing ethnic and religious-based struggles, and there are also such freelance activities such as those that resulted in the seizure of the oiler *Sirius Star* some 450 miles southeast of Mombasa, in the Indian Ocean, on 15 November 2008. Definition of such activity is somewhat difficult. In a very obvious sense, it cannot be classified as war in any meaningful sense any more than domestic conflict—in the form of the often-murderous activities of various gangs, complete with their culture of violence and separation—can be realistically classified as a level of conflict *per se*. But in the case of the Somali episode, the group responsible for the seizure of this vessel owes its immediate origins to political events in the form of the collapse and fragmentation of the Somali state, and its operations would seem to be part of a struggle that may not fully accord with basic state definitions but nonetheless would seem to be partially so, even if these, and the ransom, comes complete with a very sizeable price tag.[3]

With reference to war and the state at the present time, and separate from the "other" levels of conflict, we in Western societies have terms of reference with respect to the nature and context of war that are provided not by any trinity but by a number of separate influences. One hesitates to assert five influences lest this be considered toadying to the U.S. military establishment but most certainly a pentagon could be listed thus: the international community, the diplomatic, the economic, the military, and, in a class of its own, Information Technology. War most definitely could be portrayed as the product of the inter-play of these factors, or indeed an inter-play of any number of factors, the precise number defined by personal calculation and preference. For example, one could consider war in terms of perception and that could include international as well as domestic persuasion, and such matters as money, credit, manufacture, and access to resources could each be afforded single status; likewise specifically military dimensions, such as weaponry, and matters of perception, proper knowledge and appreciation of the theater of operations, numbers-to-space problems and factors of time and distance, can be listed as complete in their own right. The problem herein is endless in the sense that subjects and their numbers abound, but here, in this first chapter of the fourth book, Clausewitzian elements of war can be concentrated, and, perversely, in a Jominian checklist. But if one seeks to establish the parentage of war then one of the many possible double helical structures of its Deoxyribonucleic Acid could be as is shown in the accompanying chart.

Such representation must represent a final word in the sense that, by definition, the next DNA layer would involve 16 great-great-grandparents, which would be altogether too much, and indeed, it may very well be that the definition given here, with two layers and the equivalent of three DNA generations, would have been more seemly had it selected just four rather than eight through either a distinct separation of the nature and the conduct of war or a merging and reclassification of items, for example the international with domestic context, immutabilities with perceptions, war with the war and the campaign with the battle. But the basic point is simple enough. There is no way in which the Clausewitzian trinity can be replaced for it is possessed of both simplicity and accuracy that ensures continued relevance, but the factors that have made for change in the last 200 years demand proper acknowledgement and recognition, and to cite but one example: at the time of Clausewitz, the written word was possessed of an importance that one would suggest now has been largely lost, but the revolution in communications means that events at the point of battle can now be placed before electorates in real time, not days,

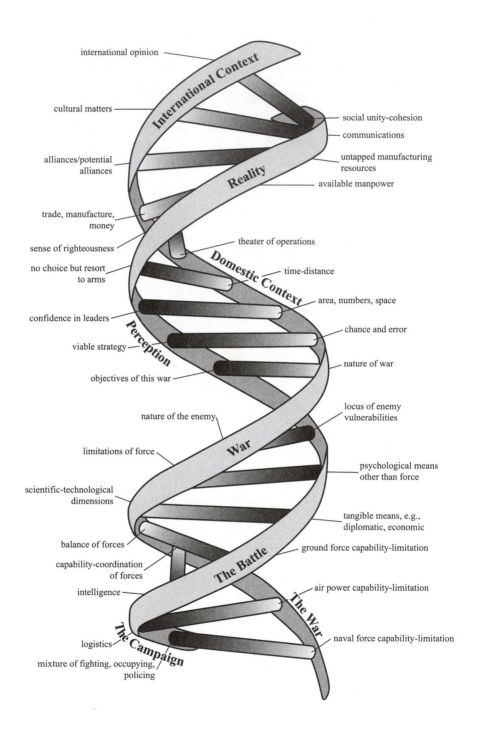

international opinion

International Context

cultural matters

social unity-cohesion

communications

alliances/potential alliances

untapped manufacturing resources

Reality

available manpower

trade, manufacture, money

sense of righteousness

theater of operations

Domestic Context

time-distance

no choice but resort to arms

area, numbers, space

confidence in leaders

Perception

chance and error

viable strategy

nature of war

objectives of this war

locus of enemy vulnerabilities

nature of the enemy

limitations of force

War

psychological means other than force

scientific-technological dimensions

tangible means, e.g., diplomatic, economic

balance of forces

ground force capability-limitation

capability-coordination of forces

The Battle

intelligence

air power capability-limitation

The War

logistics

The Campaign

mixture of fighting, occupying, policing

naval force capability-limitation

weeks, or months after proceedings and then only after suitable treatment on the part of the state, witness the start of the Gulf campaign in 1991 and the television broadcast from Baghdad that placed on screens across the world live images of the first strikes and anti-aircraft fire to electorates and the military alike. And with reference to such matters, timing can be very important, for example, in the 1970s the Provisional I.R.A's deliberate timing of many of its actions between 1600 and 1800 in order to ensure maximum coverage on early evening news programs but before British and local authorities had time to act and to set in place authoritative accounts of proceedings.

The elements of war identified in the double helical structure may be defined with relative ease. First and foremost are the international and the domestic contexts, and with reference to the first the need for international support and approbation is obvious in terms of institutions but also in terms of popular endorsement. The significance of such organizations as the United Nations, regional organizations, and standing alliances need little in way of explanation although the latter, with the inter-play of privilege and benefit of membership and the consequential aspect of obligation, requires explanation. The importance attached to membership of an alliance or coalition is virtually synonymous with credibility as an ally, how the other members of an alliance or coalition assess value and credence (*bündnisfähig*). International opinion, which may involve such matters as race, religion, culture, and sense of historical grievance, is much more difficult to define and evaluate but most obviously possess self-evident importance and, given the reach of the Information Revolution, represent a constant: consideration of how a course of action might be seen by outsiders most definitely is not new but perhaps today has an immediacy and potency that are unprecedented. By way of example of the importance of international opinion, and specifically grass-roots opinion, in the arrangement of states, the Iraqi conflicts of 1991 and 2003 provide pertinent illustration. The Iraq seizure of Kuwait in August 1990 achieved what previously would have seemed impossible, namely the lining up of the Arab world alongside the United States and her associates to the extent that military forces from 13 Islamic states, plus the *Taliban* from Afghanistan, were in the coalition order of battle in January 1991,[4] but in March 2003 military forces from just six countries, five of them members of N.A.T.O., were involved in the invasion of Iraq. The only Arab countries that fell into line were those so closely identified with the United States that they had no real alternative, and most certainly the overall lack of sympathy and support from the Arab world in part explains the continuing problem that Iraq represents at the present time (2009).[5]

The international community provides a crucial dimension in terms of political endorsement or otherwise, but no less importantly it provides, in an international economic system where no single state or groups of states is self-sufficient, the basis of war in terms of trade, manufacture, and credits. The changed patterns of industrial production, trade, and finance of recent years make for an inter-dependence that was unthinkable less than two generations ago. In terms of wherewithal and means, the United States at the present time could not fight the Vietnam War as once she did. This does not mean that the United States could not fight a war in southeast Asia again, but it would have to be a different war, and the ordering of supplies and money would represent problems that simply could never have been countenanced for a moment in the late 1960s. One admits to special difficulties of understanding of international finance, specifically with present levels of debt that were unthinkable even a generation ago, and especially with reference to the United States at the present time. In November 2008, the United States public debt was increasing by $1,442 per second, and a third of that was financed from abroad, but with public debt more or less doubling between 2000 and 2008, the United States has persisted with very costly military commitments in Afghanistan and Iraq and the financial crisis that manifested itself in the last quarter of 2008 would seem to have made for discipline of the United States creditors rather than the United States herself. In a situation that defies ready comprehension, it is perhaps worth recall that the trough is finite, at some time or another.

The domestic context is very similar to its international counterpart in terms of public opinion and resources, but with two matters of self-evident importance. The unity and cohesion of government, and its ability to provide leadership and control, possess obvious importance, but while the *materiél* needed for war imposes demand upon sources of production and distribution, perhaps one matter, the availability of trained manpower, possesses an importance seldom afforded proper consideration. The massive decline of the birth rate throughout Western societies in the 1970s meant that Britain, by the end of the Cold War, needed to recruit something like one in four 18-year-old males simply to maintain the armed forces at their then-existing strength, and the end of the Cold War came none to soon in this respect. The process whereby European N.A.T.O. armies shared or pooled support formations was in very large measure the result of enforced economy of manpower that was the result of smaller intakes by the year, while the move from conscript to regular armies on the part of many European N.A.T.O. countries can have but one result in terms of the *numbers-versus-commitment* problem. Inevitably this matter is but one aspect of wider problems relating to costs and the availability of adequate numbers of aircraft, warships, and military equipment, their proper maintenance, and adequate proper levels of supply and timely distribution, though this is a matter discussed separately.

The matter of perception reaches across all eight elements of war identified in the double helical structure and very obviously is closely related to the second, the domestic context, in terms of public perception and support. The first two matters—the sense of righteous endeavor and the sense of the inevitable—do leave themselves exposed to denunciation on the grounds that they represent a most mediocre summary of St. Augustine of Hippo (354–430), St. Thomas Aquinas (1225–1274), and Just War theory, and most certainly the whole matter of perception must embrace *jus ad bellum* and *jus in bello* and with it various of these details, most obviously the exhaustion of all means short of war prior to the use of force, proportionality, and the minimum use of force commensurate with aim and need, observation of the laws and ethics of war, and the search for a better peace.[6] The sense of righteous endeavor and the sense of the inevitable do embrace these points and perhaps the surest guarantee of domestic and international accord and support is the reluctance to resort to force, the sense that war has come but has not been sought, and quite clearly leaders seen or believed to have explored all means short of war necessarily possess a certain credence, but the problem herein is the obvious one; past leaders such as Hitler commanded faith on the part of his people, and was possessed of a militant philosophy that most certainly embraced and abrogated for the German people the concept of righteous endeavor.

The last element at what historically would have been termed the grand strategic level relates to constancy in terms of the nature of war and the conduct of operations. At this level—the highest level of planning involving as it does definition of aim and settling of policy objectives, the resultant organization of state, society, and military, and the subsequent supervision of effort—the distinction between the political and the military is very largely meaningless, and this definition includes both personnel and policy. In the settling of policy, the civil and military may well use the arguments that would seem to be prerogative of the other, but crucial for both to understand are certain basic realities about war and specifically about the war at hand. A basic understanding of the enemy in terms of a working knowledge and correct appreciation of the theater of operations, such matters as time, distance, area, and numbers-to-space ratios represent the *sine qua non* of endeavor, to which needs to be added the imponderables of error and chance.

Below this level lie the elements of war and the war, involving as it must first a basic understanding of the nature of war, of the limitations of force and of the nature of the enemy and an appreciation of the scientific and technological dimensions of war. To these are added the detail of the war in terms of the definition of objectives, most obviously in terms of capability of realization and the identification of what in American *militarese* are Clausewitzian centers of gravity but which really lend themselves more readily to definition as potential points of critical vulnerability, be these political, military, societal, or economic.[7] These would constitute targets the destruction of which would represent very serious damage to the enemy's ability to maintain the state, economy, and armed forces in the field though it is possible to argue that the only real center of gravity with the capacity to incur permanent and real damage or loss would be key personnel, and specifically the head of state or government and senior ministers and military personnel. At the other end of the scale, with reference to forces in the field, various means other than direct attack may be employed in order to demoralize. In 1991, coalition air operations, day after day, brought home to Iraqi military personnel the hopelessness of their position and this without their being subjected to direct attack, and desertion had become widespread by the time that the ground offensive began. The deliberate dropping of leaflets, and specifically leaflets warning of future targets to be attacked, have been employed in various wars, and what amounted to notice of the bankruptcy of counter-measures again has been instrumental in the spread of defeatism, from Japan in 1945 to Iraq in 1991.[8] But these various means of taking the offensive to an enemy necessarily go alongside other, more conventional means such as the diplomatic, economic, and psychological (i.e. straight broadcasting).

At the level of the war itself, which in effect relates to the campaign and the conduct of war rather than the nature of war, the primary factors relate to the balance of forces and the size and capability of forces, and specifically matters relating to the air force. In such matters, the United States, in terms of the U.S. Air Force and U.S. Navy, is in a class of its own, possessed of capability well beyond any other single state, but in any war air superiority, or at least the absence of enemy air superiority, has proved of crucial importance as being the primary pre-requisite for major offensive operations on the ground. Air power in the form of the employment of massed formations in round-the-clock offensive operations represents one of the major factors in the planning of the campaign and the battle, but strategically probably only the U.S. Air Force has the numbers and capability to attempt Inside-out Warfare, while only the U.S. Navy has numbers and capability that in 1991 revealed themselves in terms of unprecedented inland reach. Naval cruise missiles were employed extensively in this campaign, as were carrier aircraft, but primarily in association with land-based aircraft. Subsequent improvements in carrier aircraft capability pointed in the direction of a genuinely independent capability, but the decline of carrier numbers, and future problems of in-flight refueling for carrier aircraft, place certain question marks against such present and future capability. Navies also have brown-water capability, though it needs to be noted that during the war in southeast Asia, the U.S. Navy employed direct fire, in the form of rocket-assisted projectiles, against targets in Laos.

At the level of battle, basic requirements are the need for proper and effective command and control, specifically with reference to the proper co-ordination of joint and combined forces and the timely and proper use of intelligence material that has been properly processed through the collection-examination-analysis-distribution cycle. In addition, of course, there must be full and proper allocation and distribution of supplies and the concentration of lines of communication troops and units and formations detailed to occupy, it being one of Clausewitz's most famous lines, "It is easy to conquer: it is hard to occupy."

This rendition of the elements of war is somewhat different from that given by Clausewitz in *On War* and for one reason. As noted elsewhere, in book 1, chapter 1, a great deal of *On War* is devoted not to the subject of war but to campaigning, to soldiering in the field. These comments in effect have concerned themselves with the grand strategic, the strategic, and what may be termed the operational levels of war because in recent decades the distinction between them has become blurred on account of the fact that modern means of communication allow a superior authority to reach down to units and formations in the field in a way that was wholly impossible even 40 years ago.[9] Evidence of this exists in the fact that the 1991 campaign operations by certain U.S. battalions were supervised and directed by a corps commander, that is, three levels of command above the unit in the field. The elements of war thus presented here bring together these levels because this is a present reality that is likely to manifest itself even more obviously in future. The ability to map and navigate even in the most difficult of terrain as a result of satellite technology, to effect immediate orders as a direct result of surveillance of the battlefield by various televised means on a 24-hour basis, and the increased need for care in terms of planning with reference to the requirements of allies all suggest that any examination of war must encompass a proper consideration of the various levels, imponderables and constants of the war, the campaign and the battle. The elements of war identified herein would seem to provide the basis of examination of past and future conflicts though one point would seem to be all-important and which, arguably, places every other calculation in proper perspective, namely the correct observation of what is in American terms the 11th and in British terms the 13th principle of war: never get involved in a pissing match with a skunk. All states have fought the wrong war at the wrong time and been worsted by an enemy that should have been defeated if not with ease then without undue difficulty, and when stripped down to basics what would seem to be beyond dispute is that the correct understanding of the enemy, of the physical dimensions of the theater or theaters of operation, and of the limits of possibilities represent the *sine qua non* of successful military undertakings, though it needs be added that clear designation between the different levels—and specifically between the nature of war and the conduct of operations—remains essential to success.

A Clausewitzian trinity of the political, the economic, and the military may serve as the possible basis for the analysis of war and wars, but, at the present time and in terms of the state and its prosecution of a war, the crucial element must be the political in terms of the willingness of society and military alike to undertake a course of action that is certain to be expensive in terms of time and resources and that may well prove costly in terms of lives. The domestic elements herein possess self-evident importance but scarcely less important must be the correct appreciation of the nature of the war that will be fought and the nature of the enemy and the identification of objectives that are capable of realization. To give but one obvious example, in 1991 there was fought in the Middle East a campaign and the fact that the U.S. leadership did not know the difference between a campaign and a war was the primary reason why the one was won and the other was lost, and the basic error was repeated after November 2001 with reference to Afghanistan and after March 2003 with reference to Iraq. In 2001, the campaign was won by year's end and the war began in January 2002 while in 2003 the conduct of operations presented little if any real difficulty but the real war began with the overthrow of the incumbent Iraqi regime. In all three cases, there was proclamation of the war having been won at the time the campaigns drew to their respective conclusions, but the fact that the conflicts in Afghanistan and in post-2003 Iraq have already lasted longer than the Second World War in Europe is indicative of the fact that those with the power of decision in Washington did not understand the nature of war and the nature of the conflict they initiated; they did not understand either the nature of the enemy or the nature of the problems that the removal of that enemy would create. As is so frequently if not always the case, the problems presented by victory are more difficult than the problems of fighting a war in the first place. Expressed a slightly different way, victories in campaigns do not necessarily result in victories in wars, and the deliberate targeting of a regime or individual may well result in the release of forces that may be local but do not permit the restoration of order. And, of course, these arguments and their attendant definitions have been set out as the basis of understanding primarily in terms of the provoking of questions rather than the provision of answers.

CHAPTER 2

To the Present Time: The Offensive and Defensive and the *Vernichtungsschlacht*

Perhaps one of the more surprising assertions of Clausewitz was that the superiority of the defensive (over the offensive) is very great, and much greater than may appear at first sight[1] though one must add a related point: that statement is about the only piece in the relevant sections dealing with the conflicting claims of the defensive and the offensive that is readily comprehensible. Be that as it may, the statement is surprising not least because of Clausewitz's own experience of war, which in part provided the basis of his analysis. The French Revolutionary and Napoleonic Wars, *prima facie,* would seem to point in a very different direction; most of the battles, campaigns, and individual wars were won by the Army taking the offensive.[2]

A very careful reading of the relevant sections of *On War* points to the fact that the Clausewitzian assessment is reasoned and reasonable.[3] Certainly there is no denying that, as Clausewitz argued, "it is easier to hold ground than take it" just as "it is easy to conquer: it is hard to occupy," but, of course, the point is that war is not about one-on-one and about equal means,[4] in which situation the power of the defensive, established on a river line, on high ground, or in woods is greater than the power of the offensive. In real terms, the offensive, operating across a smaller frontage than the defensive, can concentrate overwhelming fire power and break the latter, but in so doing it is then presented with the problems of maintaining the breach, the timely commitment of second-echelon formations in order to ensure exploitation, and the proper provision of lines-of-communication troops and forces of occupation. Given the rapid exhaustion of supply, the culminating point, the point in time and distance where the force of the offensive is spent and a rough balance between the offensive and the defensive is restored, is reached relatively quickly.[5] But recognition of this fact of life is really only a description of the battlefield rather than explanation of the battle's outcome, and most certainly does not explain advances and conquests in two world wars that do not fully and immediately accord with the concept of the superiority of the defensive over the offensive.

So much of historical writing about the First World War has concerned itself with the Western Front, which in military terms was where events were decided, that it is very easy to lose sight of the fact that in the First World War German formations reached as far to the east as Rostov-on-Don while Turkish formations reached Baku; in the Second World War, German forces reached the North Cape, Brest, eastern Libya/western Egypt, and Mozdok, which is seven degrees of longitude east of Moscow.[6] The fact that in the Second World War German armies conquered a continent while Japanese forces secured control of an area twice the size of Europe does not square readily with the concept of the superiority of the defensive over the offensive. Explanation lies in the fact that whereas the Clausewitzian analysis is abstract, primarily concerned with a theoretical situation, the two world wars of the 20th century presented very different realities. For both Germany and Japan, the greater part of their conquests were registered in successive campaigns against individual enemies inferior in terms of demographical, economic, and military resources to themselves, and in the case of the First World War and the extent of German and Turkish conquests the greater part of these gains came after the collapse of Russia and her exit from the war. Germany's gains on the Eastern Front in the First World War prior to October 1917 were relatively modest, in large measure because her commitments elsewhere—in 1915 in the Balkans, in 1916 in front of Verdun, on the Somme, in Galicia, and against Romania, and in 1917 on the Western Front generally—precluded major and sustained offensive operations in the east. Between May and September 1915, German and Austro-Hungarian armies were involved in an offensive that carried the tide of war from the border areas, in the area of Plock on the Vistula below Warsaw, some 200 miles to the east, to the Dvinsk-Pinsk-Tarnopol line.[7] The relative slowness of the summer 1915 campaign in very large measure stemmed from the fact that the German success was registered in Poland, which in terms of area, roads, and railways was really the equivalent of the Western Front. This was a part of Russia that equated in size to northern France but it was less well served in railways and supply centers and consequently could not support the military numbers that were deployed in Belgium and north France, either defensively or offensively. The lack of an adequate road system meant that any advance necessarily was very difficult, but the success of the Central Powers in this offensive stemmed from possession of the initiative and local superiorities that enabled their forces to launch a series of attacks that turned successive Russian positions. The overall result of this campaign was a series of local Russian defeats and withdrawals and the loss of one of the most heavily industrialized parts of the Russian empire, but even allowing for the Brusilov Offensive—which for all its fame and attention registered a maximum advance north of the Pruth of some 40 miles—the front line barely changed over the next 18 months.[8] There was, for the Russians, the disastrous extension of front and commitments brought about by Romania's entry into the war and all but immediate and comprehensive defeat and occupation, but the Kerensky Offensive and the German operations in the Gulf of Riga in autumn 1917 excepted,[9] there was very little movement on the Eastern Front after September 1915.

In terms of physical conditions on the ground and limited offensives, a very similar situation repeated itself on the Eastern Front in 1943–1944 in terms of the very limited advances recorded by Soviet formations. A lack of roads and their armies' lack of mechanization, and a very deliberate Soviet caution that stressed limited advances and security rather than deep penetration and risk, combined to ensure that, in real terms, the front really did not move over great distances between November 1942 and November 1943, the area south of the Don into the Caucasus excepted. Between between November 1943 and April 1944 again the movement of the front line was not great and to some extent was exaggerated by the scale of the offensive and the subsequent advance south of the Dnepr to the Romanian border area in March–April 1944.

But more important than any consideration of the conflicting claims about the defensive and the offensive, and the two are basically complimentary and complementary, are two matters relating to the two world wars of the 20th century and the campaign *per se*. First, and very simply, in the two wars there was but one campaign that saw the defeat of a great power. There were a number of individual campaigns that saw the conquest of individual states, and in certain cases more than one state, but only the 1940 campaign in northwest Europe saw the defeat of a great power, France. Second, and the reverse side of this argument, both wars saw the issue of war, of victory, and defeat, decided in protracted wars of attrition, but very oddly the two world wars, at least in their attrition phases, were short wars, wars that by historical standards were very short indeed, and of a duration that in previous times could never have resulted in exhaustion and defeat of a great power.[10]

Perhaps one of the more interesting observations about the First World War is a prophetic comment, written in 1887, which bears examination, in terms both of its apocalyptical anticipation of future war and the basis of its correctness:

This would be a universal war of unprecedented scope, unprecedented force. From eight to ten million soldiers will destroy one another, and in the course of doing so will strip Europe clean in a way that a swarm of locusts could never have done. The devastation caused by the Thirty Years War telescoped into three to four years and spread over the entire continent . . . hunger, epidemics, the universal engagement of both troops and masses, brought about by acute need and hopeless jumbling of . . . trade, industrial and credit mechanisms . . . all this ending in general bankruptcy . . . the collapse of old states and their vaunted wisdom . . . the utter impossibility of foreseeing how this will end and who will emerge victorious from this struggle. Only one result is absolutely beyond doubt—universal exhaustion and the creation of conditions for the final victory of the working class.

The observation, made by Friedrich Engels,[11] owes its percipience to the fact that rather than it being a Marxist analysis and interpretation of war, it is a Clausewitzian analysis and interpretation of the state and society as they would be affected by the demands of war; its understanding of the changing nature of war stems from Engels having understood the forces of change within society as these were to effect the conduct of war.[12] The very same matters, *mutatis mutandis*, were at work in determining the course and outcome of the Second World War but the toll exacted was at least four times the total military and civilian dead of the First World War, yet the point was in both wars the protracted process of exhaustion of resources, manpower, and *materiél* were very much the same, and very oddly the lengths of the wars were similar. The period of attrition and exhaustion in the European part of the Second World War was between June 1941 and May 1945, that is, after the German conquest of Europe and with the start of the Nazi-Soviet conflict, and this period of duration is very close to that of the First World War, and not that different from the length of the Japanese war after December 1941. The basic point, if these arguments are indeed correct, may be that industrialization has not resulted in the lengthening of wars but in their shortening, that the greater the industrial strength of a state the less it can prosecute a long war, or at least a protracted total war.

Certainly with reference to this latter argument, the example of the Second World War would seem to provide supporting evidence primarily in terms of the speed with which Germany and Japan collapsed once the tide of war came to their respective borders and coasts. It was really not until September 1944 that the tide of war reached Germany's pre-war borders,[13] and thereafter Germany's defeat was registered relatively quickly, with due allowance for winter and its restrictions on operations, while in real terms the tide of war reached across the western Pacific to the Japanese home islands in February–March 1945.[14] The weakness of this argument is obvious: the tide of war reached the homelands because Germany and the Japanese had already been defeated. The situation in which Germany and Japan found themselves had been some five years in the making, and the point was that in September 1944 both found themselves presented with all the bills that they had incurred and the promissory notes that they had issued and which they could not honor. What is very interesting about these events is the fact that Germany and Japan in a sense owed their initial successes to the simple fact that they separately fought a series of campaigns rather than wars, campaigns in which they fought enemies inferior in resources to themselves, and, most certainly in the case of Germany, it is possible to argue that no single enemy that she faced after September 1939 was able to fight a battle on its terms prior to November 1942.[15] But by the final phase of the German war, there was something in place that had been absent for all but the last two or three months of the previous global conflict. Apart from these final weeks of war, the First World War was fought by alliances and states that were roughly in balance with one another, and, for the Second World War, this most certainly was not the case, most certainly not in this final phase after September–October 1944. The defeat of Germany was not limited to September 1944–May 1945, but the speed of events in terms of Allied operations and Germany's collapse, especially in the period

January–May 1945, was noteworthy in terms of the superiority of the offensive regarding the speed of advance and depth of penetration, and the comprehensiveness of the victory. One codicil concerning the power of the defensive needs to be added though: in the face of desperate, last-ditch resistance, the Soviets lost more dead—some 300,000 troops—in taking Berlin than the United States lost in the whole of the European war.

This last phase of the second German war could be presented, wrongly, as evidence of the proven worth, the continued validity, of the *Vernichtungsschlacht*. Most certainly both the Soviet and the Anglo-American offensives of March 1945 do possess certain aspects that accord with the *Vernichtungsschlacht* but clearly, given wars that had lasted years, identification of these offensives in such terms would be at best wholly mendacious. But the fact is that if the two world wars were short wars by historical standards and, 1940 excepted, great powers could not be defeated in single campaigns, perhaps the most significant development of recent decades has been the development of means to conduct the *Vernichtungsschlacht* and to complete the defeat of an enemy within a single campaign.[16] The problem with such an assertion, however, is the obvious one. None of the three self-evident examples that could be used to demonstrate that the *Vernichtungsschlacht* is alive and well embrace the defeat of a great power and all three are peculiar to the Middle East, with all that might entail in terms of perception and realities. And, of course, the putting forward of such a view could not be done without the inevitable addition of a counterview. The first such example would be the June 1967 war, which saw the Israeli military defeat her three neighbors in a war that lasted, depending on perspective, either three hours, six days, or, more accurately, 42 years to date.

The other two examples both relate to Iraq, the first in January–February 1991 and the second in March 2003, and the significance of the *Vernichtungsschlacht* lies not so much in Iraq's double defeat but the comparison and contrast between these wars, particularly the 1991 campaign, with the war between Iraq and Iran (9 September 1980–20 August 1988). The latter is a conflict sometimes referred to as the two combatants' First World War most obviously in terms of length, losses, and exhaustion but also on account of the battlefield. After June 1982, by which time the Iranians had recovered virtually all the territory that had been lost in the Iraqi offensive that opened the war, trench warfare *à la* Western Front was in place complete with trench systems and defense in depth, massive barbed wire entanglements, and the (Iraqi) use of chemical weapons. But in 1991 and again in 2003, a coalition led by the United States achieved within a matter of days what had proved beyond the Iranians in eight years of war.

Obviously what distinguishes the campaigns of 1991 and 2003 from the 1980–1988 war is the very nature of Iraq's enemy. Iran simply did not begin to compare to a coalition headed by the country that was the greatest power (and possessed of what was technologically the most advanced military) in the world. In terms of the 1991 campaign, Iraq found that she had conjured into existence, and against herself, an alliance possessed, via a technological capability and massive advantage of numbers, such overwhelming superiority that it did not need to fight for air supremacy. The winning of air supremacy was simultaneous and synonymous with the exercise of supremacy, and in 1991, and again in 2003, the Iraqi Air Force was incapable of even a token challenge to coalition control of the skies. In 1991 and again in 2003, as was the case in 1967, the ground offensive began in conditions of devastating air superiority against a demoralized enemy, the resultant campaign on the ground famously lasting less than 100 hours (24–27 February). But it has been suggested, specifically by captured Iraqi prisoners, that the air campaign after 17 January had all but brought about a collapse of logistical support for the Iraqi formations inside Kuwait and that a ground campaign was unnecessary. Had the air effort been continued, perhaps for another one or two weeks, the collapse of the logistical system in theater would have forced Iraq formations to withdraw from Kuwait.[17] Be that as it may, the events of 1991 (and 2003) would suggest a restoration of the power of decision within a single campaign—in a major international context a return to the wars of German unification or to the Balkan Wars—but quite clearly this must be a conclusion tempered by one reality. The United States believed it had such power and capability in 1965, which was one of the reasons why her political leadership, her military, and indeed American society itself was prepared to wage war in southeast Asia.

The Vietnam War very clearly provides reason to pause for consideration, and indeed the Korean War before it embraced a lesson that the United States seemingly never grasped. The idea of "hug-and-hold" may be paraded at the present time as the means of countering an otherwise unassailable American superiority of firepower and mobility on the battlefield, but the basic tactic was there in both the Korean War and the Vietnam War. In Korea, the Chinese communists' offensive of November–December 1950 represented the close-quarter battle with perhaps the single most effective attack being that directed, at night, against an American regiment in front of Unsan (November 1). The main communist efforts materialized on 24–25 November in front of Anju-Tokohon and Hagaru, and such was their effectiveness that United Nations forces, which had secured Chosan on the Yalu in the last week of October, found themselves astride the 38th parallel, and fighting inside South Korea by mid-December.[18] But while the communists were able to advance the length of North Korea in this time, two matters need be cited. For all their success in driving their enemy southward, and ultimately to the 37th parallel, the communists were unable to complete the destruction of major American and allied formations in the north. The Americans were able to use their air and naval superiority to full effect in terms of the evacuation of formations from first Wŏnsan and then Hŭngnam. Perhaps more pertinently, the extent of the U.N. reverses in large measure stemmed in very large measure from an overweening, condescending American confidence that discounted Chinese presence and capability.[19] In terms of the war in southeast Asia, the latter commodities were there in abundance but so was a North Vietnamese refusal to abide by

an American script. The same recourse to the close-quarter battle, when tied
to an astute awareness of the power of the media and the need to neutralize
American power by political means, was never more obvious than with the Tet
Offensive (January–February 1968) and the siege of Khe Sanh (January–April
1968), but was present in a whole series of operations especially in or near the
Demilitarized Zone in the border area in the period, 1968–1972. The communist spring offensives of February–March 1969 and April 1970 bracketed
the series of actions that were fought for the control of Ap Bia/Hamburger
Hill before and in May 1969, and finally there was the siege of Quảng Tri
after March 1972 that resulted in the North Vietnamese capture of the city on
1 May,[20] the basic communist aim in this period being to break American will
to continue the war, which was very largely realized in this time. In this process, the Tet Offensive possessed obvious significance, not just in the short-
term regarding its impact upon public opinion in the United States in 1968
but also as a pointer to the future. The communist offensive was urban-based,
to ensure maximum publicity and immediate impact and to set at naught the
enemy's superiority of firepower and movement in the field.

The idea that the *Vernichtungsschlacht* may well have returned to the military
repertoire cannot be denied. Air power and with it Inside-out Warfare may
well have to be restored to the inventory of the greatest of the powers though
it needs to be noted that even middle-ranking military powers, such as the
leading European N.A.T.O. countries, do not possess this capability. They may
acquire such capability only by the pooling of their forces in order to be able
to afford the numbers and specialist aircraft that alone can provide such capability. But the *Vernichtungsschlacht* and Inside-out Warfare may only have relevance and applicability in certain very specific instances, and preparations
to retain or acquire such capability may well represent preparation for the
last war.

The world may well have moved beyond the point where wars between
states represent the *sine qua non* of war and wars, and it may very well be that
such campaigns as those fought in 1991 and 2003 represent the drawing of the
final line in the sand, the point in time when the business of war most definitely moved away from conflicts between coalitions and states and concerned
itself primarily and overwhelmingly with conflicts below the level of the state.
States will still be involved in wars but not so much with one another as with
other enemies, and in this context the hug-and-hold/close-quarter battle will
possess the same importance and significance as it did in the Korean and Vietnam conflicts but with two obvious points of difference. The global market,
modern means of travel, and the inter-nationalization/trans-nationalization of
conflicts have combined to spell the end of invulnerability, as events in New
York (11 September 2001), on Bali (12 October 2002 and 1 October 2005),
and in Madrid (11 March 2004) and London (7 July 2005) have demonstrated
only too clearly. Moreover, the speed of communication in terms of both the

image and spoken word has provided the esoteric, whether individuals or cause, with access to international public opinion in a manner and at a speed that was unthinkable even 20 years ago.

What has emerged is a most potent mix, specifically with reference to fundamentalist belief and the waging of war against non-believers by all means, and specifically by hug-and-hold in the form of the suicide attack. Western society, with its very selective accounts of its own history, has little understanding of either the use of women and children in the suicide role or the identification of women and children as legitimate targets. But, for example, the *al-Qa'ida* concept of the just war against non-believers, with its aim of creating a new Islamic society cleansed of pollutant Western contacts and influences, embraces the idea of the purging of society of those who have transgressed religious and societal norms, and this is a process that can be set in place once victory has been won or as part of the struggle for victory—either as an end or one of the means. In both cases, fundamentalist belief provides comfort against conscience, but most certainly this form of warfare, and particularly in Iraq since 2003, has placed Western society and military in exactly the opposite position. The belief that war should not be waged either by or against women and children goes alongside the moral dilemma presented by suicide attacks against civilian targets and people. The identification of targets on the basis of their association, real or alleged, with non-believers naturally presents the latter with the choice of continuing or abandoning the struggle, and with reference to the latter an abandonment of the struggle would entail an abandonment of people who had looked to Western military for protection and support, and in not a few cases means of livelihood—and there is the additional small matter that the argument that ending involvement in theater would somehow absolve oneself of any form of responsibility for what then follows is, to put it mildly, somewhat unconvincing. And, of course, in the context of Afghanistan post-2001 and Iraq post-2003, there is the problem of wars that supposedly were won years ago reaching into the indefinite future.

In both Afghanistan and Iraq, the basic problems that existed were how to convert a successful campaign into a won war and, on the reverse side of this same coin, how to complete the occupation and a return of these countries to a status of stability and international respectability. It is quite obvious that the fragmentation of these countries and the emergence of militias and resistance to Western control, ideas, and systems, all of which were never anticipated, illustrates that imposing forms of Western government and mores have not provided the answers to these countries' needs. In these matters, and specifically the unavailing attempts to set in place an acceptable system over the last five years, one is reminded of the content of a speech, made almost a lifetime ago:

First, no people on earth can be held, as a people, to be an enemy, for all humanity shares the common hunger for peace and fellowship and justice.

Second, no nation's security and well-being can be lastingly achieved in isolation but only in effective co-operation with fellow-nations.

Third, any nation's right to form a government and an economic system of its own choosing is inalienable.

Fourth, any nation's attempt to dictate (to) other nations their form of government is indefensible.

And fifth, a nation's hope of lasting peace cannot be firmly based upon any race in armaments but rather upon just relations and honest understanding with all other nations.[21]

One wonders specifically about the third and fourth points and how they would be received in Washington D.C. during the period after 2001 had Eisenhower been alive and in fit state to repeat his 1953 speech. As it is, the problems that have beset the coalition's operations in both Afghanistan and Iraq since 2001 and 2003, respectively, stem in large measure from a failure on the part of those in the political and military leadership in Washington with the power of decision to understand the distinction between a war and a campaign, to understand the limits of force and to understand the nature of the countries and societies with which they were involved. A campaign that was won was not a war that had been won, and an ability to win a campaign presented questions rather than provided answers.

CHAPTER 3

The Illusion of Certainty

One of the ironies of 20th-century military thought is that whereas Mahan had his counterpart in Sir Julian Corbett (1854–1922) and land warfare came into possession of many schools, Giulo Douhet (1869–1930) only had disciples; the Five Circles and Inside-Out Warfare concepts form part of an unbroken, singular, air culture that has existed for almost as long as the use of the aircraft in war. As such, these concepts labor under the legacy of persistent failure since air power in various wars has never been able to deliver upon the promises of its advocates, and these present concepts, and even more obviously the concept of Parallel Warfare, lay themselves open to the charge that they are merely failure recycled under a new name—the one-more-effort-down-the-old-path-and-we-will-make-Douhet's-ideas-work argument that independent air forces have employed before, during, and since the Second World War.

Given that the rationale for independent air forces lay and perhaps continues to lie in an strategic bombing role, perhaps this line of argument is inevitable, but in considering the Desert Storm and Kosovo campaigns and the present doctrinal debate, one is left to wonder how much of these ideas represent rational argument and how much dogmatic assertion, articles of faith. But this question obscures the real ones, whether new technology really does offer the opportunity to make Douhet's ideas work, whether new technology will alter the very nature of war. Concepts such as the Five Circles, Inside-Out Warfare, Parallel Warfare, Rapid Dominance and, most recently and all but unbelievably, Shock and Awe, have as their base the assumed effectiveness of modern weaponry of unprecedented accuracy and destructive power, and certainly this unprecedented accuracy and destructiveness of modern weaponry cannot be disputed. But what can be disputed is the assumption that new-found and future capability will produce results that hitherto have proved elusive, and the basis of doubt on this particular score lies in the reality that whereas technology in the form of the destructiveness of weaponry is linear and predictable in terms of cause and effect with reference to *matériel*, the same does not hold true for societies and the elusive will to make war. The new concepts of warfare have as their premise a view of an enemy state and society unchanged and unchanging other than the damage inflicted upon both by one's own offensive action, and such a concept as Shock and Awe is explicit in its faith in technology, its successful application, and an ability to control the process, witness:

The ability to impose massive shock and awe . . . to be able to "turn the lights on and off" of an adversary as we choose, will so overload the perception, understanding and knowledge of that adversary that there will be no choice except to cease and desist or risk complete and total destruction,[1]

and presumably, being rational, mend its ways, as, of course, the Japanese did when faced with such a choice in 1941. Resisting the temptation to question the circumstances that might lead a superpower to threaten a lesser society with complete and total destruction and the various limitations that the possession of the means to turn the lights on and off would inevitably entail, any consideration of warfare, and specifically warfare over the last 100 years, suggests that societies possess enormous capacity for adaptation and endurance and that the main impact of bombing campaigns has been to strengthen the will to resist. The simplicity of this statement of argument conceals a profound point of change that such concepts as Inside-Out Warfare and Shock and Awe present. It is not so much that Inside-Out Warfare claims to be able to affect an enemy capacity that will result in air power being able to achieve what has hitherto been elusive whereas critics of this claim would hold to the belief that the concept of strategic bombing will never be brought to fruition because the basic idea is inherently flawed, but that the air lobby argument has blurred the distinction between the nature of war and the conduct of war and its basic premise, technological effectiveness, runs counter to the fundamental characteristic of war: war is a human activity, not a laboratory exercise in applied technology, and doctrine is the servant, not the determinant, of war. Herein lies the gravest problem presented by the current obsession with doctrine, even more serious than that represented by the absurdities of Shock and Awe. The latter, at least in part, does start from a premise based upon the changing nature of society and technology as they might affect the conduct of war. Present doctrine, from the insularity endowed by assumed orthodoxy, would dictate a concept of operations that in turn would determine a vision of the nature of war. This is explicit in the concept of Parallel Warfare, which comes complete with a basis of knowledge and correct anticipation of every aspect of an enemy's capabilities and intentions. By inverting what is the natural order of a relationship that is not singular but embraces both the nature and the conduct of war and one in which the various parts are mutually dependent and related, present doctrine, in its certainty and purpose, represents nothing but "danger on the utmost edge of hazard."

Any consideration of warfare over the last 200 years, and particularly in the 20th century, points to societal capacity to endure that is not to be underestimated. Human resilience, and the capacity of peoples bound together by common identity, language, culture, and institutions to adapt and to continue to offer resistance even in the most appalling of circumstances has been demonstrated not just in the two world wars of the 20th century but also, and perhaps even more significantly, in other conflicts since 1945. This fact, and the ability of non-Western societies to survive conditions that would deeply divide democracies, represents a clear indication of the critical importance of moral as opposed to material factors in the conduct of war. Any suggestion that the ability to destroy the capacity to resist on a scale and at a pace that are unprecedented will profoundly alter the will and ability to resist would seem to have little historical basis—Kosovo in 1999 would seem to the exception rather than the rule—while the level of expectation and demand in terms of war being portrayed as clean, swift, minimal in its claims on life, and, critically, carries with it the certainty of victory may well present those who insist upon the efficacy of modern doctrine and weaponry with all but impossible problems of fulfilling wholly unrealistic public expectation.

The idea of Inside-Out Warfare may be proven by future events, but in its present context it would seem to be part of a much wider concept that suggests, indeed insists, that war can be controlled. The insistence on the defined end-state of conflict by the U.S. military in the last decade has its origins in the Vietnam experience, yet it begs a number of questions even it is based upon the need to soothe a potentially volatile electorate. If Roosevelt in 1941 had been subjected to such requirements, the United States probably would still be waiting to enter the Second World War, but the more pertinent point about this end-state demand is its being indicative of a desire to control the peace or at least set the agenda for peace, yet the conduct of peace necessarily presents greater problems than the conduct of war. The experience of 20th-century warfare would suggest that the ability of any single nation or associated group of nations to control the terms of reference of war is illusory. As Clausewitz had taught us, in war everything is uncertain, and wars invariably assume courses and outcomes very different from that intended by their authors. The whole notion of being able to control warfare, whether it be definition of end-state or offensive operations of surgical precision, runs directly counter to the fundamental Clausewitzian element in war: chance. War is not the preserve of the intellect and is not intrinsically rational or scientific. Man made war in his own image, complete with all the elements of human failure, mis-judgment, and incompetence therein, and, hopefully, thus it will remain. Current doctrine and predictions for the future of war that are now on the table would seem to assume otherwise, that somehow the certainties provided by technology will provide certainties in the conduct of war that will in themselves transform the nature of war. Doctrine cannot be divorced from the past, but if, as Alexander Svechin (1878–1938) is credited as having written, doctrine is the daughter of History, some of the more recent doctrinal papers would seem to leave the individual to ponder the identity of the father, and also the question of whether or not the parents were married. Current doctrine would seem to represent neither the daughter nor the product but the end of history, and the end of the primacy of man in terms of the nature and conduct of war.[2]

POSTSCRIPT

And, one would add, not just the U.S. Air Force. The recurring theme in American military thinking has been a certainty provided by technology and disproved by events, the pre-war Norton bomb-sight and firepower *à la* Vietnam being obvious examples. Most certainly the belief in the efficacy of firepower in securing victory survived Vietnam, witness the observation that the United States "should capitalize on American technological prowess and not think that we can win by sending out small counter-insurgent teams to beat the guerrillas at the type of war they know best." It is hard to understand what this means, given the failure of the "technological prowess" approach that was applied in Vietnam and the fact that guerrilla wars cannot be won unless the guerrillas are beaten in the type of war they know best. See Samuel P. Huntington, "American Military Strategy," *Policy Papers in International Affairs, Number 28*, pp. 3–17.

These, and certain of Huntington's other assertions, would seem to embrace some highly dubious assumptions, not least the belief that the United States, by virtue of technological superiority, would be able to fight wars on her own terms. With reference to this latter point, Huntington asserted that the military could impose its own mark on guerrilla wars by offensive action, and he alleged that "the offensive aimed at the center of enemy power was the core of American strategy. It has, unfortunately, been lost during the last thirty years." The implications of this remark would seem to be untenable. Since Huntington marked 1951 as the watershed in U.S. thinking regarding the offensive and defensive, it would seem that Huntington was suggesting that both the Korean and Vietnam Wars could have been won by offensive action, presumably by widening the respective wars into China and North Vietnam.

Leaving aside the merits of an argument that must be highly questionable, the Huntington thesis, and indeed the whole of the technological determinist argument, would seem to be most hazardous in that if applied it would appear to put the United States approach to warfare in an intellectual straight-jacket, with an all-or-nothing choice in consideration of the use of force and the employment of force in exactly the same way as massive retaliation did in the 1950s.

CHAPTER 4

The Approach of Absolute War

Possibly one of the most celebrated single parts of the Clausewitzian analysis of war is the concept of Absolute War and the "vast array of factors, forces and conditions in national affairs that are affected by war" and which at various times, singly and in combination, "modify the principle of enmity." What this came to mean to most students was that the tendency toward what might be termed total war would always be subject to modification, both in terms of the nature and the conduct of war, and that war would not again reach the state of absolute perfectionism achieved by Napoléon in the early years of the wars that bear his name.[1] The process of industrialization, the spread of exclusive nationalist and racist concepts, and the growth of the modern state meant that by the 20th century the state, society, and war had assumed dimensions and capabilities that the Westphalian system had been deliberately crafted to prevent, and the two world wars of that century, and most certainly the second, brought to the fore a totality, in terms of aims and conduct, which represented a complete and entire whole of a kind that Clausewitz would never have considered possible.

In terms of the nature and the conduct of war, the Second World War clearly possessed an obvious significance that compared, in many ways, to the situation that had prevailed in the aftermath of the Thirty Years' War. In the aftermath of the Napoleonic Wars with the concert of Europe and the First World War with the League of Nations there were very deliberate attempts to guard against any future repetition of these wars, but the Second World War was different from these earlier wars in terms of deliberate killings of civilian populations in German- and Japanese- occupied territories and the Final Solution program, and also on account of its ending; the use of atomic weapons against Hiroshima and Nagasaki (respectively 6 and 9 August, respectively) clearly pointed to a conduct of operations that necessarily had to be controlled and indeed avoided in the future. With the creation of a United Nations as part of the attempt to craft a new world order and either to prevent war or to ensure its limitation, for some three or four decades there was a general restraint, most obviously in terms of policies of deterrents by the super-powers but also at a different level in terms of the conduct of operations. Inevitably certain of the wars that were fought, and most obviously the (third) Chinese civil war (26 June 1946–December 1949), were bloody affairs that exacted major civilian losses,[2] but for the most parts wars were, if not exactly of the Limited Wars of the Age of Reason genre, more or less "proper" wars. The only war of national liberation in which security forces really broke the rules was fought in Algeria and France (November 1954–March 1962), but while every war produces its incidents and wrongdoings, the wars of liberation for the most part saw security forces observe rules of limitation and justness in terms of treatment of civilian populations, and such conflicts as the Korean War, where there was massive displacement of population and many deaths *en passant*, generally saw levels of military behavior that accorded with propriety. In many of these conflicts, the treatment of civilian and captured military personnel by the other side was not what it might have been (e.g. in Algeria, specifically in the early years of this conflict). But, of course, there were wars such as those that affected the Congo/Zaire between January 1961 and November 1965 when the state fell apart and spawned a number of bitter separatist and civil wars that defy ready explanation, understanding, and classification, and which had more than their fair share of incidents and wrongdoings.

The campaigns that have been fought over the last three decades, and to which reference has already been made in these pages, have generally exhibited a viciousness that was notably absent, or perhaps more accurately less pronounced, in the campaigns fought over the previous three decades. But in assessing future prospects, it is very difficult to escape the conclusion that what will be at stake in future conflicts make for a totality that has been absent from wars, in terms of nature and conduct, since 1945, and that such wars could possibly extend to employing bacteriological weaponry against not just individuals and holdings but societies *per se*, and, of course, attempts to wreck societies and organizations will involve full recourse of cyber warfare.

Those causes of strife that have come to center stage in recent years have been primarily concerned with identity and have taken the form of racial, ethnic, and religious differences, and these are certain not to pass from the scene in the future. Perhaps the form of struggle that has assumed the highest profile has been religious, primarily Islamic and specifically identified with *al-Qa'ida*, and there is little doubt that these, and specifically *al-Qa'ida*, have some time to run. There is among adherents to this militant Islamic cause a singular hold on truth in the form of the Koran and Moslem teaching and a focus on immediate enemies, most obviously Western countries and Israel. With reference to the latter, it is very hard to escape the conclusion that her campaign in Gaza (27–28 December 2008/18 January 2009) in the long term can only result in increased recruitment for Palestinian militancy. But apparently three-quarters of *al-Qa'ida* personnel and recruits are Saudis, which is comment enough on the state of affairs in a country that has been looted of wealth by a ruling hierarchy to the extent that in 1991, in the prelude to the Iraqi campaign, Saudi Arabia was not A.1 credit-worthy in terms of international finance while between 1991 and 2003 the living standards of the ordinary Saudi fell by a quarter. The country has been in the process of being milked dry by a corrupt, self-interested, self-indulgent royal dynasty that has become identified with Western interest. Revolution, when it comes, will most certainly be anti- Western in orientation and effect, but the basic point is that any revolutionary struggle will be trans-national and most certainly will not be limited to a single country or even a single area. But, of course, Saudi Arabia is not alone in being a potential target of righteous revolutionary endeavor. The other Gulf states likewise lay themselves open to charges of corruption, self-indulgence, and a wholly wrongful association with the West, but more basic is the simple fact that the whole basis of struggle for *al-Qa'ida* is religious and therefore is opposed, in the final analysis, to all Moslem states and their governments because each and every one of them, obviously, has been guilty of not following Islamic standards and ethics as laid down by revolutionary doctrine. For example, the country with the largest Moslem population in the world is Indonesia but it has a constitution in which there is no reference to Islam. *al-Qa'ida* and its concept of struggle represent the ultimate in contradiction of terms in that together they embrace a concept of permanent total war, an unending commitment to struggle to ends that remain undefined.

But if the religious dimension has assumed the highest profile in terms of forms of struggle over recent years, what has been crucial in providing *al-Qa'ida* with international standing, perhaps the most serious and persistent form of struggle has been racial and ethnic, and in Africa specifically tribal. Within sub-Saharan Africa are three main groups of peoples, the Bantu, Nilotes, and the para-Nilotics, and, it would seem, there are more than 400 Bantu groupings spread from southeast Nigeria south and east over southern Africa. The divisions between these peoples—witness the Bantu Hutu and para-Nilotic Tutsi—and the no less obvious divisions within these groups linguistically and by tribe[3] represent an obvious and potential source of conflict, or perhaps more accurately a proliferation of conflicts, and in countries such as Kenya this has become increasingly apparent in the last decade.

Africa inevitably attracts attention in terms of problems of identity and racial and tribal conflicts but, without in any way belittling these matters, race and identity are matters that potentially could produce any number of crises and wars in other parts of the world. The largest parliamentary democracy in the world, India, has for 30 years been faced with militant separatism in Assam and since November 1990 has been involved in an ongoing campaign against two major and at least four lesser militias,[4] while in South America the largest country, Brazil, most definitely has a racial problem in the making in terms of the fact that the country has one of the largest gaps in income distribution in the world. The wealthiest 10 percent of the population have incomes 28 times that of the poorest 40 percent of the population; one-third of the population lives under the poverty line, while black and other non-white people make up 70 percent of the poor.[5] With countries such as Bolivia playing host to Amerindian organizations that are intent on overcoming the primacy of a white, Hispanic hierarchy that has been in place since the Spanish conquest,[6] it may very well be the problem of identity will produce crises and wars across several continents. And, it need be added, the disintegration of Yugoslavia and the wars of Croatia (March 1991–December 1995) and Slovenia (June–July 1991) and the Kosovo episodes[7] provide evidence that Europe has not rid herself of such problems.

Racial, ethnic, and religious differences are certain to reach into the future and to provide the basis for future wars but there are developments presently in the making that over the next 20 to 30 years must come to center stage and will ensure a return to the totality of war at its worst. In one sense, these developments can be summarized under one label: shortages of food, which tied to major population growth, may well become issues for conflict, either caused by regional population growth in excess of the area's capability to support a population or from localized famines exacerbated by distribution or simply by distribution issues owing to war-lordism. Regardless of the cause, the type of conflict and fighting will likely be the same.

In the course of the 20th century, the world's population more than tripled, indeed all but quadrupled, rising from about 1,650,000,000 in 1900 to about 5,978,000,000 in 1999, and various estimates suggest that this number will grow to around 8,900,000,000–9,000,000,000 between 2040 and 2050.[8] These figures would suggest an increase of population by about one-half over the next four decades, or, more simply, an increase of population by about 60,000,000—more or less equal to the population of Iran or France or Thailand or the Democratic Republic of the Congo or Britain at the present time—year on year. But by the meanest, least exacting standard, the world at the present time is incapable of providing properly for its peoples. Famines and massed deaths from starvation may have been shelved over the last century—the Bengal Famine of 1943–1945 and the east Africa famines of 1980–1984 may well have been the last major famines in the 20th century—but most certainly in recent years there has been increased occurrence of malnutrition. How major increases of population are to be managed given the slenderness of the margins by which starvation and famine have been kept at bay in recent years is not clear, but the problem is one that extends beyond mere numbers. The greatest increases in population in recent years have manifested themselves primarily in countries that historically have been the least prepared in terms of means to accommodate such growth. To give but a couple of examples, according to the 1981 census India had a population of 683,810,051, and in less than three decades (to January 2009) this had increased by two-thirds to a total of 1,143,670,000 and it seems that she will overtake China as the most populous state in the world in the next decade. Bangladesh and Pakistan, which in 1983 had populations of 94,650,000 and 88,000,000, now, in 2009, have populations of 158,665,000 and 165,475,000, respectively, and in the case of Bangladesh this represents a total of 2,854 persons per square mile.[9] Such figures can be repeated all but endlessly and to no real purpose, suffice it to indicate that no fewer than 18 countries have populations of more than 70,000,000. Indonesia, Brazil, Nigeria, and Mexico all have population totals of more than 100,000,000 and the Philippines, Vietnam, Ethiopia, Egypt, Turkey, and Iran present themselves in the next grouping with more than 70,000,000.[10] Historically, none of these countries could be deemed to have possessed industrial diversity and general economic self-sufficiency.

The problem presented by major population growth is compounded by the fact that the process of industrialization in certain countries that has gone alongside major population growth has been accompanied by urbanization that has resulted in major loss of arable land. Major population growth over the next three or four decades thus would run alongside declining food production unless there was some major advance in terms of yield, a second Green Revolution in a hundred years, which would at least keep agricultural output at its present level. But while such a change would seem unlikely, or at least unlikely on a scale that would meet increasing demand, the problem of maintaining present yields is necessarily compounded by climate change, the fall in the level of water tables, and problems that are associated with fertilizers. With reference to the first, changing patterns of rainfall with attendant drought were certainly at work in producing widespread crop failures in east Africa after 1978, specifically the Ethiopian disaster of 1984, but the basic point is that increased demand on water, when tied to failure of the rains, will lead to a further depletion of water tables with inevitable results in terms of a decreased ability of societies to provide food for their peoples. This problem would seem to be at its worst in Africa, the desiccation of the continent pointing to the fact that this is not simply a local or even regional problem but one that, even at the present time, affects a continent.

What this will mean in terms of war and wars, and what this will mean in terms of war and wars as distinct from general criminal activity, is very difficult to discern, but as noted elsewhere the advance of the desert necessarily means enforced movement of populations into areas already occupied and worked, with all that such a situation would imply in terms of civil unrest and strife. The loss of working land, with the resultant loss of means of livelihood, inevitably must mean massively increased price of land and produce, and at a time when an increasing part of society—specifically in the countryside but in both the countryside and urban areas—lacks the means to buy the basic necessities of life.[11]

To these matters must be added the certainty of increased price and scarcity of oil, a certainty that goes alongside the lack of any final, authoritative figures about known reserves. It would appear, however, that while the world reserves have an estimated life of some 54 years, such countries as Algeria, Brazil, China, Mexico, Russia, and the United States have reserves that will last less than 20 years.[12] Most certainly massive increases in the price of oil must be expected in the future, both short- and long-term, what happened briefly in 2008 in this matter can only be a harbinger of the future. But the fact that the greater part of the world's reserves are vested in six countries, five of which are in the Middle East,[13] would seem to invoke, on the basis of past historical experience, the notion of wars of acquisition on the part of more powerful states that lacked or exhausted their own reserves. But such wars, should they occur, could never be more than temporary, short-lived palliatives. Any conquest would be set at naught in less than a lifetime.

But oil, whether reserves, production, or price, necessarily is but one part of what is certain to be major problems confronting the existing international system. Major increases in the price of oil can only result in increased costs in every aspect of production, but in one matter such increases are certain to compound the basic problems confronting agriculture. Major increases in the price of fertilizers cannot be avoided, yet the impact of even modest increases on such countries as Zimbabwe has been little short of disastrous. Of course with reference to Zimbabwe, the increasing cost of fertilizers has been but one aspect of problems facing agriculture, and in very large measure fertilizers have become prohibitively expensive primarily as a result of what is virtually the collapse of the economy as a direct result of the incompetent and corrupt rule of the dictatorship of Robert Mugabe (1924–). Moreover, the failure of the rains has compounded problems. But the basic point is that present levels of agricultural output have been possible only by intensive use of fertilizers, and it would seem that generally, but specifically for developing countries, these are likely to become very expensive, perhaps even prohibitively expensive, in years to come.

These various matters, namely increasing population in a world incapable of major increases of agricultural output and beset by increasing prices and growing shortages of oil and other resources, would most certainly have their initial impact on developing countries, and the sort of wars that we have seen in Liberia and Sierra Leone would seem to have a place marked out for them in the future. How these developments might affect more advanced Western countries is not clear although in one specific area there may well be a development not afforded much in the way of present calculations. The depletion of stocks in the sea has clearly assumed disastrous proportions and has been the direct result of increasingly irresponsible conduct on the part of some of these fishing nations, but whether the sea, the seabed, and the mass below the seabed can yield new sources that may be used for food, fuel, or other manufactured material would present the obvious problem of jurisdiction and definition of the role of navies. Since the end of the Cold War, navies have lost a great deal of their *raison d'être*. The strategic deterrence has largely passed—what remains seems to be no more than the playing out a role that is no more—and at best a genuine blue-water alternative to the U.S. Navy would seem to be one or two generations away. It will take perhaps two or three decades for China to acquire and bring into service a genuine carrier force. The main operational role of navies, and specifically the U.S. Navy, since the end of the Cold War, has been brown-water, but it may be that the search for increased offshore resources may well provide navies with extra responsibilities relative to other navies and to revolutionary militia groups. Even at the present time there is, in terms of claims and counter-claims, one potential area of conflict at sea, and that is over the Spratly Islands in the South China Sea.[14] No fewer than six countries — Brunei, China, Malaysia, the Philippines, Taiwan, and Vietnam — have claims on these islands that reach back to 1973 and saw Chinese and Vietnamese warships fight one another in March 1988. Various islands in the group host garrisons drawn from the Philippines, Taiwan, and Vietnam, but in recent years there seems to have been a general move away from confrontation claims in favor of pooled development. But the issue of sovereignty and rights has not been either resolved or even the subject of international mediation and arbitration has defied agreement.[15] Other islands or groups that may well be the subject of future dispute remain (predictably) the Falkland Islands/Islas Malvinas, the South Georgia group and South Sandwich Islands, Ascension, St. Helena, Tristan da Cunha, and other islands in southern waters, in part because of their remoteness, would seem to present little cause for dispute and war though there are various claims on Antarctica.[16]

Other naval matters that are currently on the table primarily involve pollution—in South Korean waters, and in the Black, Baltic, and North Seas—and, more seriously, the tasks that should have been assigned to history, namely the suppression of piracy, slavery, the drug trade, and human trafficking/illegal entry by sea. By the very nature of things, the greater part of the effort on these scores necessarily must be the gathering, evaluation, and timely and effective use of intelligence since mere patrols contribute but little in such matters. Very clearly what navies need is both blue- and brown-water capability, warships that can reach across the seas with weapons to match, and inshore units with speed and support to deal with the situations in which they might find themselves.

In one sense somewhat curiously and in another sense perhaps predictably, the matters raised in these pages primarily involve states and society, armies and navies, claims and counter-claims, and quite clearly have no place for air forces, Inside-out Warfare, and the *Vernichtungsschlacht*. But air forces nonetheless remain, at least for Western states, at the cutting edge of any major military endeavor, and very clearly have a major role to play not least in lessening the risk of casualties among ground troops. Certainly the manner in which politicians and the media in Western countries have portrayed losses in Afghanistan and Iraq borders on the absurd—British losses in Afghanistan in eight years prior to January 13, 2009 equate to 10 minutes 32 seconds of Soviet losses on the Eastern Front in the Second World War. The B.B.C. in a report of 13 July 2008 stated that the Americans had suffered heavy losses in what had been the most costly single incident in Afghanistan since 2001; nine soldiers were killed— 41 seconds of Soviet losses—and by the standard of real losses scarce worthy of a mention. But the point is any losses, in the age of the Information Revolution, now possesses very real political clout, and most certainly the close public supervision of events has immense significance in terms of accountability.

Air forces have changed very significantly since the end of the Second World War, most obviously in terms of aircraft, propulsion, and performance but also in terms of role. In the Second World War, the British and U.S. Air Forces were general air forces, unlike their German and Japanese Army counterparts. The latter were basically committed to the close support role whereas over time their enemies came into possession of aircraft for five very different roles, namely defense, strategic bombing, close support, naval support operations, and transport. Very obviously, over the last 50 years the distinction between the defensive, bombing, and close support roles has been blurred with successive generations of new aircraft, of unprecedented performance, capable of operating in all three roles, and as noted elsewhere, in 2003 the United States proved able to destroy an enemy state but did not need to mobilize in the sense that this term came to be used in the two world wars of the 20th century in order to do so, and she did so primarily by air power. But, of course, such capability would be largely discounted in a situation in which the United States found herself involved in a series of conflicts below the level of the state, and very clearly the United States would have very limited capacity in a situation that spawned any number of wars at this level. Put another way, if it is a case that "no country, no matter how powerful or prosperous, can control the forces of globalisation on its own,"[17] then the same most definitely applies in terms of the powerful and prosperous, whether singly or in combination with others, and war, witness the evidence of Afghanistan and Iraq at the present time.

If in 2004 there were indeed some sixty-odd wars around the world then very clearly the international system that was put in place in the two generations after the end of the Second World War came complete with any number of flaws of both commission and omission. But given the diversity of peoples, cultures, and religions within individual countries, reaching across borders and embracing whole regions, this number of conflicts is unlikely to decline given worsening social conditions for the majority of peoples throughout the world. The problems of increasingly scarce resources, and specifically food shortages that will be the consequence of the coming together of problems that would defy ready solution, will all but certainly lead to turf wars that will be fought for the sake of existence itself, and the losers would face starvation and death, while advanced countries would be faced with impossible dilemmas; to help one people would mean, given the scarcity of resources, the condemnation of another while their ability to intervene in such wars would necessarily be limited even if the will to intervene was there. Costs and numbers would necessarily limit the capacity of outside powers to intervene in many conflicts while the obvious lesson of the present commitments in Afghanistan and Iraq may well not be lost upon electorates in future. These two commitments have both lasted longer than the Second World War and primarily because the American political and military leadership that ordered these undertakings simply had no understanding of what these commitments would entail. At the present time, they seem to be open-ended commitments in pursuit of the unobtainable. If that is indeed the point learned by domestic electorates then the capacity of the United States and her associates to undertake future military commitments except in direct response to attack is likely to be very limited indeed. The wars that will determine allocation of land, food, and resources will nonetheless be fought, and to very bloody ends. In the situation that is now taking shape, all those factors that made for the avoidance of Absolute War in favor of the limitation of Real War would seem to be in retreat. What we as an international community face is diffusion of power with proliferation of issues critical to survival, of peoples and people, with no international order capable of dealing with issues and their resultant conflicts. Such wars, fought about fundamentals, can only be appalling in terms of their conduct and ubiquity, but specifically parts of Africa, are very likely to see a re-primitivization of war with reference to weaponry, means of killing, and general treatment of populations. The displacement of Real War by Absolute War would seem to be in train.

BOOK VI

Conclusion

CHAPTER 1

To the Gods
Belongs Tomorrow

To-day is ours; what do we fear
To-day is ours; we have it here:
Let's treat it kindly, that it may
Wish, at least, with us to stay.
Let's banish business, banish sorrow
To the gods belongs to-morrow.

—Abraham Cowley

In these few pages what has been placed before the reader is not an alternative to *On War* but what is hopefully complementary. Clausewitz's tome is possessed of a status that stems from its comprehensiveness and its age, and most certainly is not going to be shouldered aside by any other work on this subject; its place in history, and on future reading lists, is assured and properly so.

In these pages what has been placed before the reader is an analysis of war and wars since the end of the Thirty Years' War with the major part of attention placed upon the wars since Clausewitz's time, and for obvious reason. By definition, Clausewitz could not concern himself with such matters as air power and strategic nuclear deterrence, and while he would have recognized elements of constancy and continuity in the concept of limited war that emerged in the period of the Cold War when set alongside war in the Age of Reason, there were also elements of change that had been set in place over the intervening period. Moreover, while *On War* is concerned very largely with campaigning in the field, various other matters such as technology, industry, navies, and the sinews of war were afforded only *en passant*—and occasionally baffling—reference.[1] Very obviously there are arguments and definitions set down by Clausewitz that have continuing relevance but equally there have been developments in the last 200 years that have changed the political, societal, and military landscape and which demand consideration in their own right.

The basic themes developed in these pages may be defined simply. The Clausewitzian concept of war was simplistic. War was the preserve and prerogative of the state and was possessed of one single, simple nature, but that, most definitely, was not the case before 1618 and also has not been the case in recent years, is not the case at the present time, and seemingly will not be the case in the foreseeable future. War has become diffuse and seemingly ever less manageable, and in several different ways. Certainly post-campaign settlements have not necessarily been wholly in accord with what happened on the ground, and that most certainly is a point that Clausewitz would have recognized immediately, but the fragmentation of a defeated polity, and the subsequent elusiveness of settlement would not necessarily have received the same treatment by the Prussian general. Moreover, the diffusion of war and the elusiveness of victory have gone hand-in-hand with developments that have enabled the world's greatest power to acquire means of conducting war at a pace and on a scale that are unprecedented, and perhaps largely irrelevant. And, of course, the operative word in that sentence is perhaps.

There have emerged in recent years organizations that, with due allowance for points of difference, correspond perhaps to the *condottieri* of 15th-century Italy in terms of their freelance activities spreading conflict across areas with a form of armed struggle that was very different from that in place. These new organizations, and specifically *al-Qa'ida*, present something that is very new, namely a philosophy of revolutionary struggle based on religious principles and not limited by country or geographical area, and this at a time of massive change in terms of the speed of travel of both persons and the word. In terms of the latter, the Information Revolution has meant that the political and military hierarchy, while many matters remain under its remit, is not necessarily better placed than the ordinary man in the street in terms of access to news that may well shape public attitudes and opinion. In terms of the future conduct of war, such a development possesses obvious significance.

In terms of present and future developments, these pages have embraced one basic point, that the present international system in terms of states and borders is necessarily flawed. Many states lack genuine national identity on the part of their very diverse peoples, while borders, in all too many cases, do not accord with racial, cultural, linguistic, or religious divides. In itself such a situation provides the basis for many wars across the world and these wars, with identity the key factor, are likely to be of particular nastiness in terms of methods of operation and identity of targets. Recent wars in the Congolese republics, Rwanda, and Burundi most definitely would seem indicative of this development.

This basic theme has been extended into the future by reference to such matters as population increase, climate change, and desiccation, a state of affairs that provides the basis for many other wars, wars for control of resources, and particularly for control of arable land and food. The proposition herein is that these wars would seem likely to be very violent indeed, and if indeed the world proves unable to meet the food demands of the next 40 years, what is likely to impose itself on the international system is a series of successive and concurrent wars that, with the very basis of livelihood at stake, would embrace a meaning to totality that most certainly has not been set in place since 1945. But, of course, the obvious riders apply; predictions of population growth and its effects have been proven wrong in the past, witness Thomas Robert Mathus (1766–1834), and prediction as per these lines represents a most hazardous and imperfect undertaking and certain to be disproved almost as soon as the ink is dry. It is to be hoped that with respect to the arguments set down in these pages, events unfold to a different end and if there is to be conflict then it accords with dictates of moderation that made for the limitation of Real War rather than the totality of Absolute War.

Notes

BOOK I, CHAPTER 1

1. Edward Earle Meade (editor), *The Makers of Modern Strategy. Military Thought from Machiavelli to Hitler.* Chapter 5, "Clausewitz" by H. Rothfels, p. 93.

2. Proper family name was Ulyanov. The name Lenin was adopted in 1901.

3. Carl von Clausewitz, *On War.* Book I. *The Nature of War.* Book I. Chapter I. Section 27.

4. And, it should be noted, this is a comment that can be used as the basis of explanation of any and every victory. One would suggest, however, that defeat usually provokes more questions than victory, and perhaps the greater relevance of this Clausewitzian comment applies to defeat.

5. The Japanese navy also lost 2 escorts, 3 armed merchant cruisers, 11 destroyer-transports, 2 fleet and 4 auxiliary minelayers, 9 fleet and 10 coastal minesweepers, 33 gunboats and 8 motor gunboats, and 16 submarine chasers and 6 net-layers from its escort, local, and auxiliary formations.

6. The American losses were not just those incurred in the Pacific but in the Pacific and in home waters, the Caribbean, North Atlantic, and Mediterranean, and to all causes, including accident and mis-identification.

7. Dante Alighieri, more properly Durante degli Alighieri, c.1265–1321.

8. Johannes Gutenberg, born 1398 and died 1468.

9. The papal decree, which in effect exclusively divided the world outside Europe between Portugal and Spain, was issued on 4 May 1493: the Portuguese and Spanish then re-negotiated various details and a treaty was signed at Tordesillas on 7 June 1494: it was ratified by Spain on 2 July and by Portugal on 5 September.

10. Technically this was not quite true. With the expedition had been a number of Asians from the Spice Islands who had been taken to Spain in previous expeditions and who were pressed into service with Magellan's expedition as interpreters. It would seem that with Magellan killed short of the Spice Islands, one or more of these Asians

was/were the first to circumnavigate the world but, of course, not in a single voyage (as per the *Victoria*).

11. At Brussels, Charles V formally handed to his son, Philip (1527–1598), the sovereignty of the Netherlands. On 16 January 1556 Charles V formally handed to Philip the sovereignty of the Spanish kingdoms and Sicily, and shortly thereafter that of Burgundy. It is sometimes represented that Charles V abdicated as Emperor at Brussels on 25 October 1555 but this was not the case; Charles announced his intention to abdicate as emperor at the Diet of Augsburg in 1555 and at this time in effect passed over all power and responsibility to his successor and younger brother, Ferdinand I (1503–1564), but the formal election of the new emperor, and Charles V's abdication, awaited February 28, 1556.

12. Ferdinand Magellan or Fernão Magalhães in Portuguese and Fernando de Magallanes in Spanish, b. 1480 and killed on Mactan, in the Philippines, in 1521. Five ships and a total of 277 officers and men sailed; just one ship and 17 officers and men survived to return to Spain.

The five ships involved in this expedition were the flagship *Trinidad* and the *Concéption, San Antonio, Santiago,* and *Victoria.* The *Santiago* was wrecked between La Plata and the Cape and the *San Antonio* deserted at the Cape and returned to Spain. The *Concéption,* the least seaworthy of the ships that reached the Philippines, was abandoned and burnt, and the *Trinidad* was abandoned in the Spice Islands.

13. Jean (–1463) and Gaspard Bureau (1393–1469). Jean was in charge of French artillery and commanded at the final battles in the Hundred Years' War in front of Bordeaux (1453).

14. For example, Alvin and Heidi Tofflers' *War and Anti-War: Survival at the Dawn of the 21st Century* and Andrew F. Krepinevich's *Cavalry to Computer: The Pattern of Military Revolutions.* Amid a mass of publications on the subject one would note just a number of perhaps the more important works: Jonathan Bailey's *The First World War and the Birth of Modern Warfare;* Michael Duffy's *The Military Revolution and the State, 1500–1800;* Geoffrey Parker's *The Military Revolution: Military Innovation and the Rise of the West, 1500–1800;* and Clifford J. Roger's *The Military Revolution Debate: Readings on the Military Transformation of Early Modern Europe.*

15. Thomas A. Keany and Eliot A. Cohen, *Gulf War: Air Power Survey. Summary Report,* p. 238.

16. Errors and Omissions Excepted.

17. The date of 1470 is almost certainly incorrect but identification of this phenomenon proved more than a little difficult. It would seem that the discovery of the means to sail against the wind came well before 1470, and perhaps, in the interest of accuracy and simplicity, it may have been better to cite (a) the founding of the Sagres navigational school and observatory in 1418 by (b) Prince Henry the Navigator (1394–1460) or (c) the rounding of the Cape of Good Hope in 1487 by Bartolomeu Dias as the relevant point in time and not 1470. Another option might be the citation of Ptolemy's *Geography,* which reached Christian Europe in 1407 and had been widely distributed even as early as 1409.

The point of relevance lies in the fact that in 1400 Europe was in retreat. The Viking settlements in the New World had long gone, and by 1400 the links with China had been largely lost in the wake of the Mongol conquest and Islamic control of trade routes throughout the Middle East and points south and east. By 1500 Europeans were on the brink of opening direct maritime links with India and, of course, had found North America, the Caribbean, and Brazil. The world of 1500 was very different from that of 1400 but what date one chooses. . . . Felix and Anthea Barker. Ross MacDonald and Duncan Castlereagh, *A History of Discovery and Exploration. The Search Begins. Part 3. The Great Age of Exploration.*

18. William Shakespeare (1564–1616). The histories excluded, the plays that are not set wholly or in part in the Mediterranean are *Love's Labour's Lost* (1591), *As You Like It* (1599), *Hamlet* (1602), *The Merry Wives of Windsor* (1602), *Measure for Measure* (1604), *King Lear* (1606), and *Macbeth* (1606). The dates relate either to first printed form or first production on stage and are taken from the entry in *The Concise Dictionary of National Biography.* Volume III, pp. 2707–2709.

Elizabeth I was born in 1533, became queen in 1558, and died in 1603.

19. René Descartes (1596–1650). His main publications were *La Géométrie* in 1637, *Meditationes de prima philosophia* in 1641, and *Principia philosophiae* in 1644.

BOOK I, CHAPTER 2

1. General Sir Rupert Smith, *The Utility of Force. The Art of War in the Modern World*, pp. 1–3.

2. See, for example, John Keegan, *The Face of Battle*, pp. 320–342.

3. The sack of Magdeburg is always afforded singular treatment but in the interest of historical accuracy two points may be noted. First, the fact that in April 1631 Protestant armies sacked Frankfurt-an-der-Oder—and behaved toward the Catholic garrison and an overwhelmingly Protestant civilian population in a manner that certainly stands in comparison with what was to happen at Magdeburg less than six weeks later—is very seldom acknowledged: see John Childs, *Warfare in the Seventeenth Century*, p. 53 and C. V. Wedgwood, *The Thirty Years War*, p. 384 (and its six antiseptic lines). In terms of historical treatment, the point of comparison between the sacks of Frankfurt and Magdeburg possibly lies in geographical position in the sense that (the more famous) Magdeburg was central whereas Frankfurt, to the east and on the Polish border, was peripheral, but it may also be the product of a distinctly Protestant rendition of proceedings. Second, it might be noted that it was really after 1631, and more specifically after the French intervention in 1635, that the exhaustion of Germany, and with it the increasingly ferocious dimensions in terms of the nature and conduct of the war, assumed the proportions that one normally associates with the Thirty Years' War: see Friedrich Heer, *The Holy Roman Empire*, p. 208.

4. There seems to be much confusion reference to the treaties that ended the Thirty Years' War, negotiations for which were conducted in Münster and Osnabrück in and after 1644. The first Treaty of Münster, concluded on 30 January 1648, was between Spain and the United Provinces, and ended the Dutch Revolt with the Spanish recognition of Dutch independence. The second Treaty of Münster and the Treaty of Osnabrück, concluded on 24 October 1648, represented a general peace concluded among Austria, France, Sweden, and the estates of the Empire. These treaties are generally known incorrectly as the Treaty of Westphalia, more accurately the Peace or Treaties of Westphalia. It seems that the ratification of these two treaties was afforded on 8 February 1649. Thereafter the war between France and Spain continued until the Treaty of the Pyrénées, concluded on 7 November 1659 on the Ile des Faisans, which is in the river Bidassoa that, to this day, belongs to neither France nor Spain.

For good measure, it could be argued that the process of ending the Thirty Years' War was not really completed until the Treaties of Olivia and Copenhagen in

May and June 1660. In these treaties various disputes involving Brandenburg, Denmark, Poland, and Sweden—witness the First Northern War of 1655–1660—were finally resolved, the Treaty of Kardis of June 1661 notwithstanding.

5. Care needs be exercised on this matter for one reason: the concept of the *commonwealth* was in place. Enforced regency, particularly relating to matters of insanity of rulers, naturally pointed to an obvious distinction between ruler and realm. Such matters were known but generally were set aside as small change and not of significance *per se*.

6. It seems that the first national flag was Danish and dated back to the 13th century. Legend is that the Dannebrog fell to Earth during the battle of Lyndanisse, present-day Tallinn in Estonia, on 15 June 1219 and gave the Danes victory. It seems, however, that the battle was fought in 1208 and the 1219 date is traditional.

It would seem that the Danish lead was not followed and that regimental colors pre-dated national flags. By c. 1700 among the major powers there were perhaps five national flags, those of Spain (red), France (white), United Provinces (orange), England-Britain (the flags of England and Scotland superimposed), and Austria (black and yellow).

7. The process of ensuring proper control of formations, units, and individuals was necessarily a part of the process of codification of military law and it is generally agreed that the first statement to such effect, and the start of the process of codification, was in 1665. Between 1680 and 1706, the process of codification by the French Army resulted in something like 19 volumes in the French Army manual.

8. John III Sobieski, King of Poland and Grand Duke of Lithuania (1629–1696): the Polish march, along with Sobieski's undisputed reputation, has ensured that the Polish dimension of this action, the relief of Vienna, and the defeat of the Turkish Army on 12 September outside the city's walls at the Kahlenberg have always commanded attention. Less noted has been the fact that Sobieski, and his army of somewhere between 20,000 and 27,000-strong, met first with Charles V of Lorraine (1647–1690) and Austrian troops and then John George III Elector of Saxony (1647–1691) and Imperial troops, who between them numbered some 40,000 officers and men.

The Polish force left Cracow on 15 August and joined the other formations at Hollabrunn (some 20 miles to the north of Vienna), in the first days of September, and thereafter the combined army advanced and established itself on the Kahlenberg on 11 September from which it "swept down . . . to deliver Christendom forever from the specter of Moslem conquest which had haunted it for three centuries." Clearly, it was the juncture of the Austrian, German, and Polish forces that was the basis of the Christian victory and provided the European dimension of this victory. F. L. Carsten (editor), *The New Cambridge Modern History*. Volume V. *The Ascendancy of France, 1648–88*, pp. 497, 513–517.

9. One would make the point that obviously much more was at work in this process than Galileo's treatment before the Inquisition and that France, of course, was a Catholic country, particularly after the revocation of the Edict of Nantes. It is perhaps worth noting, if only in passing, that the Edict of Nantes of 13 April 1598 did not extend toleration to Jews and Moslems and that Moslems were expelled from France in 1610. What is generally called the Revocation of the Edict of Nantes was in fact the issuing of the Edict of Fontainebleau on 22 October 1685.

10. Poland of the late 16th and early 20th century embraced a religious tolerance massively at odds with what was happening elsewhere in Europe. Perhaps the most famous single incident in this tolerance was the comment by Sigismund I (1506–1548)—

"Permit me . . . to be the king of both the sheep and the goats"—but it is worth noting the twin facts that a Catholic Pole permitted the building of Armenian and Greek churches and a synagogue at Zamość and Szarogród and that an Orthodox Pole helped in the establishment of a Protestant church and a mosque at Ostróg at this same time. It is perhaps surprising to note that a mosque remained at Brest until 1939. Norman Davies, *God's Playground. A History of Poland.* Volume I. *The Origins to 1795*, p. 145. R. B. Wernham, *The New Cambridge Modern History.* Volume III. *The Counter-Reformation and Price Revolution, 1559–1610*, p. 392.

11. The word quartermaster apparently entered the English language about 1600 and the duties of such an officer were primarily concerned with the finding of accommodation, that is, quarters. The original *Generalquartiermeister* was an operations officer with a staff responsible for plans, operations, and logistics (i.e., everything other than those personnel matters that came under the authority of the Adjutant-General).

In the Prussian system, this system basically remained in place until the end of the First World War, hence Ludendorff, who as a major-general in August 1914 had been *Generalquartiermeister* of the 2nd Army, took the title of First Quartermaster-General in 1916 when his commander, Hindenburg, became chief of the general staff. In these positions the *Generalquartiermeister* was the equivalent of deputy commander and by this time, at corps level and above, the *Generalquartiermeister* was no longer responsible for logistics. This was vested in the *Quartiermeisterabteilung*. Moreover, in the Prussian Army the reforms put in place after Jena included the organization of a general staff responsible for plans, operations, and related matters. After 1871 this system was applied to Germany's four armies with a general staff corps largely drawn from *Kriegsakademie* graduates.

After 1871 the major powers, following the Prussian example, introduced staff systems and there were various differences, most obviously the British 1906 system with its three-fold division of responsibilities between the G branch, which was responsible for plans, operations, and training; the A branch, which was the Adjutant-General's staff responsible for personnel, disciplinary, and related matters; and the Q branch, which was the Quartermaster-General's staff responsible for logistics, base facilities, barracks, and kindred matters.

In the British Army, the unit quartermaster, normally an officer commissioned from the ranks, is an appointment distinct from the quartermaster-general staff with the G-4 designation and formation headquarters.

12. Blenheim, or more accurately the village of Blindheim, is on the Danube some 10 miles southwest of Donauwörth in Bavaria, Germany. The battle is also known as the battle of Höchstädt. Austerlitz is some four miles east of Brunn in Moravia, present-day Brno in the Czech Republic.

BOOK I, CHAPTER 3

1. The distance between Moscow and Paris is 1,550 miles/2,495-kms., and the advance took the Russian Army from 19 October 1812 to 31 March 1814, which was the equivalent of 86.11 miles per month/2.94 miles a day. The distance between Lisbon and Toulouse is 644 miles/1.037-kms., and the advance took the British Army from 1 August 1808 to 10 April 1814, which was the equivalent of 9.47 miles per month/0.31 miles or 543 yards a day. And, of course, there is also the associated question of the relative size of enemy armies.

2. Moreover, it should be noted that the French victory at Ulm was at least the equal of any victory recorded by any army over the previous 200 years. A total of some 30,000 Austrian troops were obliged to surrender at Ulm, and this without full-scale battle though there were certain actions as the French closed on the city; of the 72,000-strong Austrian Army that had crossed the Inn, more than 60,000 were killed or captured. Scott Bowden, *The Glory Years of 1805–1807*. Volume I. *Napoleon and Austerlitz*, p. 245.

3. Apparently there were four Chappe brothers involved in the devising of a semaphore system but normally credit is reserved for Claude Chappe (1763–1805); Ignace Chappe (1760–1829) is acknowledged as important in the process of building (and specifically the first Paris-Lille line) on account of his being a member of the Legislative Assembly that authorized and paid for the project.

4. See, for example, a range from Edward Shepherd Creasy, *The Fifteen Decisive Battles of the World: From Marathon to Waterloo*, of 1851 to recent times, Robert A. Doughty and Ira D. Gruber, *Warfare in the Western World*. Volume I. *Military Operations from 1600 to 1871*, p. 184.

5. Figures vary, depending on sources, but H. W. Koch, *The Rise of Modern Warfare, 1618–1815*, pp. 200–202 indicates that the French state raised a force of some 1,200,000 men but that this total included men drafted into the armaments industry and that the military component numbered some 800,000 men (in 11 armies) of whom 600,000 saw combat. This source also indicates that, in addition, some 150,000 troops were involved in the suppression of the rising in the Vendée. On pp. 206–207 Koch states that the French Army consisted of 250 infantry demi-brigades and 83 cavalry regiments, the latter roughly numbering some 500 squadrons of 140 men. The demi-brigade consisted of one regular battalion and two volunteer battalions.

J. Christopher Herold, *The Age of Napoleon*, p. 44 gives totals of 1,500,000 men and 14 armies raised in two years after the passing of the law of 23 August 1793.

6. Nonetheless the British undertook a second attack on the Danish fleet at Copenhagen in the first week of September 1807 when it seemed as if Denmark might be obliged to join a Franco-Russian alliance. The bombardment of Copenhagen saw the first employment of rockets.

7. The battle fought at Eylau on 8 February 1807 was not quite in the same class as the other battles.

8. Koch, *The Rise of Modern Warfare*, p. 253.

Prince Klemens Wenzel Nepomuk Lothar Fürst von Metternich-Winneburg zu Beilstein (1773–1859): first minister at Vienna between 1809 and 1848. Otto Eduard Leopold von Bismarck-Schönhausen (1815–1898): Prussian Minister-President 1862–1890, Chancellor of the North German Confederation 1867–1871, Chancellor of Imperial Germany 1871–1890.

9. Mann, *The History of Germany since 1789*, p. 41.

BOOK II, CHAPTER 1

1. Michael Howard, *The Franco-Prussian War. The German Invasion of France, 1870–1871*, p. 60. Helmut von Moltke, *The Franco-German War of 1870–71*, pp. 403–404, states that the German armies in France in February 1871 numbered 630,736 men and 1,742 guns with a 207,972-strong reserve in Germany.

2. The obvious example of these rivalries was the Anglo-French differences that manifested themselves at Fashoda in southern Sudan between July and November 1898,

which assumed the significance it did in part because of rivalry in the wake of British success in the third and fourth Ashanti wars (1893–1894 and 1895–1896, respectively) and conquest of what is presently northern Nigeria (1897) and the French defeat in the second Mandingo war (1894–1895). There were various differences in the area of the Ivory, Gold, and Slave Coasts, and, of course, after 1884 there was a new arrival in this area in the shape of German possession of Togoland (and also the Cameroons). The French conclusively won the third Mandingo war (1898) but it was the British conquest of northern Nigeria that brought Anglo-French rivalries to the fore, but, in the final analysis, at this time France, given her position relative to Germany, was never going to risk war with Britain over extra-European matters.

3. Published in Britain as *The Nation at War* in 1936.

4. To these matters one would add another, namely the fact that the First World War undid the aristocratic systems within Europe. The casualties that were incurred meant that aristocracies could not cover officer losses, and while the increased size of armies over the previous four decades had resulted in armies reaching down to the emerging middle class for extra officers, the First World War, with hostilities-only officers, pointed in the direction of an emergent meritocracy. There was also the parallel development whereby increasing numbers of women entered employment in industry, trade, and commerce, and, in contributing to the national war efforts, in effect ensured their acquisition of rights on the basis of equality.

5. If the reference is to a novel it was Friedrich de la Motte Fouqué (1777–1843); if the reference is to an opera it was Ernst Hoffmann (1776–1822).

BOOK II, CHAPTER 2

1. There are problems in terms of numbers, with German casualties varying considerably, and much would seem to depend if included within German casualty figures are peoples from Austria and the various other territories that were incorporated within the *Reich*. One can be sure that whatever figure chosen is certain to be wrong. The 587 figure is deduced on the basis of some 3,000,000 military dead, but the latter would be between 3,250,000 and 3,500,000 if the other areas and casualties are included in the German total.

2. Whatever source is checked the numbers are different. The figures used here are those checked over many decades by Willmott with sources long forgotten, but it should be noted, for example, that the Wikipedia page on the Internet gives very different figures, both overall totals and totals by individual countries, viz., "The total estimated human loss of life caused by World War II was roughly 72 million people. The civilian toll was around 47 million, including twenty million deaths due to war related famine and disease. The military toll was about 25 million, including the deaths of about five million prisoners of war in captivity. The Allies lost about 61 million people, and the Axis lost 11 million."

Source: http://en.wikipedia.org/wiki/List_of_World_War_II_casualties_by_country.

Russian 1994 estimates give the number of Soviet soldiers who died in German captivity as 6,000,000.

3. In fact the Charter had 50 signatory states, but the Soviet Union had triple representation in the form of Belorussia, Russia, and Ukraine. Poland was not one of the original 50 but joined later in 1945. One of the 50 was India, which, of course, was not independent in June 1945, and two states within Europe never have been members

of the United Nations—perhaps surprisingly, Switzerland, and less surprisingly, the Vatican. At the present time (April 2007), the United Nations has 192 member states.

4. In Book VI. *Defence*. Chapter XXVI. *Arming the Nation*. But one admits to an inability to find the translation that provided this quotation, which one has used for years without thinking about source. Certainly some of it seems to have come from the first English-language translation of *Vom Kriege*, by J.J. Graham, and was published in London by N. Trüber in 1873. An alternative rendition is provided on p. 480 of the Howard and Paret (editors and translators) edition of *On War*.

5. One would acknowledge that Britain had conceded the principle of independence for the colony of the Gold Coast on 11 May 1956 with the result that the colony received its independence as Ghana on 6 March 1957. The same principle with reference to Nigeria was conceded on 27 October 1959. With these events preceding the Macmillan speech, the point made here can be disputed but one would suggest that even after the ceding of independence to Ghana and Nigeria, there was no general realization in Britain that the independence of the remaining British possessions in Africa had to follow in short order.

6. Marcello Caetano (1906–1980) was dictator of Portugal between 26 September 1968 and the 1974 coup. He succeeded Antonio Salazar (1889–1970) who had been *de facto* ruler of Portugal/dictator of the *Estado Novo* after 5 July 1932.

7. This comment is made in the full knowledge that the date can be disputed with reference to overseas territories. The Spanish relinquished the western Sahara on November 1975 and French Somaliland, Djibouti, on 27 June 1977. Of course, there remained a number of overseas territories such as the Falklands and Hong Kong, and a number of possessions that were exposed to the imperialist label, for example, the Soviet position with reference to Eastern Europe and the Russian position with reference to first the Soviet Union and then its successor Russian state. In addition, there are various territories not reconciled to local sovereignty, for example, within Indonesia and in various Third World countries.

BOOK II, CHAPTER 3

1. The five states concluded an alliance with the Treaty of Brussels of 17 March 1948.

2. It remained in place until 11 May 1949 though the western the airlift continued until 30 September. In total, 278,228 flights delivered 2,326,406 tons of food, goods, and supplies, including more than 1,500,000 tons of coal, to West Berlin's airfields.

3. These 12 states were joined by Greece and Turkey in 1952, Germany in 1955, Spain in 1982, and then, after the Cold War and the collapse of the Soviet Union and the Warsaw Pact, on 12 March 1999 by the Czech Republic, Hungary, and Poland and, on 29 March 2004, by Bulgaria, Estonia, Latvia, Lithuania, Romania, Slovakia, and Slovenia. West German membership lapsed with German re-unification, 3 October 1990. Germany thereafter was a member of N.A.T.O. with the four great powers formally ending their reserved rights and privileges within Germany on March 15, 1991.

4. The first Soviet ICBM test was in August 1957: the Soviets put the first man, Yuri Gagarin (1934–1968), into space on 12 April 1961.

5. But it was not until June 1992 that the Strategic Air Command, the formation with responsibility for the Air Force's strategic role, was dissolved.

6. These totals were as per 15 August 1945. By year's end, another four fleet and five escort carriers had been commissioned.

7. Polmar, *Aircraft Carriers*, p. 519, states that in mid-1950s, there were three fleet and two escort carriers in the Pacific while in the Atlantic, the U.S. Navy had three *Midways* and one fleet, four light, and two escort carriers.

8. Speech in January 1997 at the Henry L. Stimson Center, Washington DC, as reported in the *International Herald Tribune*, 23 January 1997.

9. East Germany was not involved as a separate nation in the Olympic Games until 1968 and, of course, comparative figures do not exist in reference to the 1980 and 1984 Olympic Games. But at the summer games, the returns (gold-silver-bronze/total) were as follows: 1968 the United States 45-28-34/107, the Soviet Union 29-32-30/91, and East Germany 9-9-7/25; 1972 the Soviet Union 50-27-22/99, the United States 33-31-30/94, East Germany 20-23-23/66; 1976 the Soviet Union 49-41-35/125, East Germany 40-25-25/90, the United States 34-35-35/94; 1988 the Soviet Union 55-31-46/132, East Germany 37-35-30/102, and the United States 36-31-27/94. It is also worth noting, perhaps, that in 1988 Hungary, Bulgaria, and Romania were in the top eight countries regarding medals.

10. SALT I. The ABM treaty allowed both the Soviet Union and United States to put in place two anti-ballistic missile systems, separate from one another, and neither individually nor together the basis of a defensive system that covered the entire homeland. The accompanying treaty limited the United States to a maximum of 710 submarine-launched ballistic missiles and 44 submarines and the Soviet Union to 950 submarine-launched ballistic missiles and 62 submarines, plus other arrangements that limited new building of various systems.

11. The treaty provided for the Soviet Union and United States both having no more than a total of 2,400 inter-continental ballistic missiles, submarine-launched ballistic missiles, heavy bombers, and air-to-surface ballistic missiles, this total to be reduced to 2,250 by the end of 1981. Both states were to be limited to a maximum total of 1,320 MIRV-ed ballistic missiles and heavy bombers to cruise missiles, of 1,200 launchers of MIRV-ed ballistic missiles, and of 820 launchers of MIRV-ed inter-continental ballistic missiles.

12. And after the INF Treaty of 8 December 1987 that provided for the scrapping of intermediate- and shorter-ranged nuclear weapons.

13. The main provisions of this treaty were the reduction of the American and Soviet-Russian nuclear arsenals to totals of 1,600 strategic nuclear delivery vehicles, 6,000 warheads, 4,900 ballistic missile warheads, and, for the Soviets 1,540 nuclear warheads on 154 inter-continental ballistic missiles. Such reductions, between three-tenths and two-fifths of the existing armories, were to be achieved by 2001; Belorussia, Kazakhstan, and the Ukraine were to become parties to the non-proliferation treaty and were to surrender the weapons on their soil to Russia.

14. One always thinks of Jimmy Carter (1924–) and Herbert Hoover (1874–1964) together; both engineers, both decent, honorable men who achieved so much when they were not in office, and both defeated by things they did not understand and for which no one at the time had any answer.

15. Willy Brandt, born Herbert Ernst Karl Frahm in 1913, died in 1992.

BOOK III, CHAPTER 1

1. S. W. Roskill, *The Strategy of Sea Power. Its Development and Application*, pp. 15, 18–19.

2. For the purposes of completing the record, filling the gaps, German U-boat losses totaled 17 in June 1943 and 10 in both September and December 1943.

3. Kit C. Carter and Robert Mueller, *U.S. Army Air Forces in World War II. Combat Chronology, 1941–1945*, p. 505. Samuel Eliot Morison, *History of U.S. Naval Operations in World War II*. Volume XIV. *Victory in the Pacific, 1945*, p. 10.

4. Certain of the islands had quite large settler populations and hence could provide armed manpower in some numbers, and therefore quite sizeable military forces were needed for operations, small though these latter might appear to be.

It also bears to recall that slavery was a problem in the sense that a British defeat of French and Dutch forces in the Caribbean could not but put the issue of slavery in these colonies on the table, and, of course, the example would not be lost upon British possessions.

5. Alan *Burns, History of the British West Indies*, p. 587. Marcel Reinhart, *Histoire de France*. Volume II. *1715–1946*, p. 187.

6. Henry Newbolt, *Naval Operations*. Volume V. Appendix A. Table III. *Distribution and Employment of Destroyers during Inauguration of Convoy System*, pp. 387–391.

7. See John Winton, *Convoy. The Defence of Sea Trade 1890–1990*, pp. 115–122.

8. At and off Truk on 17 February American warships, submarines, and carrier aircraft sank 8 warships of 23,733 tons and 33 naval transports and support ships of 199,525 tons, and at and off Koror on 30 March, 11 warships of 5,484 tons and 21 service transports and support ships and 1 merchantman of 126,817 tons.

The returns of 17 February 1944 must represent this date as the most destructive single day in naval history, and before the outbreak of war this total of losses represented what the Imperial Navy had calculated might be nearly three month's losses. By way of comparison, the amount of Japanese shipping lost represents, on a rough rule of thumb, nine days' output on the part of American shipyards between 1942 and 1945.

9. The source of this latter suggestion was (then Lieutenant) John Andreas Olsen, Royal Norwegian Air Force, in letter to H. P. Willmott of 27 May 1997.

BOOK III, CHAPTER 2

1. The first ascent by a (unmanned) hot-air balloon was on 5 June 1783 at Annonay (a small town south of Lyon) in France, and the first manned flight in a Montgolfiere hot-air balloon was on 21 November 1783 over Paris. The first manned flight in a hydrogen balloon was on 1 December 1783. The first fatal crash occurred on 15 June 1785 near Boulogne. The first successful manned parachute descent was in 1793.

The first flight was by Orville Wright (1871–1948), the second minutes later by Wilbur Wright (1867–1912). The two brothers both had two flights on this same day, the first one of 120 feet in some 12 seconds (6.8 m.p.h.), the second and third of 175 and 200 feet, respectively, and the fourth and last one of 852 feet in 59 seconds (19.69 m.p.h.). Maximum height attained seems to have been about 10 feet.

2. The L. 59 was 743 feet (227.21-m.) in length whereas the Boeing 747 is 231 feet 10 inches (70.9-m). The airship's average speed during this 95-hour flight was 44.45 m.p.h.

On the question of inter-continental flight some aircraft must have flown between the Balkans and Anatolia and between the Sinai and Egypt proper before November 1917 but the significance of this one flight cannot be gainsaid by pedantic definition.

What is interesting about this flight was that it was the third time she attempted to reach East Africa and a sister airship had already been lost, and it seems that the mission was abandoned as a result of the receipt of a false signal sent by the British.

3. The *Hindenburg*, with a length of 804 feet (245.87-m.), a diameter of 135 feet (41.28-m.), and lift of 112 tons (114 tonnes), remains the largest flying machine ever to have taken to the air; in terms of length, she was longer than the contemporary *Yorktown*-class aircraft carriers and *North Carolina*-class battleships.

4. On 20 July 1921 the *Ostfriesland* was the target of 69 bombs (between 230 and 600 lbs. in weight) of which 13 were hits. On the following day she was hit by 3 of 11 1,100-lb. bombs, and was then subjected to an attack, with 2,000-lb. bombs, which resulted in six near-misses, one extremely close, that split open the battleship and resulted in her sinking within a matter of minutes.

Interestingly, and seldom noted in accounts, is that the near-misses were deliberate and in some measure the result of the advice of a Russian *émigré* and airman, Alexander Seversky. Moreover, the *Ostfriesland* trials and sinking were not isolated; the old pre-dreadnought *Alabama* was used as a target but not sunk in bombing trials on 27 September that same year and the pre-dreadnoughts *New Jersey* and *Virginia* were sunk off Cape Hatteras on 5 September 1923.

5. The naval airship *Shenandoah* crashed in a storm on 3 September 1925 at Caldwell, Ohio. Mitchell was court-martialled in December 1925 for comments about senior service personnel whom he blamed for the crash. He resigned from the army the following month.

6. The six cities were Tokyo (five raids: 10 March; 13, 15 April; 23 and 25 May), Nagoya (four raids: 12, 20 March; 14 and 16 May), Osaka (four raids: 14 March; 1, 7 and 15 June), Kobe (two raids: 17 March and 5 June), Yokohama (two raids: 15 April and 29 May) and Kawasaki (the raid of 15 April). The areas of these cities and area destroyed were as follows: Tokyo 110.8 and 56.3, Nagoya 39.7 and 16, Osaka 59.8 and 15.6, Kobe 15.7 and 8.8, Yokohama 20.2 and 8.9, and Kawasaki 11 and 3.6 square miles.

The glow from the fires of the Tokyo Raid could be seen at a distance of 150 miles.

7. The total of 57 cities do not include Hiroshima and Nagasaki, their respective figures being 6.33 and 4.70 square miles and 5.60 and 2.24 square miles.

8. A total of 633 Superfortresses were involved in the operations of 14 August but of these, 39 were involved in mining operations and not bombing.

9. Tokyo had population densities of 135,000 people per square mile in certain areas and the average for Japan's secondary cities was about 49,300. Of Tokyo's total surface area 8 percent consisted of parks and streets compared to a figure of 26 percent for London.

10. Of this total, an estimated 13,000,000 people were rendered homeless and 8,000,000 were evacuated from inner city areas.

BOOK III, CHAPTER 3

1. Providing a statement of losses is fraught with difficulty, in large measure because the various parties to this and later wars had good reason to seek to understate their losses. Perhaps the most reliable figures are those provided by Anthony W. Cordesman and Abraham R. Wagner in *The Lessons of Modern War. Volume I. The Arab-Israeli Conflicts, 1973–1989*, in part because of their distance in time from events. On page 19, losses are given as 965 Arab and 200 Israeli tanks and 444 Arab and 40 Israeli aircraft. Victor Flintham, *Air Wars and Aircraft. A Detailed Record of Air Combat, 1945 to the Present*, p. 59, gives air losses as 338 Egyptian, 29 Jordanian, 61 Syrian, 23 Iraqi and 1 Lebanese aircraft, and 35 Israeli aircraft.

The 1968 Israel Defense Ministry publication, *Israel Defence Forces: The Six Day War*, p. 13, set out the claim of having destroyed some 300 aircraft in the first three hours of the war.

2. Flintham, *Air Wars and Aircraft*, p. 66, states that reliable estimates suggest Israel lost 115 aircraft, while Egypt, Iraq, and Syria lost 242, 21, and 179 aircraft, respectively.

3. It should be noted, however, that the first amphibious landings involving major use of helicopters were during the Suez operation of 1956.

4. Mark Clodfelter and *The Limits of Air Power: The American Bombing of North Vietnam* notwithstanding. The war was also synonymous with Joan Baez and "There but for Fortune."

5. Lieutenant-General John J. Tolson, *Airmobility, 1961–1971*, pp. 97–101, 209–214.

6. And not just the Air Force. Among missiles then being developed or entering service at this time were the SLAM anti-ship AGM-84E Harpoon, the AGM-109 Tomahawk II MRASM, the Phoenix, the constantly-being-updated AIM-7 Sparrow and AIM-9 Sidewinder, the laser-guided Paveway and the AGM-62 Walleye electro-optical bomb, the AGM-88 HARM, and the Hellfire anti-tank missile. E.&.O.E.

7. The costs of the F-14 were such as to provoke a search in 1974 for a cheaper alternative, the F-18 Hornet, which flew for the first time in 1978.

8. John Andreas Olsen, *Strategic Air Power in Desert Storm*, p. 158.

9. This section on Warden and Deptula has been drawn primarily from Olsen, *Strategic Air Power in Desert Storm*, pp. 77, 79–87.

10. One could add two other points: the first that the impact of the Information Revolution and the massive acceleration of communications rather than pointing in the direction of diffusion resulted, at least in the 1991 conflict, in an ever closer supervision of formations and units by superior command to the extent that in 1991 one U.S. corps commander was supervising the operations of battalions, again, private information. The other point is the conduct of the battle of encirclement that never materialized, and the fact that the attempts to synchronize movements and to ensure close and effective co-ordination of advancing formations ran completely counter to maneuver warfare doctrine—a state of affairs that does raise a number of matters, but not in these lines.

BOOK III, CHAPTER 4

1. Benjamin S. Lambeth, *NATO's Air War for Kosovo: A Strategic and Operational Assessment*, p. 78.

2. The source of the first three demands no identification in these pages; the source of the fourth was von Moltke the Elder.

3. The source of these two comments was Rear Admiral P. W. Brock, who wrote them on a paper prepared with great pleasure and pride by Willmott in 1968. The comments have never been forgotten.

4. H. P. Willmott, *When Men Lost Faith in Reason: Reflections on War and Society in the Twentieth Century*, pp. 8–9, 237.

5. This episode that culminated with the meeting of Chernomyrdin and Milošević and the latter's decision to seek an arrangement that would meet N.A.T.O. demands has commanded a great deal of attention, witness Ivo H. Daadler and Michael E. O'Hanlon, *Winning Ugly: NATO's War to Save Kosovo*, pp. 140, 155–161, 165–175, 191, Lambeth, *NATO's Air War for Kosovo*, pp. xiv–xv, 67–86, 219–250, and Stephen T. Hosmer, *The Conflict over Kosovo: Why Milosevic Decided to Settle When He Did*, specifically chapter 11, "Concluding Observations," pp. 123–131.

6. Clark (1944–) was the supreme allied commander in N.A.T.O. between 1997 and 2000; Ellis (1947–) was Commander-in-Chief, U.S. Naval Forces, Europe, with headquarters in London, and Commander-in-Chief, Allied Forces, Southern Europe, at Naples, after October 1998.

7. Daadler and O'Hanlon, *Winning Ugly: NATO's War to Save Kosovo*, pp. 140, 155–161, 165–175, 191; Lambeth, *NATO's Air War for Kosovo*, pp. xiv–xv, 67–86, 219–250; and Hosmer, *The Conflict over Kosovo: Why Milosevic Decided to Settle When He Did*, pp. 123–131.

8. Lambeth, *NATO's Air War for Kosovo*. p. 86.

BOOK IV, CHAPTER 1

1. Either wholly or partially within Europe were four empires—Austria-Hungary, Germany, the Ottoman Empire, and Russia. The European states with overseas empires were Belgium (by virtue of royal possession of the Congo), Britain, Denmark, France, Italy, the Netherlands, Portugal, and Spain. The non-European empires were Abyssinia, China, Japan, and Persia, to which should be added the United States on account of her possession of the Philippines and other holdings in the Pacific and Caribbean.

2. http://news.bbc.co.uk/2/hi/africa/country_profiles/1024563.stm. The population and life expectancy figures were United Nations calculations made in 2005; the income figures were World Bank figures.

The Kenyan figures are remarkable in terms of something like a six-fold increase of population in some 50 years and a decline of life expectancy as a result of AIDS, Malaria, Yaws/Framboesia, and the various other public health problems that abound, but what is perhaps no less remarkable about Kenya is that to date it has not experienced dictatorship, civil war, or a military coup since independence, and it may well be that the Mau Mau rebellion cast a long shadow in this respect. The very nastiness of that insurgency may well have served to ensure restraint and moderation. But, of course, the codicil is obvious: "to date".

3. http://en.wikipedia.org/wiki/Sierra_Leone and /Sierra_Leone_Civil_War.

It needs to be noted that the process of peace-enforcement was conducted primarily by British forces that were in Sierra Leone after a British statement of long-term disinterest in remaining in the country and a declaration of accountability to the United Nations. The latter's initial efforts in Sierra Leone, involving armed forces from various countries that simply had no knowledge of the country and its problems and that had troops who acquired a certain reputation regarding their behavior toward local women, were singularly unfortunate and ineffective.

4. Lieutenant-General Roméo Dallaire (with Major Brent Beardsley), *Shake Hands with the Devil. The Failure of Humanity in Rwanda*. Murder of Hutus in Rwanda.

5. Please note that these comments were penned before the financial, industrial, and economic crises that gripped the world in and after September 2008.

6. Francis Fukuyama, *The End of History and The Last Man*, pp. xiii–xiv.

7. For example, in terms of real purchasing power, the value of tea declined by some 97 percent in the course of the 20th century and, perhaps surprisingly, in March 1998, and after a year in which its price declined by a third, oil was cheaper in real terms than it had been in 1948. In this latter case, the consequences for such countries as Saudi Arabia are very serious but for such countries as Nigeria and Indonesia the consequences bordered on the disastrous.

8. The rise of homelessness and diseases that had been all but eradicated in the generation after the Second World War has been features of the 1980s and 1990s, and it is perhaps worth noting that whereas the life expectancy of the homeless in London in 1990 was 47 years, by 1996 this had fallen to 42 years, which was male life expectancy in Britain in 1900. In very large measure, the phenomenon of increasing homelessness in Britain was the result of deliberate abolition of welfare provisions in the 1980s. The problem of disease stems from the fact that antibiotics, which have saved millions of lives since the Second World War, were in danger of becoming powerless to fight off new strains of super-resistant bacteria. In hospitals throughout the West, one strain—*staphylococcus aureus*—even in the 1990s became legendary for its ability to collect resistance traits against anti-bacterial agents. In such cases, doctors were able to turn to the "last resort" antibiotic called vancomycin—until the mid-1990s while another bacterium—*enterococcus faecium*, which causes wound and urinary tract infections—was discovered in a form completely resistant to vancomycin; doctors found that some strains of *enterococcus* could not be killed by any known antibiotic. In the 30 years after 1964, 40 diseases were identified for which there was no known cure.

9. And to this one would add the increasingly divisive impact of the state education system in various countries in Europe and the United States. What was a system of quality but inequality has been replaced by one of mediocrity and equality, while in privileged schools there would seem to have been an attention to personal well-being and enrichment that can only be described as particularly divisive.

10. The G.I.A. campaign in Algeria began in 1992. It was notable for the violence of its operations—in 1997 it conducted no fewer than 14 major massacres of village populations though there seems to be no agreement about numbers killed, for example, the official death toll as a result of the Rias massacre of 29 August 1997 was 238 but unofficial reports suggest a total more than three times that number—but was curbed in the period 1998–2002; most of its members accepted amnesty and for the most part the campaign died. But break-away factions and other groups moved into place, the most notable (and notorious) being the *al-Qa'ida in the Islamic Maghreb* (A.Q.I.M.).

11. Witness Margaret Thatcher: "There is no such thing as society. There are individual men and women, and there are families." *Woman's Own* magazine article, 1987.

12. And, it may be noted, in 2009 Britain had more people over 65 years of age than children 16 years and younger. Source: B.B.C. television news report of 27 January 2009.

13. It may be, however, that in the wake of the present economic crises affecting the world, the trends of the last three decades may be reversed. The rolling back of the state in terms of powers and controls that was set in place by the Reagan and Thatcher administrations may now belong to history.

14. And permanent, endemic warfare as has occurred in such countries as El Salvador, where the Farabundo Marti National Liberation Front has been active since 1979, and Guatemala, where the American intervention in 1954 against a democratically elected government paved the way for intermittent warfare over some four decades.

15. In Britain in 1970, the balance between productive and non-productive families—the latter being defined as families in which no member was in receipt of payment for work and which therefore includes retired people—was 5:1. In 1990, the balance had changed to 3:1 and it is projected that by 2010 the balance will be 2:1.

16. Captain J. Welch, RN, "The International Money Market: A Weapon in Waiting?" *Royal United Services Institute Journal*, April 1996. Walter Laqueur, "Postmodern Terrorism," *Foreign Affairs*, September–October 1996.

17. In the center of Groznyy on 31 December 1994 the Russian 131st Motor Rifle Regiment is reported to have lost 20 of its 26 tanks, all but 18 of its 120 BMPs and all 6 of its 2S6 Tunguska air defense vehicles, mostly to RPG-7s. The 81st Motor Rifle Regiment, also in Groznyy, is alleged to have suffered similar losses at the same time. The Russian conduct of this operation was not all it might have been but the actions nonetheless demonstrated the effectiveness of general-purpose, low-technology weaponry in the close-quarter battle.

18. An Amnesty International report in June 1997 indicated that in the previous reporting year, torture and maltreatment resulted in deaths of people in custody in no fewer than 46 countries, while a total of 150 countries were found to have acted questionably with respect to individuals held in custody.

19. Source unknown. The comment was believed to have been taken from Friedrich Nietzsche's *Thus Spake Zarathustra*, but the reference cannot be found. But the comment is too nice to be omitted.

20. From John Kenneth Galbraith, *A Journey Through Economic Time* and the review of the same by Richard J. Barnet that appeared in *Book World*, 19 June 1994.

BOOK IV, CHAPTER 2

1. Robin Hallett: *Africa since 1875: A Modern History*, pp. 38–39. The term state would embrace the ancient kingdoms of Morocco, Abyssinia, and Benin and the more recent Ashanti (Gold Coast/Ghana), Sokoto Fulani (northern Nigeria), Ganda (the Burundi-Rwanda-Uganda general area), Ndebele, and Zulu (southern Africa) kingdoms; certain of these latter kingdoms were roughly the same size as the British Isles.

2. These were *The Mini-manual of Urban Guerrilla Warfare* and *For the Liberation of Brazil*, which were published in 1969 and 1970, respectively.

3. Proper name Mohammed Abdel Rahman Abdel Raouf Arafat al-Qudwa al-Husseini; alternatively given as Mohammed Abdel Raouf Arafat al-Qudwa Al-Husseini. Even without the extras, Yasser Arafat is somewhat easier.

4. While on such matters it has been alleged that the attack on the World Trade Center in New York on 26 February 1993 was organized on the basis of C.I.A. manuals that had been made available to *Mujahedeen* by the Americans.

5. It need be noted, however, that whatever corruption was present in the Liberian system—and the corruption that had emerged in a century of True Whig Party rule was very real, as was the harm done to the state in political and social terms—was minor compared to the corruption that has been set in place in various African countries. The most notorious was the dictatorship of Mobutu Sese Seko (1930–1997 and president between 1965 and 1997) in Zaire but Kenya, Nigeria, Zambia, and Zimbabwe all have regimes notable for the fact that corruption is now a thing of the past. The brown-envelope-under-the-table has been replaced by such blatant thieving of state finances on scales that go beyond mere looting that a new word entered the language to describe such regimes as that of Mobutu in Zaire, and subsequently was applied to such regimes as that of Frederick Chiluba (1943–) in Zambia: kleptocracy.

6. The post-colonial Kenyan state, fashioned by President Jomo Kenyatta (1894–1978 and born Kamau wa Ngengi) was very much a personal dictatorship but not oppressive. Business was conducted less through parties and formal institutions and rather by personal meetings that embraced a patron-client arrangement. Kenyatta has been variously described as a regime- rather than a nation-builder. The system he set in place most definitely faltered under the presidency of Daniel arap Moi (born

1924 and president between 1978 and 2002) and basically has fallen apart during the presidency of Mwai Kĭbakĭ (born 1931 and president since 2002), specifically under the impact of the 2008 disturbances.

7. It is interesting to look at the names of British cruisers of the Second World War that have disappeared from the lists: the *Curacao, Cairo, Calcutta, Capetown, Colombo, Delhi, Dunedin,* and the *Durban* and the *Bermuda, Ceylon, Fiji, Gambia, Jamaica, Kenya, Mauritius, Newfoundland, Nigeria, Trinidad,* and the *Uganda;* also disappeared the names of the *Colony*-class frigates *Anguilla, Antigua, Ascension, Bahamas, Barbados, Caicos, Cayman, Dominica, Labuan, Tobago, Montserrat, Nyasaland, Papua, Perim, Pitcairn, St. Helena, Sarawak, Seychelles, Somaliland, Tortola,* and the *Zanzibar.* One imagines that in 1945 children at secondary schools would have known, within a certain tolerance, where all these places were; in 2005. . . .

8. The British took possession of the various territories that became known as British Somaliland in 1884, and initially these territories were ruled from Delhi: in 1898 they came under London. Briefly lost in 1940–1941, British Somaliland became independent on 26 June 1960 and by voluntary union became part of Somalia on 1 July 1960. The ex-British territories proclaimed the union dissolved and their separate independence in May 1991 though the latter remains unrecognized internationally.

9. The Belgian Congo achieved independence on 30 June 1960, and was engulfed in a series of wars and internal power struggles (in part supported by various Western states) until 1965 and the establishment of the Mobutu dictatorship. That appallingly and increasingly corrupt regime lasted until 1997 when the regime—abandoned by the United States after the Soviet Union was no more—collapsed, after which time the country was racked by a series of ethnic wars.

The total number of deaths as a result of Belgian royal rule is much disputed, and most estimates range between 5,000,000 and 15,000,000. The latter figure would seem to be grossly exaggerated. A Belgian government report in 1910 estimated the population of the Congo to be about this figure, which would suggest such losses over two decades to be somewhat improbable. Most recent studies suggest that the original report, by Roger Casement in 1904, with an estimated loss of population of 3,000,000 was probably near the mark, which would suggest losses over 20 years to be in excess of this figure, but it should be noted that such losses would have included disease, starvation, and other matters not directly attributable to the regime. In any event, such losses would represent one in five of the total population of the Congo, the losses of the recent conflict perhaps one in ten.

10. The *Irgun* or *Irun Zvai Leumi,* which were abbreviated forms of the name *HaIrgun HaTzva'i HaLe'umi BeEretz Yisra'el*/National Military Organization in the Land of Israel, in 1946 was headed by Menachem Begin. The Hotel housed certain Mandate secretariat organizations. 91 deaths were caused by the bombing.

11. *Ethniki Organosis Kyprion Agoniston*/National Organization of Cypriot Fighters: the campaign in Cyprus lasted between April 1955 and December 1959. Cyprus, less two British base areas, became a sovereign independent state in August 1960. It was generally understood at the time that the E.O.K.A. aim, in accordance with developments over the previous 10 years, was *enosis,* union between Greece and (Greek-controlled) Cyprus, though whether this was ever formally declared to be the aim is not altogether clear.

12. In French the *Front de Libération Nationale;* in Arabic the *Jabhat al-Taḥrīr al-Waṭanī.*

BOOK V, CHAPTER 1

1. It needs be noted, however, that truces or ceasefires may be observed even in conflicts in which Western states deny the opposition status and legitimacy.

2. Lest the arguments set out here in this paragraph be deemed simplistic, it should be noted that to a degree the arguments apply equally well to authoritarian states. Peoples must be persuaded of right cause, witness, for example, Bismarck and the process that led to the war of 1870–1871. Moreover, the elimination of forces of moderation in the aftermath of defeat has similarly affected authoritarian states, for example Russia after 1917 and Austria and Germany after 1918. Likewise, it could be argued that while the comments about the United States and the Vietnam War are in order, the United States at this time was host to a cultural revolution, or at least cultural change, which the demands of partial mobilization fuelled.

3. Interestingly, a British naval officer, commenting on anti-piracy operations in the middle of the 1920s in southern Chinese waters, observed that while some of the pirates were simply in the business for cash (i.e. were real pirates in the correct meaning of the word), for many others their activities were the product of a peasant society protest against the endemic corruption in and foreign domination and exploitation of their country. Source: *Journal of the Royal United Services Institute*, Number LXXXIV. February–November 1939. Commander W.G.A. Robson and lecture "Combined Operations with the Chinese against pirates, West River 1923–25," pp. 101–104. See also *Journal of the Royal United Services Institute*, Number LXXIV. February–November 1929. Captain L.D.I. Mackinon and lecture "The Work of the British Navy in the Far East," of December 5, 1928, pp. 96–109.

4. The armed forces from Islamic countries that were involved were those of Bahrain, Egypt, Kuwait, Morocco, Oman, Qatar, Saudi Arabia, Syria, and the United Arab Emirates; Bangladesh and Pakistan; Niger and Senegal; plus the *Taliban* from Afghanistan: from the N.A.T.O. countries those of Belgium, Canada, Denmark, France, Greece, Italy, the Netherlands, Norway, Portugal, Spain, Turkey, the United Kingdom, and the United States; the remaining forces were from the Philippines and South Korea; Argentina and Honduras; Australia and New Zealand; and from four member countries of the Warsaw Pact (which in effect no longer existed but was not formally dissolved until 1 July 1991), namely Czechoslovakia, Hungary, Poland, and Romania.

Germany and Japan did not send forces to the Middle East and after the campaign were presented with massive bills by the United States. India provided refuelling facilities in the Arabian Sea (i.e. in the approaches to the Persian Gulf).

5. The armed forces were from Australia and from Denmark, Poland, Portugal, the United Kingdom, and the United States.

A certain corrective needs to be included, and that is that another 33 countries at various times provided forces for the occupation duties that were the consequence of this campaign, but the real point would seem to be not those that were involved in occupation but the departure of their forces. The countries that withdrew formations and units were Nicaragua in February 2004, the Netherlands by March 2004, Spain after April 2004, the Dominican Republic and Honduras in May 2004, the Philippines in July 2004, Thailand in August 2004, New Zealand in September 2004, Portugal in February 2005, the Ukraine in December 2005, Bulgaria in January 2006, Japan in July 2006, Italy in December 2006, and Slovakia in February 2007.

6. In recent times, a third element has been added, namely *jus post bellum*, but which is not considered here: see http://en.wikipedia.org/wiki/Just_War.

7. Or should it be points of potentially critical vulnerability? One suspects that this is how it should be expressed.

8. See Richard B. Frank, *Downfall: The End of the Imperial Japanese Empire*, pp. 153–154, 233, 324–315.

9. And because human beings invariably concern themselves primarily about immediate probabilities rather than future possibilities: a comment taken (and slightly changed) from Clausewitz's analysis of policy: Book V. Chapter VI. (B) *War as an Instrument of Policy*.

BOOK V, CHAPTER 2

1. The quotation is drawn from Book I. Chapter I. Section 17. *The effect of polarity is often destroyed by the superiority of the defence over the attack, and thus the suspension of action in war is explained.* But even after nearly 40 years, Book V. Chapters IV and V dealing with *Ends in War more precisely defined* do not seem to have improved in terms of understanding; see, for example, Section 16, which, one would suggest, is utterly incomprehensible. Reading these seemingly interminable sections reminds one of the lines from Gilbert and Sullivan's *The Mikado*: "All prosy dull society sinners, Who chatter and bleat and bore, Are sent to hear sermons From mystical Germans Who preach from ten till four."

2. The significance of Waterloo in terms of a victory of the defensive is obvious but a certain care needs to be exercised in terms of the general argument. The Austrian victory at Aspern-Essling (21–22 May 1809) was clearly a defensive victory outside the three-year timeframe. In terms of campaigns, the 1812 campaign clearly had a major defensive and successfully defensive aspect for the Russians, as did various campaigns in the Peninsular War after 1809, and there were a number of actions in 1813 and 1814 in which the French secured a series of local defensive victories, though the campaigns and war were lost.

3. But almost certainly wrong.

4. Book IV. Chapter I. Section 2. *Advantages of Defence*.

5. See Book VII. *The Attack*. Chapters IV. *The Diminishing Force of the Attack*. Chapter V. *The Culminating Point of the Attack*.

6. Mozdok, taken by German forces on 25 August 1942 (i.e. before the main battle in and for Stalingrad began), is in 43°45'North 44°43'East; Moscow is in 55°45'North 37°42'East.

7. Płock, capital of Poland between 1079 and 1138, is on the Vistula in 52°33'North 19°42'East, some 58 miles below Warsaw. The offensive came to an end with German and Austro-Hungarian formations on the Dvinsk-Pinsk-Tarnopol line. Dvinsk, present-day Daugavpils in Latvia, is in 55°53'North 26°32'East; Pinsk, in Belorussia, is in 52°07'North 26°06'East; Tarnopol, present-day Ternopil in Ukraine, is in 49°34'North 25°36'East.

8. The Brusilov (1853–1926) Offensive, which began on 4 June 1916 and continued through various phases to the end of September, is generally regarded as Russia's supreme military achievement in the First World War. The offensive resulted in the Russian capture of some 200,000 Austro-Hungarian troops and is normally portrayed as a major factor in the unraveling of the Hapsburg state and military. In terms of scale and results, the offensive clearly had a certain importance but not in terms of miles covered on the ground. It is perhaps worth noting that something like 60,000 Russian

troops deserted in the course of the Brusilov Offensive, which itself tells a story about the state of the armies that conducted this campaign. And, it needs to be noted, Austria-Hungary nominally remained in the war though stiffened on the Eastern and Italian Fronts with German formations, units, and personnel. As it is, Austro-Hungarian casualty figures are subject to some dispute, and it would seem that the 200,000 figure relates to prisoners taken by the Russians in the first three days of the offensive. The official history, *Österreich-Ungarns letzter Krieg*, Volume 4. *Das Kriegsjahr 1916, erster Teil. Die Ereignisse vom Jänner bis Ende Juli.* p. 663, gives losses of 10,756 officers and 464,382 men, but more recent studies (as per Holger H. Herwig, *The First World War. Germany and Austria-Hungary 1914–1918*, p. 209) indicate losses as high as 750,000 officers and men, with some 380,000 taken prisoner.

9. Alexander Kerensky (1881–1970): head of the Russian provisional government in the summer of 1917.

10. The major wars within Europe after 1648 were the first Northern War, spring 1655–May 1660 (five years); the Russo-Polish War, July 1654–January 1667 (12 years but with truces and peace negotiations that extended over two years); the Dutch War, March 1672–June 1679 (seven years), the War of the League of Augsburg, September 1688–October 1697 (nine years); the Great Northern War, April 1700–August 1721 (21 years); the War of Spanish Succession, March 1701–September 1714 (13 years); the War of Austrian Succession, December 1740–October 1748 (almost eight years); the Seven Years' War, August 1756–February 1763 (six years); the French Revolutionary Wars, April 1792–March 1802 (almost 10 years), and the Napoleonic Wars, May 1803–June 1815 (12 years).

11. Quoted by William C. Frank, Jr. and Philip S. Gillette (editors), *Soviet Military Doctrine from Lenin to Gorbachev, 1915–1991*, p. 65.

12. What is perhaps the most interesting part of this prediction are the last 12 words. Engels did not predict proletarian victory (though obviously it was assumed) but the conditions for the victory of the working class. The subtlety of the difference is easily missed, and there is little doubting the correctness of the Engels view, witness the state of central and eastern Europe, 1918–1919.

The irony of the observation is not immediately obvious, but the fact is that by the same token the Second World War should have produced the same conditions "for the final victory of the working class," but, in western Europe and the United States, a social revolution was set in place via the democratic process while in Eastern Europe the victory was one imposed by force of arms, and it was a victory of Stalinist henchmen and not the working class.

13. There or thereabouts. Soviet forces reached East Prussia, in the area of the border with Lithuania (and in the general area of Augustów that had been in Poland in 1939), on 17 August 1944 but with the main Soviet efforts unfolding in the Balkans and with other commitments in front of Warsaw and the Carpathians and German forces in position on the Courland peninsula, it was not until 10 October that Soviet forces arrived in the Memel area, and the Germans nonetheless remained on the line of the Niemen at this time. American forces closed with the western border of Germany in September, Aachen being taken in the battle of 2–21 October.

14. The February–March 1945 slot is based upon two separate events, the U.S. carrier operations of 16 February off Honshu that were directed primarily against Tokyo, and 12 March which was the first massed U.S. bomber raid, again directed against Tokyo. Heavy bomber raids had begun in November 1944 but it was not until March 1945 that the Americans acquired the numbers to mount a sustained bombing offensive.

15. This can be disputed with reference to the battles in front of Moscow in December 1941 and in front of Kharkov in May 1942. With reference to the former, the Soviet Army really had little choice but to attempt to prevent the fall of the capital. With reference to the latter, the assertion is perhaps in need of certain correction though it may be argued that at Kharkov a thoroughly ill-conceived and badly conducted operation was hardly the battle the Soviet Army wanted to fight.

16. That is, to pick up, and to return to, the argument noted in book 2, chapter 5.

17. See, for example, Williamson Murray, *Air War in the Persian Gulf*, p. 300.

18. Ch'osan, on the Yalu, is in 40°45'North 125°52'East. Anju, near the mouth of the Chongchon river, is in 39°36'North 125°44'East; Tokohon is some 40 miles to the east of Anju and is not on the Chongchon. Unsan is north of the Chongchon and is some 30 miles from Anju. Hagaru, or Hagaru-ri, at the southern end of the Changjin (or Chosin) Reservoir, is some 45 miles up river from the coast near Hŭngnam, which is in 39°50'North 127°67'East. Wŏnsan is in 39°11'North 127°21'East.

19. And which, in very large measure, was possessed of personal matters regarding the American commander in theater best not considered in these pages.

20. Quảng Tri was the first major city to be taken by the communists after the Tet Offensive, and was held until the South Vietnamese Army offensive from 28 June–16 September that resulted in the recapture of the city. Thereafter, the communists retained control of much of the province but not the capital itself.

21. These were the five key points that formed the main part of the "Chances for Peace" speech made on 16 April 1953 by President Dwight D. Eisenhower (1890–1969).

BOOK V, CHAPTER 3

1. Harlan Ullman, "A New Defence Construct: Rapid Dominance," *Royal United Services Institute Journal*, October 1996.

2. This text has been drawn, largely verbatim, from *When men Lost Faith in Reason. Reflections on War and Society in the Twentieth Century*, pp. 250–253.

BOOK V, CHAPTER 4

1. Book VIII. *War Plans*. Chapter II. *Absolute War and Real War*.

2. The series of civil wars that engulfed China after 1916 included one between the incumbent Kuomintang regime and the communists that began in 1926. This conflict was halted after December 1936 in response to Japanese designs in northern China, but there were a series of clashes between K.M.T. and communist forces in the latter years of the Japanese war and in the immediate aftermath of the Japanese surrender as both sides vied for position. After an American-brokered truce, full-scale civil war was resumed on 26 June 1946 and resulted in the progressive communist conquest of the country. Peking was captured on 22 January 1949, Nanking on 22 April two days after communist forces crossed the Yangtze, Canton on 15 October and Chungking (the wartime K.M.T. capital) on 30 November. The K.M.T. government established itself on Formosa on 7 December, its forces having been withdrawn to Formosa and certain other islands. The communist republic had been proclaimed at Peking on 1 October.

Estimates of losses vary but the military deaths for both sides are generally reckoned to be around 1,200,00, and overall losses around 4,000,000, which would make this civil war the most costly conflict for at least 50 years after the end of the Second World War.

3. The diversity of these groups may be gauged by reference to the fact that in southern Africa, the Bantu peoples divided into two main sub-groups, the Nguni and the Sotho-Tswana. The Nguni included such peoples as the Swazi and the Zulu, and the Hutu in Rwanda. The Nilotes include such tribes as the Luo in Kenya but are also present in Uganda and southern Sudan, while the para-Nilotics include such groups as the Maasai in Kenya and the Tutsi in Rwanda, Burundi, and the Congo; the latter are predominantly Catholic but with a Moslem minority and have a minimum of three languages.

The parallel is not exact but the division between Bantu, Nilotes, and para-Nilotics could be compared to the division between Teuton, Latin, and Slav within Europe. Sources: A. H. LeQ. Clayton and various conversations and readings, specifically that of 23 January 2009 and http://en.wikipedia.org/wiki/Bantuand/Bantu_ expansion.

4. The United Liberation Front of Asom/Assam was formed in 1979 and the National Democratic Front of Bodoland in 1986; the former started its operations in May 1990. These campaigns have attracted very little outside attention but have been marked by captures, assassinations, and car bombings. The proliferation of different separatist groups within what was British Assam, with the resultant proliferation of minor militias to go alongside rising nationalist aspirations, has made the search even for local truces fraught with difficulty. Sources: http://en.wikipedia.org.wiki/Assam,/ United_Liberation_Front_of_Asom and /National_Democratic_Front_of_Bodoland.

The other militias involved in the struggles in this area are the United People's Democratic Solidarity, which has sought to advance the cause of a Karbi state, the Dima Halam Daogah, which is fighting to create a Dimaraii state, the Kamtapur Liberation Organization, which was formed in December 1995 and has been seeking to establish a state that would include parts of West Bengal and Assam, and the Hmur People's Convention-Democracy 1986, which sought to create a state in Mizoram. It should be noted, however, that one file on the Internet lists nine militant organizations within Assam in addition to the two fronts. This file is: http://www.satp.org/satporgtp/coun tries/india/states/assam/terrorist_outfits/Klo.htm

5. Source: http://en.wikipedia.org/wiki/Black_people.

6. In December 2005, a presidential election in Bolivia unusually produced a candidate with an overall majority on the first vote, Juan Evo Morales Ayma (1959–) taking 53.9 percent of the overall vote. He had been the candidate in the 2002 election when he had come second with 20.9 percent of the vote. Morales stood as a socialist and as a native peasant, was an Aymara-speaking Amerindian, and was the first Amerindian to become Bolivia's head of state. The various Amerindian groups, of which the Quechuas-, Aymara-, Chiquitano- and Guarani-speaking are the largest, make up some 55 percent of the population; mixed Spanish-American *mestizo* make up some 30 percent of the population with Europeans, overwhelmingly Hispanics, making up the remainder. The proven strength of Amerindians in this election, which was the first in which Amerindians prevailed and which prompted Morales to claim that his election marked the end of 500 years of colonialism, may well provide the basis for the continuing militia campaigns in the country. Source: http://en.wikipedia.org/wiki/Bolivia.

7. The initial Kosovo fighting took place between April 1996 and October 1998 and was followed by a series of incidents that set in train the N.A.T.O. intervention, 24 March–10 June 1999: see Book II. Chapter VI, this volume. The Slovenian war was a 10-day affair and not seriously pressed but most certainly some of the operations in the wars involving Croatia and Bosnia-Herzegovina (and to which reference has been

made in Book III. Chapter IV, this volume), specifically the deliberate killing of civilians and ethnic cleansing, were as bad as the worst in other recent conflicts.

8. Sources: http://en.wikipedia.org/wiki/Human_population: World Population; http:schools-wikipedia.org/wp/w/World_population.htm: World Population.

9. The Bangladesh totals, and specifically the population density, mean that it is now more crowded than Java, which always used to be the most congested place in the world. Java, with an area of 48,919 square miles and a present population of around 130,000,000, has a population density of 2,657 persons per square miles.

10. The populations figures are as follows: (1) China 1,335,962,132 (2) India 1,143,670,000 (3) the United States 305,695,000 (4) Indonesia 229,331,501 (5) Brazil 190,585,000 (6) Pakistan 165,475,000 (7) Bangladesh 158,665,000 (8) Nigeria 148,093,000 (9) Russia 141,864,046 (10) Japan 127,704,000 (11) Mexico 106,682,500 (12) the Philippines 90,457,200 (13) Vietnam 87,375,000 (14) Germany 82,062,200 (15) Ethiopia 79,221,000 (16) Egypt 75,808,000 (17) Turkey 71,517,100 (18) Iran 70,495,782 Source: http://en.wikipedia.org/wiki/List_of_countries_by_population.

11. The figures given here and the basic argument that has been developed represent worse-case pessimism, and various counter-arguments and data need to be provided here in the interest of balance.

It needs to be noted that not too long ago demographers feared that the world population would rise to at least 10,000,000,000, and in recent years the general wisdom is that the world's population should level off at or slightly below the 8,000,000,000 figure. It could be argued, if this latter figure is correct, the shortages and strife of the future (as per the text) will not come to pass, and most certainly there seems to be one argument of note, namely that the basic problem is not one of output but of distribution, and that this has been compounded by deliberate storage in order to maintain prices.

In addition, it cannot be denied that there could be a second Green Revolution in coming years, and this argument would seem to suggest that genetic engineering is likely to be the answer rather than the problem. Moreover, the loss of arable land might be reversed by what would seem draconian measures in terms of forced movements of population, as has happened in recent years in China. In terms of fuel, the use of nuclear power for heat and power would free sufficient fossil fuel to last two or three generations, and there can be no prediction as to what technological innovation might conjure into existence in the meantime.

These matters need to be presented in order to balance the argument expounded in the text.

12. The returns are Algeria 15 years, Brazil 14, China 11, Mexico 9, Russia 17, and the United States 8 years.

Interestingly, on 26 January 2009 in one of his first public speeches after inauguration, President Barack Obama (1961–) stated that American dependence on foreign oil "bankrolls dictators, pays for nuclear proliferation and funds both sides of our struggle against terrorism." It is not exactly clear about the payment and funding but past bankrolling cannot be denied, and the obvious point being made, to reduce U.S. dependence on foreign oil, is worthy of note and for reasons that need no elaboration.

13. These countries (with reserves in billions of barrels and life at present rates of production) are Saudi Arabia 267 and 72 years, Canada 179 and 149, Iran 138 and 95, Iraq 115 and 150, Kuwait 104 and 110, and the United Arab Emirates 98 billion and 93 years. Source: http://en.wikipedia.org/wiki/Oil_reserves.

14. Spratly Island is in 08°38'North 111°55'East.

15. Taiwan holds Itu Aba, at 17.76 square miles the largest single island in the group, and has done so since 1956; the Philippines has held seven islands since 1968. Vietnam has occupied six islands since 1975 when the North Vietnamese occupied islands that had been claimed by South Vietnam. China has held nine reefs, with one airstrip built on Fiery Cross Reef, since 1988. Source: http://en.wikipedia.org/wiki/Spratly_Islands.

16. Antarctica is the subject of claims on the part of Britain (1908), New Zealand (1923), France (1924), Norway, Australia (1933), Chile (1940), and Argentina (1943) with Norway having two separate claims (1929 and 1939) and one part, Marie Byrd Land, which is not claimed. Five other countries, namely Brazil, Peru, Russia, the United States, and Uruguay have expressed a right to claim. The continent has been subject to international treaty—which included demilitarization—that was concluded in 1959 and became effective on 23 June 1961; it had 46 adherents. In 2004, an Antarctica secretariat was established at Buenos Aires. The only clashing claims are those of Argentina, Britain, and Chile, but issues of fishing, mining, and other matters could give cause for friction and discord. Antarctica apparently has a permanent population of one, a Roman Catholic priest.

17. Kofi A. Annan, *World Economic Form. The Davos Agenda. The Times*, 27 January 2009, p. 45.

BOOK VI, CHAPTER 1

1. See, for example with reference to navies, Book III. *On Strategy in General.* Chapter XVII. *The Character of Contemporary Warfare*, para. 3: "Obviously, wars fought by both sides to the full extent of their national strength must be conducted on different principles from wars in which policy was based on the comparative size of the regular armies. In those days, regular armies resembled navies, and were like them in their relation to the country and its institutions. Fighting on land therefore had something in common with naval tactics, a quality that has now completely disappeared."

Bibliography

GENERAL

Albrecht-Carrié, René. *A Diplomatic History of Europe since the Congress of Vienna.* London: Methuen, 1958.

Allmand, Christopher. *The Hundred Years War. England and France at War c. 1300–c. 1450.* Cambridge: Cambridge University Press, 1988.

Angell, Norman. *The Great Illusion: A Study of the Relation of Military Power to National Advantage.* London: Heinemann, 1913.

Archer, Christon I., John R. Ferris, Holger H. Herwig, & Timothy H. E. Travers. *World History of Warfare.* Lincoln: University of Nebraska Press, 2002.

Barzun, Jacques. *From Dawn to Decadence. 500 Years of Western Cultural Life. 1500 to the Present.* London: HarperCollins, 2000.

Bennett, Matthew (general editor). *The Hutchinson Dictionary of Ancient and Medieval Warfare.* Oxford: Helicon, 1998.

Braudel, Fernand, translated by Siân Reynolds. *The Mediterranean and the Mediterranean World in the Age of Philip II.* 2 vols. New York: Harper & Row, 1972.

Bregman, Ahron. *Israel's Wars. A History since 1947.* London: Routledge, 2000.

Burns, Alan. *History of the British West Indies.* London: Allen & Unwin, 1965.

Contamine, Philippe, translated by Michael Jones. *War in the Middle Ages.* Oxford: Blackwell, 1984.

Creasy, Edward Shepherd. *The Fifteen Decisive Battles of the World: From Marathon to Waterloo.* London: Bentley, 1851.

Creveld, Martin van. *Supplying War. Logistics from Wallenstein to Patton.* Cambridge: Cambridge University Press, 1977.

Creveld, Martin van. *Technology and War. From 2000 B.C. to the Present.* New York: The Free Press, 1991.

Davies, Norman. *God's Playground. A History of Poland.* Volume I. *The Origins to 1795.* Oxford: Oxford University Press, 1981.

Doughty, Robert A., Ira D. Gruber, et al. *Warfare in the Western World*. Volume I: *Military Operations from 1600 to 1871*, and Volume II: *Military Operations since 1871*. Lexington, Massachusetts: DC Heath, 1996.

Ewen, Frederic. *Heroic Imagination. The Creative Genius of Europe from Waterloo (1815) to the Revolution of 1848*. New York: New York University Press, 2004.

Finucane, Ronald C. *Soldiers of the Faith. Crusaders and Moslems at War*. London: Orion, 2004.

Fischer-Fabian, S., translated by Lore Segal & Paul Stern. *Prussia's Glory. The Rise of a Military State*. New York: MacMillan, 1981.

Freedman, Lawrence (editor). *War*. Oxford: Oxford University Press, 1994.

Fukuyama, Francis. *The End of History and The Last Man*. New York: The Free Press, 1992.

Fuller, J.F.C. *The Conduct of War 1789–1961. A Study of the Impact of the French, Industrial, and Russian Revolutions on War and its Conduct*. London: Eyre & Spottiswoode, 1961.

Geyl, Pieter. *Debates with Historians*. Cleveland, Ohio: Meridian Books, 1965.

Hanson, Victor Davis. *Carnage and Culture. Landmark Battles in the Rise of Western Power*. New York: Doubleday, 2001.

Heer, Friedrich. *The Holy Roman Empire*. New York: Praeger, 1969.

Holsti, Kalevi J. *Peace and War: Armed Conflicts and International Order 1648–1989*. Cambridge: Cambridge University Press, 1991.

Hooker, Richard D. Jr. (editor). *Maneuver Warfare. An Anthology*. Novato, California: Presidio, 1993.

Howard, Michael. *War in European History*. Oxford: Oxford University Press, 1976.

Keegan, John. *The Face of Battle*. London: Jonathan Cape, 1976.

Keen, Maurice (editor). *Medieval Warfare. A History*. Oxford: Oxford University Press, 1999.

Kelly, Jack. *Gunpowder. A History of the Explosive That Changed the World*. London: Atlantic Books, 2004.

Lukacs, John. *The End of the Twentieth Century and the End of the Modern Age*. New York: Ticknor & Fields, 1993.

Mann, Golo. *The History of Germany since 1789*. New York: Praeger, 1968.

Messenger, Charles (editor). *Reader's Guide to Military History*. London: Fitzroy Dearborn, 2001.

Oman, Chester W. C. *A History of the Art of War in the Middle Ages*. London: Methuen, 1898.

Reinhard, Marcel. *Histoire de France*. Volume II: *1715–1946*. Paris: Larousse, 1954.

Ritter, Gerhard, translated by Heinz Norden. *The Sword and Sceptre. The problem of militarism in Germany*. Volume I: *The Prussian Tradition 1740–1890*. Volume II: *The European Powers and the Wilhelmine Empire 1890–1914*. Volume III: *The Tragedy of Statesmanship—Bethmann Hollweg as War Chancellor* (1914–1917) and Volume IV: *The Reign of German Militarism and the Disaster of 1918*. London: Penguin Press: 1972, 1972, 1973, and 1973, respectively.

Showalter, Dennis. *German Military History 1648–1982: A Critical Bibliography*. New York: Garland, 1984.

Wernham, R.B. *The New Cambridge Modern History*. Volume III: *The Counter-Reformation and Price Revolution, 1559–1610*. Cambridge: Cambridge University Press, 1971.

CLAUSEWITZ

Aron, Raymond, translated by Christine Booker & Norman Stone. *Clausewitz. Philosopher of War.* London: Routledge & Kegan Paul, 1983.

Bassford, Christopher. *Clausewitz in English. The Reception of Clausewitz in Britain and America 1815–1945.* Oxford: Oxford University Press, 1994.

Clausewitz, Carl von, translated and edited with an introduction by Hans W. Gatzke. *Principles of War.* Harrisburg, Pennsylvania: Military Service Publishing Company, 1942.

Clausewitz, Carl von, translated by J.J. Graham and with an introduction by F.N. Maude. *On War.* London: Kegan Paul, Trench, Trübner, 1908.

Clausewitz, Carl von, edited by Anatol Rapoport. *On War.* London: Penguin, 1968.

Clausewitz, Carl von, edited & translated by Michael Howard & Peter Paret. *On War.* Princeton, New Jersey: Princeton University Press, 1976.

Clausewitz, Carl von. *The Campaign of 1812 in Russia.* New York: Da Capo, 1995.

Clausewitz, Carl von. *The Essential Clausewitz. Selections from On War.* Mineola, New York: Dover Publications, 2003.

Echevarria, Antulio J. II. *Clausewitz and Contemporary War.* Oxford: Oxford University Press, 2007.

Greene, Joseph I. (editor). *The Living Thoughts of Clausewitz.* London: Cassell, 1945.

Greene, Joseph I. (editor). *The Essential Clausewitz. Selections from On War.* Mineola, New York: Dover Publications, 2003.

Handel, Michael I. *Sun Tzu and Clausewitz Compared.* Carlisle, Pennsylvania: U.S. Army War College, 1991.

Handel, Michael I. *Masters of War: Sun Tsu, Clausewitz and Jomini.* London: Frank Cass, 1992.

Herberg-Rothe, Andreas. *Clausewitz's Puzzle. The Political Theory of War.* Oxford: Oxford University Press, 2007.

Howard, Michael. *Clausewitz.* Oxford: Oxford University Press, 1983.

Leonard, Roger Ashley. *A Short Guide to Clausewitz On War.* London: Weidenfeld & Nicolson, 1967.

Smith, Hugh. *On Clausewitz. A Study of Military and Political Ideas.* Basingstoke, Hampshire: Palgrave, 2005.

Strachan, Hew. *Carl von Clausewitz's ON WAR. A Biography.* Conshohocken, Pennsylvania: Atlantic Books, 2007.

Strachan, Hew, & Andreas Herberg-Rothe (editors). *Clausewitz and the Twenty-First Century.* Oxford: Oxford University Press, 2007.

Tashjean, John E. *Transatlantic Clausewitz.* Carlisle, Pennsylvania: U.S. Army War College, 1982.

THEORY AND ANALYSIS

Addington, Larry H. *The Patterns of War since the Eighteenth Century.* Bloomington: Indiana University Press, 1984.

Asprey, Robert B. *War in the Shadows. The Guerrilla in History.* London: Macdonald and Jane's, 1975.

Bailey, Jonathan. *The First World War and the Birth of the Modern Style of Warfare.* Camberley: Strategy & Combat Studies Unit, Occasional Paper No. 22, 1996.

Clutterbuck, Richard. *Protest and the Urban Guerrilla*. London: Cassell, 1973.

Creveld, Martin van. *The Art of War. War and Military Thought*. London: Cassell, 2000.

Delmas, Philippe, translated by Camilla Hewitt. *The Rosy Future of War*. New York: The Free Press, 1995.

Duffy, Michael. *The Military Revolution and the State, 1500–1800*. Exeter: University of Exeter Press, 1980.

Earle, Edward Meade (editor). *Makers of Modern Strategy. Military Thought from Machiavelli to Hitler*. Princeton, New Jersey: Princeton University Press, 1971.

Echevarria, Antulio J. II. *After Clausewitz. German Military Thinkers before the Great War*. Lawrence: University Press of Kansas, 2000.

Fairbairn, Geoffrey. *Revolutionary Guerrilla Warfare. The Countryside Version*. London: Penguin, 1974.

Falls, Cyril. *The Art of War. From the Age of Napoleon to the Present Day*. London: Oxford University Press, 1961.

Gat, Azar. *The Origins of Military Thought from the Enlightenment to Clausewitz*. Oxford: Clarendon Press, 1989.

Gat, Azar. *The Origins of Military Thought from the Enlightenment to the Cold War*. Oxford: Clarendon Press, 2001.

Gott, Richard. *Guerrilla Movements in Latin America*. London: Nelson, 1970.

Gray, Colin S. *Another Bloody Century. Future Warfare*. London: Weidenfeld & Nicolson, 2005.

Handel, Michael I. *Masters of War. Classical Strategic Thought*. London: Frank Cass, 1992.

Hanson, Victor Davis. *Ripples of Battle: How Wars of the Past Still Determine How We Fight, How We Live and How We Think*. New York: Doubleday, 2003.

Howard, Michael (editor). *The Theory and Practice of War*. London: Cassell, 1965.

Huber, Thomas M. (editor). *Compound Warfare. That Fatal Knot*. Fort Leavenworth, Kansas: U.S. Army Command & General Staff College Press, ND.

Hundley, Richard O. *Past Revolutions, Future Transformations. What Can the History of Revolutions in Military Affairs Tell Us about Transforming the U.S. Military?* Santa Monica, California: Rand Corporation, 1999.

Ignatieff, Michael. *Virtual War. Kosovo and Beyond*. London: Chatto & Windus, 2000.

Jones, Archer. *The Art of War in the Western World*. Urbana: University of Illinois Press, 2001.

Kagan, Donald. *On the Origins of War and the Preservation of Peace*. New York: Doubleday, 1995.

Kahn, Herman. *On Thermonuclear War*. Princeton, New Jersey: Princeton University Press, 1960.

Kaldor, Mary. *New and Old Wars. Organised Violence in a Global Era*. Stanford, California: Stanford University Press, 2007.

Knox, Macgregor, & Williamson Murray (editors). *The Dynamics of Military Revolution 1300–2050*. Cambridge: Cambridge University Press, 2001.

Koch, H. W. *The Rise of Modern Warfare, 1618–1815*. Englewood Cliffs, New Jersey: Prentice Hall, 1981.

Krepinevich, Andrew F. *Cavalry to Computer: The Pattern of Military Revolutions*. Washington, DC: *The National Interest* article, September 1994.

Laqueur, Walter. *Guerrilla. A Historical and Critical Study*. London: Weidenfeld and Nicolson, 1977.

Lynn, John A. *Battle. A History of Combat and Culture. From Ancient Greece to Modern America*. Cambridge, Massachusetts: Westview Press, 2003.

Machiavelli, Niccolò. *The Art of War.* New York: Da Capo, 2001.

Moltke, Helmuth von, edited by Daniel J. Hughes, translated by Daniel J. Hughes & Harry Bell, foreword by Gunther E. Rothenberg. *On the Art of War. Selected Writings.* Novato, California: Presidio, 1993.

Moss, Robert. *Urban Guerrillas. The New Face of Political Violence.* London: Temple Smith, 1972.

Münkler, Herfried, translated by Patrick Camiller. *The New Wars.* Cambridge: Policy Press, 2002.

Olsen, John Andreas (editor). *On New Wars.* Oslo: Instituit for Forsvarsstudies ad Fontes, 2007.

O'Neill, Bard E. *Insurgency and Terrorism. Inside Modern Revolutionary Warfare.* McLean, Virginia: Brassey's [US] Inc., 1990.

Osanka, Franklin Mark (editor). *Modern Guerrilla Warfare. Fighting Communist Guerrilla Movements, 1941–1961.* New York: Free Press, 1962.

Paret, Peter (editor). *Makes of Modern Strategy from Machiavelli to the Nuclear Age.* Princeton, New Jersey: Princeton University Press, 1986.

Parker, Geoffrey (editor). *The Cambridge Illustrated History of Warfare. The Triumph of the West.* Cambridge: Cambridge University Press, 1995.

Parker, Geoffrey. *The Military Revolution: Military Innovation and the Rise of the West, 1500–1800.* Cambridge: Cambridge University Press, 1996.

Porter, Bruce D. *War and the Rise of the State: The Military Foundations of Modern Politics.* New York: The Free Press, 1994.

Record, Jeffrey. *Beating Goliath. Why Insurgencies Win.* Washington, DC: Potomac, 2007.

Rogers, Clifford J. *The Military Revolution Debate: Readings on the Military Transformation of Early Modern Europe.* Boulder, Colorado: Westview Press, 1995.

Small, Melvin, and J. David Singer (editors). *International War. An Anthology.* Chicago, Illinois: Dorsey Press, 1985.

Smith, Rupert. *The Utility of Force. The Art of War in the Modern World.* London: Penguin, 2006.

Stoessinger, John G. *Why Nations Go To War.* New York: St. Martin's Press, 1990.

Strachan, Hew. *European Armies and the Conduct of War.* London: George Allen & Unwin, 1983.

Summers, Harry G. Jr. *On Strategy. A Critical Analysis of the Vietnam War.* Novato, California: Presidio, 1982.

Summers, Harry G. Jr. *On Strategy II. A Critical Analysis of the Gulf War.* New York: Dell, 1992.

Thompson, Loren B. (editor). *Low-Intensity Conflict. The Pattern of Warfare in the Modern World.* Lexington, Massachusetts: Lexington Books, 1989.

Tzu Sun, translated by Samuel B. Griffith. *The Art of War.* Oxford: Oxford University Press, 1971.

Tzu Sun, translated by Ralph D. Sawyer with Mei-chün Lee Sawyer. *The Art of War.* New York: Barnes & Noble, 1994.

Tangredi, Sam J. *Globalization and Maritime Power.* Washington, DC: National Defense University Press, 2002.

Toffler, Alvin & Heidi. *War and Anti-War: Survival at the Dawn of the 21st Century.* Boston, Massachusetts: Little, Brown, 1993.

Triandafillov, V. K., translated by William A. Burhans. *The Nature of the Operations of Modern Armies.* London: Frank Cass, 1994.

Weigley, Russell F. *The American Way of War. A History of United States Military Strategy and Policy.* Bloomington: Indiana University Press, 1973.

Weigley, Russell F. *The Age of Battles. The Quest for Decisive Warfare from Breitenfeld to Waterloo.* Bloomington: Indiana University Press, 1991.

THIRTY YEARS' WAR AND WAR IN THE AGE OF REASON

Asch, Ronald G. *The Thirty Years War. The Holy Roman Empire and Europe, 1618–48.* Basingstoke, Hampshire: Macmillan, 1997.

Bromley, J. S. (editor). *The New Cambridge Modern History.* Volume VI: *The Rise of Great Britain and Russia 1688–1715/21.* Cambridge: Cambridge University Press, 1970.

Carsten, F. L. (editor). *The New Cambridge Modern History.* Volume V: *The Ascendancy of France, 1648–88.* Cambridge: Cambridge University Press, 1961.

Childs, John. *Warfare in the Seventeenth Century.* London: Cassell, 2001.

Duffy, Christopher. *The Military Experience in the Age of Reason.* London: Routledge and Kegan Paul, 1987.

Goodwin, A. (editor). *The New Cambridge Modern History.* Volume VIII: *The American and French Revolutions 1763–1793.* Cambridge: Cambridge University Press, 1968.

Lindsay, J. O. (editor). *The New Cambridge Modern History.* Volume VII: *The Old Regime 1713–1763.* Cambridge: Cambridge University Press, 1966.

Luvaas, Jay, editor & translator. *Frederick the Great on The Art of War.* New York: Da Capo, 1999.

Parker, Geoffrey. *The Army of Flanders and the Spanish Road 1567–1659.* Cambridge: Cambridge University Press, 1972.

Steinberg, S. H. *The 'Thirty Years War' and the Conflict for European Hegemony 1600–1660.* London: Edward Arnold, 1981.

Wedgwood, C. V. *The Thirty Years War.* London: Jonathan Cape, 1938/New York: Methuen, 1981.

FRENCH REVOLUTIONARY AND NAPOLEONIC WARS

Austin, Paul Britten. *1812. The Great Retreat.* London: Greenhill, 1996.

Bowden, Scott. *The Glory Years of 1805–1807.* Volume I: *Napoleon and Austerlitz.* Chicago, Illinois: The Emperor's Press, 1997.

Breunig, Charles. *The Age of Revolution and Reaction 1789–1850.* New York: Norton, 1970.

Cate, Curtis. *The War of the Two Emperors. The Duel Between Napoleon and Alexander.* New York: Random House, 1985.

Caulaincourt, Armand de. *With Napoleon in Russia. The Memoirs of General de Caulaincourt, Duke of Vicenza.* New York: William Morrow, 1935.

Crawley, C. W. (editor). *The New Cambridge Modern History.* Volume IX: *War and Peace in an Age of Upheaval 1793–1830.* Cambridge: Cambridge University Press, 1965.

Herold, J. Christopher. *The Age of Napoleon.* New York: Horizon, 1963.

Nicolson, Nigel. *Napoleon 1812.* London: Weidenfeld & Nicolson, 1985.

Schneid, Frederick C. *Napoleon's Italian Campaigns 1805–1815.* Westport, Connecticut: Praeger, 2002.

Ségur, Philippe-Paul de, translated by J. David Townsend. *Napoleon's Russian Campaign*. New York: Time Incorporated, 1958.

19TH CENTURY

Ernest, R., & Trevor N. Dupuy. *The Complete History of the Civil War*. New York: Hawthorn, 1960.
Foote, Shelby. *The Civil War. A Narrative*. Volume I: *Fort Sumter to Perryville*, Volume II: *Fredericksburg to Meridian*, and Volume III: *Red River to Appomattox*. London: Bodley Head, 1991.
Howard, Michael. *The Franco-Prussian War. The German Invasion of France, 1870–1871*. London: Rupert Hart-Davis, 1961.
McPherson, James H. *Battle Cry of Freedom. The Civil War Era*. New York: Oxford University Press, 1988.
Moltke, Helmut von. *The Franco-German War of 1870–71*. London: Greenhill, 1992.
Rich, Norman. *The Age of Nationalism and Reform, 1850–1890*. New York: Norton, 1977.

20TH CENTURY

Aron, Raymond. *The Century of Total War*. Boston, Massachusetts: Beacon Press, 1960.
Conquest, Robert. *Reflections on a Ravaged Century*. New York: Norton, 2000.
Freedman, Lawrence. *The Evolution of Nuclear Strategy*. London: MacMillan, 1983.
Mowat, C.L. (editor). *The New Cambridge Modern History*. Volume XII: *The Shifting Balance of World Forces 1898–1945*. Cambridge: Cambridge University Press, 1968.
Thomson, David (editor). *The New Cambridge Modern History*. Volume XII: *The Era of Violence 1898–1945*. Cambridge: Cambridge University Press, 1960.
Tucker, Spencer C. *Vietnam*. Lexington: University Press of Kentucky, 1999.
Willmott, H. P. *When Men Lost Faith in Reason. Reflections on War and Society in the Twentieth Century*. Westport, Connecticut: Praeger, 2002.

FIRST WORLD WAR

Campbell, John, et al. (editors). *World War I*. London: Chancellor Press, 1988.
Cooper. Bryan, *The Ironclads of Cambrai*, London: Souvenir Press. 1967.
Ferguson, Niall. *The Pity of War*. London: Penguin Books, 1998.
French, David. *British Strategy and War Aims 1914–1916*. London: Allen & Unwin, 1986.
Fussell, Paul. *The Great War and Modern Memory*. Oxford: Oxford University Press, 1975.
Glaise-Horstenau, Edmund, Rudolf Kiszling, Maximilian Ehnl, & Edwin Freiherr von Sacken (editors). *Österreich-Ungarns letzter Krieg*, Volume 4: *Das Kriegsjahr 1916, erster Teil. Die Ereignisse vom Jänner bis Ende Juli*. Vienna: Verlag der Militärwissenschaftlichen Mitteilungen, 1930–38.
Gray, Randal, & Christopher Argyle (editors). *Chronology of the First World War*. Volume I: *1914–1916*, and Volume II: *1917–1921*. Oxford: FactsonFile, 1990 and 1991, respectively.
Herwig, Holger H. *The First World War. Germany and Austria-Hungary 1914–1918*. New York: Arnold, 1997.

Ludendorff, Erich. *The Nation at War.* London: Hutchinson, 1936.

Rhodes-James, Robert. *Gallipoli.* London: Batsford, 1965.

Ritter, Gerhard, translated by Andrew & Eva Wilson. *The Schlieffen Plan.* London: Oswald Wolff, 1958.

Schindler, John R. *Isonzo. The Forgotten Sacrifice of the Great War.* Westport, Connecticut: Praeger, 2001.

Stone, Norman. *The Eastern Front 1914–1917.* London: Hodder & Stoughton, 1975.

Strachan, Hew (editor). *The Oxford Illustrated History of the First World War.* Oxford: Oxford University Press, 1998.

Strachan, Hew. *The First World War.* Volume I: *To Arms.* Oxford: Oxford University Press, 2001.

Strachan, Hew. *The First World War.* London: Simon & Schuster, 2003.

Wheeler-Bennett, John W. *Brest-Litovsk. The Forgotten Peace. March 1918.* London: Macmillan, 1938.

Willmott, H. P. *First World War.* London: Dorling Kindersley, 2003.

SECOND WORLD WAR

Calvocoressi, Peter, Guy Wint, & John Pritchard. *Total War. Causes and Courses of the Second World War.* London: Penguin Books, 1989.

Cowley, Robert (editor). *No End Save Victory.* London: Cassell, 2002.

Davies, Norman. *Europe at War 1939–1945. No Single Victory.* Basingstoke, Hampshire: Macmillan, 2006.

Ellis, John. *Brute Force. Allied Strategy and Tactics in the Second World War.* London: André Deutsch, 1990.

Milward, Alan S., *War, Economy and Society 1939–1945.* London: Penguin Books, 1977.

Pacific War Research Society. *Japan's Longest Day.* New York: Kodansha, 1968.

Tohmatsu, Haruo, & H. P. Willmott. *A Gathering Darkness. The Coming of War to the Far East and the Pacific, 1921–1942.* Lanham, Maryland: Scholarly Resources, 2004.

Tucker, Spencer C. *The Second World War.* Basingstoke, Hampshire: Palgrave, 2004.

Weinberg, Gerhard L. *A World at Arms. A Global History of World War II.* Cambridge: Cambridge University Press, 1994.

Willmott, H. P. *The Great Crusade. A New Complete History of the Second World War.* London: Michael Joseph, 1989). Revised edition published by Potomac Books in 2008.

Willmott, H. P. *The War with Japan. The Period of Balance May 1942–October 1943.* Wilmington, Delaware: Scholarly Resources, 2002.

Willmott, H. P., Robin Cross, & Charles Messenger. *World War II.* New York: Dorling Kindersley, 2004.

Zeiler, Thomas W. *Unconditional Defeat. Japan, America and the End of World War II.* Wilmington, Delaware: Scholarly Resources, 2004.

COLD WAR

Ball, S. J. *The Cold War. An International History, 1947–1991.* London: Arnold, 1998.

Buzan, Barry, & Ole Wæver. *Regions and Powers. The Structure of International Security.* Cambridge: Cambridge University Press, 2003.

Dunbabin, J.D.P. *The Cold War: The Great Powers and their Allies.* London: Longman, 1994.

Friedman, Norman. *The Fifty-Year War. Conflict and Strategy in the Cold War.* London: Chatham Publishing, 2000.

Hanhimäki, Jussi, & Odd Arne Westad (editors). *The Cold War. A History of Documents and Eyewitness Accounts.* Oxford: Oxford University Press, 2003.

Leffler, Melvyn P., & David S. Painter (editors). *Origins of the Cold War. An International History.* London: Routledge, 1995.

Levite, Ariel E., Bruce W. Jentleson, & Larry Berman (editors). *Foreign Military Intervention. The Dynamics of Protracted Conflict.* New York: Columbia University Press, 1992.

Miller, David. *The Cold War. A Military History.* London: John Murray, 1998.

Thomas, Hugh. *Armed Truce. The Beginnings of the Cold War 1945–1946.* New York: Atheneum, 1987.

Walker, Martin. *The Cold War and the Making of the Modern World.* London: Fourth Estate, 1993.

Young, John, & John Kent. *International Relations Since 1945. A Global History.* Oxford: Oxford University Press, 2004.

IMPERIALISM AND THE WARS
OF NATIONAL LIBERATION

Clarke, Jeffrey J. *The U.S. Army in Vietnam. Advice and Support. The Final Years 1965–1973.* Center of Military History, U.S. Army: Washington DC, 1988.

Clayton, Anthony. *France, Soldiers and Africa.* London: Brassey's, 1988.

Clayton, Anthony. *The British Empire as a Superpower.* London: Palgrave Macmillan, 1986.

Clutterbuck, Richard. *The Long Long War. The Emergency in Malaya 1948–1960.* London: Cassell, 1967.

Dalloz, Jacques, translated by Josephine Bacon. *The War in Indo-China 1945–1954.* Dublin: Gill & Macmillan, 1990.

Fall, Bernard B. *Street Without Joy. Insurgency in Indo-China 1946–1963.* London: Pall Mall Press, 1963.

Galula, David. *Pacification in Algeria 1956–1958.* Santa Monica, California: Rand, 2006.

Heggoy, Alf Andrew. *Insurgency and Counter-Insurgency in Algeria.* Bloomington: Indiana University Press, 1972.

Horne, Alistair. *A Savage War of Peace. Algeria 1954–1962.* London: Macmillan, 1977.

Irving, R.E.M. *The First Indo-China War. French and American Policy 1945–1954.* London: Croom Helm, 1975.

Karnow, Stanley. *Vietnam. A History. The First Complete Account of Vietnam at War.* London: Century Publishing, 1983.

Lewy, Guenter. *America in Vietnam.* New York: Oxford University Press, 1978.

Majdalany, Fred. *State of Emergency. The Full Story of Mau Mau.* London: Longmans, 1962.

Moore, Harold G., & Joseph L. Galloway. *We Were Soldiers Once . . . and Young. Ia Drang. The Battle that Changed the War in Vietnam.* Shrewsbury: Airlife, 1992.

O'balance, Edgar. *The Indo-China War 1945–1954. A Study in Guerilla Warfare.* London: Faber & Faber, 1964.

O'balance, Edgar. *The Wars in Vietnam 1945–1973.* London: Ian Allan, 1975.

Palmer, Bruce Jr. *The 25 Year War. America's Military Role in Vietnam.* Lexington: University of Kentucky, 1984.

Porch, Douglas. *Wars of Empire*. London: Cassell, 2000.

Waals, W. S. van der. *Portugal's War in Angola 1961–1974*. Rivonia, South Africa: Ashanti Publishing, 1994.

Wiest, Andrew. *Vietnam's Forgotten Army*. New York: New York University Press, 2008.

POST-1975

Beck, Ulrich, translated by Mark Ritter. *Risk Society. Towards a New Modernity*. London: Sage, 1992.

Brogan, Patrick. *World Conflicts. Why and Where they are Happening*. London: Bloomsbury, 1992.

Cerasini, Marc. *The Future of War. The Face of 21st-Century Warfare*. Indianapolis: Alpha Books, 2003.

Cordesman, Anthony W., & Abraham R. Wagner. *The Lessons of Modern War*. Volume I: *The Arab-Israeli Conflicts, 1973–1989*, Volume II: *The Iran-Iraq War*, & Volume III: *Afghan and Falklands Conflicts*. Boulder, Colorado: Westview Press, 1990.

Cordesman, Anthony W. *The Iraq War. Strategy, Tactics and Military Lessons*. Westport, Connecticut: Praeger, 2003.

Daalder, Ivo H., & Michael E. O'Hanlon. *Winning Ugly: NATO's Wars to Save Kosovo*. Washington, DC: Brookings Institution Press, 2001.

Dallaire, Lieutenant-General Roméo (with Major Brent Beardsley). *Shake Hands with the Devil. The Failure of Humanity in Rwanda*. Toronto: Random House, 2003.

Gow, James. *The Serbian Project and its Adversaries. A Strategy of War Crimes*. Montréal: McGill-Queen's University Press, 2003.

Hosmer, Stephen T. *The Conflict over Kosovo. Why Milosevic Decided To Settle When He Did*. Arlington, Virginia: Rand Corporation, 2001.

The Independent International Commission. *The Kosovo Report. Conflict. International Response. Lessons Learned*. Oxford: Oxford University Press, 2000.

Judah, Tim. *Kosovo. War and Revenge*. New Haven, Connecticut: Yale University Press, 2002.

Martin, Pierre, & Mark R. Brawley (editors). *Alliance Politics, Kosovo, and NATO's War: Allied Force or Forced Allies*. Basingstoke, Hampshire: Palgrave, 2000.

McAllester, Matthew. *Beyond the Mountains of the Damned. The War inside Kosovo*. New York: New York University Press, 2002.

Murray, Williamson, & Major-General Robert H. Scales Jr. *The Iraq War. A Military History*. Cambridge, Massachusetts: Harvard University Press, 2003.

Olsen, John Andreas (editor). *Asymmetric Warfare*. Trondheim: Royal Norwegian Air Force Academy, 2002.

AIR POWER

Buckley, Mary, & Sally N. Cummings (editors). *Kosovo. Perceptions of War and its Aftermath*. London: Continuum, 2001.

Bucknam, Mark A. *Responsibility of Command. How U.N. and N.A.T.O. Commanders Influenced Air Power over Bosnia*. Maxwell, Alabama: Air University Press, 2003.

Carter, Kit C., & Robert Mueller. *U.S. Army Air Forces in World War II. Combat Chronology, 1941–1945*. Washington, DC: Center for Air Force History, 1991.

Clodfelter, Mark. *The Limits of Air Power: The American Bombing of North Vietnam.* New York: The Free Press, 1989.

Flintham, Victor. *Air Wars and Aircraft. A Detailed Record of Air Combat, 1945 to the Present.* New York: Facts on File, 1990.

Higham, Robin. *Air Power. A Concise History.* London: Military Book Society, 1972.

Keany, Thomas A., & Eliot A. Cohen. *Gulf War: Air Power Survey. Summary Report.* Washington, DC: Government Printing Office, 1993.

Keany, Thomas A., & Eliot A. Cohen. *Revolution in Warfare. Air Power in the Persian Gulf.* Annapolis, Maryland: Naval Institute Press, 1995.

Lambeth, Benjamin S. *NATO's Air War for Kosovo. A Strategic and Operational Assessment.* Arlington, Virginia: Rand Corporation, 2001.

Melinger, Phillip S. (editor). *The Paths of Heaven. The Evolution of Airpower Theory.* Maxwell AFB, Alabama: Air University Press, 1997.

Mets, David R., & William P. Head (editors). *Plotting a True Course. Reflections on U.S.A.F. Strategic Attack Theory and Doctrine. The Post-World War II Experience.* Westport, Connecticut: Praeger, 2003.

Murray, Williamson. *Air War in the Persian Gulf.* Baltimore, Maryland: The Nautical and Aviation Publication Company of America, 1995.

Olsen, John Andreas. *Strategic Air Power in Desert Storm.* London: Frank Cass, 2003.

Overy, Richard. *The Air War 1939–1945.* New York: Stein & Day, 1981.

Owen, Robert C. *Deliberate Force. A Case Study in Effective Air Campaigning.* Maxwell, Alabama: Air University Press, 2003.

Pape, Robert A. *Bombing to Win. Air Power and Coercion in War.* Ithaca, New York: Cornell University Press, 1996.

Stokesbury, James L. *A Short History of Air Power.* New York: William Morrow, 1986.

Tolson, Lieutenant-General John J. *Air Mobility 1961–1971.* Washington, DC: Department of the Army, 1973.

Warden, John A. III. *The Air Campaign. Planning for Combat.* New York: toExcel, 1998.

NAVIES

Corbett, Julian S. *History of the Great War. Naval Operations.* Volume I. 3 vols. London: Longman, Green, 1920, 1921, and 1923, respectively.

Corbett, Julian S. *Some Principles of Maritime Strategy.* Annapolis, Maryland: Naval Institute Press, 1988.

Halpern, Paul G. *A Naval History of World War I.* Annapolis, Maryland: Naval Institute Press, 1994.

Marolda, Edward J., & Robert J. Schneller Jr. *Shield and Sword. The United States Navy and the Persian Gulf War.* Annapolis, Maryland: Naval Institute Press, 2001.

Morison, Samuel Eliot. *History of U.S. Naval Operations in World War II.* Volume XIV: *Victory in the Pacific.* Edison, New Jersey: Castle Books, 2001.

Newbolt, Henry. *History of the Great War. Naval Operations.* Volumes IV and V. London: Longman, Green, 1928 and 1931.

Roskill, S. W. *The Strategy of Sea Power. Its Development and Application.* London: Collins, 1962.

Willmott, H.P. *Sea Warfare. Weapons, Tactics and Strategy.* Chichester: Antony Bird, 1981.

Winton, John. *Convoy. The Defence of Sea Trade 1890–1990.* London: Michael Joseph, 1983.

Index

About the Authors

H. P. WILLMOTT is one of the foremost military historians in England, having taught at the Royal Military Academy Sandhurst, as well as at the U.S. National War College, the University of Memphis, Temple University, and The Citadel, and is now a Research Associate with Greenwich Maritime Institute, University of Greenwich. The author of over a dozen books on military history, his most recent work is the three-volume series *The Last Century of Seapower*. His book *The Battle of Leyte Gulf: The Last Fleet Action* was a Society for Military History prize-winner.

MICHAEL B. BARRETT is a professor of history at The Citadel, Charleston, SC, retired brigadier general in the U.S. Army Reserve, and author of *Operation Albion: The German Conquest of the Baltic Islands.*